D1271380

PAPA DOC

Portrait of a Haitian Tyrant

1907-1971

JOHN MARQUIS

Edited by Julia Tan
Cover Design by Sanya Dockery
Book Design, Layout & Typesetting by Sanya Dockery

Published by: LMH Publishing Limited
7 Norman Road,
LOJ Industrial Complex
Building 10
Kingston C.S.O., Jamaica
Tel: 876-938-0005; 938-0712
Fax: 876-759-8752
Email: lmhbookpublishing@cwjamaica.com
Website: www.lmhpublishing.com

Printed in U. S. A.   ISBN: 978-976-8202-49-9

This book is dedicated with love to my wife Joan and the children who have enriched our lives - Beth, David, Rhys, Piers, Hermione, Laura, Johnny and Annabella.

And of course, the people of Haiti, with the sincere hope that they will find peace and harmony.

CONTENTS

FOREWORD

Papa Doc, the dictator of Haiti between 1957 and 1971, was a source of fascination for me, even before I had the dubious privilege of meeting him in the late summer of 1968. I was working as a journalist in the Bahamas in the mid-1960s, and often wondered why his countrymen kept arriving in such large numbers in Nassau, all with frightened, haunted faces and skeletal limbs. From time to time, I was assigned to meet these tormented souls as they were herded ashore by the Bahamas police, who seemed to treat them as less than human. I never forgot the looks of helplessness and bleak resignation on their faces. The refugees who risked their lives to flee Haiti in crude, overloaded sloops were in retreat from unimaginable horrors. Poverty was certainly part of the story, but their plight was a good deal more sinister than that. Their decision to sink whatever meagre resources they had, into a perilous voyage to freedom, was prompted by the vile excesses of their ruler, a former country doctor called Francois Duvalier. Statistically, Papa Doc, as he was known to his people, was a bit player set alongside the worst ogres of the 20th Century like Adolf Hitler, Joseph Stalin and Pol Pot. Even Saddam Hussein and the Ugandan madman, Idi Amin, eclipsed him in terms of body counts, but there was something about Duvalier's wickedness that transcended mere numbers. Of course, all the above-mentioned were thoroughly evil men, and at least two of them were probably certifiably insane, but none seemed more thoroughly dedicated to the dark forces of death than the tiny man in pebbled specs who ruled Haiti so ruthlessly for 14 years.

I first began to understand Haiti under Papa Doc after reading Graham Greene's fascinating novel, *The Comedians*. In it, Greene tried to capture the atmosphere of this strangely captivating land, and throw light on the macabre nature of the Duvalier regime. He dwelt on those unfortunates who were spirited away in the night, never to be seen again, and the pervasive presence of the secret police, the Tonton Macoute, whose brutality in the president's name earned them a certain status among connoisseurs of terror. Greene's mission was to expose Papa Doc in a work of fiction which, working outside the constraints of close research, would probably say more about Haiti's nightmare than a hundred academic studies. In my view, he succeeded, even though he conceded that it would be impossible to plumb the true depths of Haiti's suffering. But, horrific though it seemed, Haiti appealed to the romantic in me and, far from being repulsed by Greene's disclosures, I became increasingly determined to go there. Strangely, this fascination persists even to the present day and in the course of this book I hope you'll discover why.

Papa Doc, in geopolitical terms, was a small-time ruler. His country was, and still is, a thoroughly inconsequential little land, where natural beauty sits alongside harrowing poverty amid pervasive feelings of hopelessness. Apart from its great tradition in the arts, Haiti's two claims to distinction are that it became the world's first negro republic in 1804 and to this day remains the western world's poorest nation, after two centuries of political upheaval and presidential mismanagement. From the time Haitians staged the world's first successful slave revolt, and snatched power from the mighty French Empire of Napoleon, they have known no political peace. Instead the country has moved from one despotic ruler to the next, a persistent cycle of exploitation and brutal oppression interspersed with periods of foreign occupation and military rule. In the process, it has made no headway in the world, enjoys little status and is seen even regionally as a sad and hopeless case, with a severely depressed economy and widespread poverty. Yet Papa Doc, during 14 years of misrule and unimaginable brutality, raised Haiti's profile to such an extent that, in his own perverse way, he became an instantly recognisable 1960s figure alongside Elvis Presley, Bob Dylan and Muhammad Ali, with the same capacity to inspire awe and (misguidedly) wonderment. In an age of images, his image was as vivid as any, characterised by those same pebbled specs, his black bowler hat, his sombre visage and deeply enigmatic demeanour. In addition, there was voodoo and his own direct involvement in its strange rites, his supposed supernatural powers and reputed immortality. Papa Doc was more than a mere President, the dictator of an economically crippled country full of sullen apprehension; he was the embodiment of evil in its most sinister form. It was evil given new dimensions by the superstition and naiveté of his people, who had hoped for salvation from their President but received only cruelty and oppression. The country doctor, trained for a career of caring and compassion, was transmuted by power into a monster.

In the course of this book, I hope to explain how and why this happened. What gave Papa Doc his charisma? Perhaps it was the sharp contrast between his physical form and the deeds attributed to him. Papa Doc, always dressed in dark suit, dark waistcoat, and highly-polished black shoes, appeared forever like the respectable medical practitioner he had once been, albeit somewhat funereal for someone who had been trained to preserve life rather than promote death. Outwardly, there was little sign of the ghoul within. He liked his people to view him as a father-figure (hence his soubriquet) and anyone, not knowing anything of the gruesome reality of his life, might easily have mistaken him for a frail, vulnerable, slightly dotty but totally blameless old man. It was his deep mystique which enthralled an entire generation. What exactly was he all about?

Incredibly, given his obsessive paranoia and extreme reticence, I was actually able to meet Papa Doc in his study in the National Palace in the Haitian capital, Port-au-Prince, and we chatted for the best part of an hour about the pressures of political power in a notoriously volatile land, where life was cheaper than rum and much more dispensable. Throughout the interview, he was courteous, quietly spoken and reasonably forthcoming, given the fact that journalists were not generally seen as friends and newspapers of the day were relentlessly hostile towards him. I was with four colleagues and between us we managed to glean something of his political philosophy and presidential objectives, though very little of the machinations within. All the time, I was acutely conscious of my prevailing impression, that Papa Doc's meagre physical presence concealed huge, unfathomable secrets, and that the paternal veneer camouflaged a grotesque reality. After all, this tiny man had not long before, personally supervised the execution of 19 young army officers, every one despatched by a firing squad of 19 fellow officers, all of them in turn acting out of fear of their President. No-one need under-estimate Papa Doc's power to intimidate:

his propensity for Machiavellian intrigue and ruthlessness was almost without limit. Much bigger men quivered in his presence.

The man whose fate, in a sense, led me to Papa Doc's study was a South African-born fantasist called David Knox. He had been the Director of Information for the Bahamas Government of the day and, after vanishing for several weeks while supposedly on a weekend trip to Jamaica, eventually turned up as a prisoner of the fearsome Tonton Macoute in Port-au-Prince. While Papa Doc and I spoke in the National Palace, an enfeebled Knox was languishing in his cell in the nearby Dessalines Barracks military hospital, working on his defence for the trial then in progress, in which he faced five espionage charges which carried the death penalty. In relating the horrors of Papa Doc's regime, I begin with the story of David Knox, for no other reason than it's a tale well worth the telling, and in itself throws light on the peculiarities of Haiti and its infamous tyrant.

CHAPTER 1

A KIND OF GENTLEMAN

David Knox, to the uninitiated, was most people's idea of the slightly raffish English gentleman of a type produced by Britain's minor public schools. He was urbane, a little lofty in manner, vaguely dismissive of social underlings and charming when it suited him. He was an erect figure, briskly moustachioed and elegantly attired, who carried himself like a member of the rural gentry. He would not have been out of place in an officers' mess of the old Raj of India, or at an old boys' reunion at Rugby or Repton. The lawns of Henley or Ascot might easily have been his natural territory, high-bred fillies his choice in women. His speech was as neatly clipped as an old Havana and his voice as mellifluous as a bassoon. As Director of Information for the Bahamas Government of the late 1960s, he was both an incongruity and, finally, an embarrassment.

In 1967, the black government of the London-trained lawyer, Lynden Pindling came to power, bringing majority negro rule to the British colony for the first time in its 300-year history. The young Prime Minister achieved prominence by exploiting the race issue, decrying the excesses of the white merchant clique who had ruled the colony alongside the Royal governors since the 1600s, and espousing the long-frustrated cause of political freedom for a population descended from African slaves. Pindling was shrewd enough to play black against white with telling effect, while never advocating anything so rash as violence or civic disorder. His strength, as with many Bahamians, was an ability to talk plausibly – and what he said made more and more sense to a people growing increasingly disillusioned with the patronage and exploitation of a white oligarchy.

The election victory of January 10, 1967, was wholly unexpected. Pindling's Progressive Liberal Party was convinced that at least five more years would have to elapse to allow them their "bloodless revolution" and the ruling merchant class, known without affection as "The Bay Street Boys", were utterly convinced that their charmed lives had at least another term to run. The white United Bahamian Party went into the campaign with characteristic arrogance, believing the black masses would shrink once again from the radical mindset of Pindling and his black lawyer friends. This proved to be a calamitous misjudgement. Promising a 'Square Deal' for the people, and urging them to go 'All the Way' in removing the whites from power, Pindling achieved the unimaginable. On January 14, 1967, with the support of two independent MPs who broke a tie at the polls, Pindling was asked to form the government and the whites, as a political force, were consigned to history. This seismic convulsion in Bahamian political history might have seemed an irrelevance in global terms but it was, in fact, highly significant for several reasons. Firstly, it was very much in tune with the times. With the Civil Rights Movement in America at full tilt, and former territories of the British Empire striving for self-determination in the post-colonial era, the Bahamas was seen as a beacon of hope by blacks everywhere. Pindling was, in a sense, a mini-Mandela at a time when the great South African president-to-be was still in prison. He was the darling of white liberals and an icon among oppressed negroes everywhere. His 'revolution' — and that is hardly too strong a term for it — was achieved bloodlessly and democratically during an era when such things could not be taken for granted. Considering the Bahamas had a population of under 300,000, his victory was recognised throughout the Commonwealth as something quite remarkable, and probably more significant than the country itself in political terms. It was widely reported everywhere as symbolic of the age.

At the time, I was working freelance for several international news agencies in addition to occupying my staff position on *The Nassau Guardian*, the morning paper which for many years had espoused the white cause. The appetite abroad for copy on the election and its aftermath was virtually insatiable. By-lined news stories and features of mine found their way into titles as far-flung and diverse as *The Boston Globe* — one of the US's most prestigious titles — *The London Evening Standard* and *The Times of Malta*. Clippings came in from newspapers in India, Australia, Malaysia and Sarawak, from small town American newspapers in cosy communities like Joliet and Amarillo, and bigger journals like *The Philadelphia Bulletin, The*

Sacramento Union and *Dallas Morning News*. The involvement of high profile personalities of the time like film actor Sidney Poitier – a boyhood friend of Pindling, who was in Nassau to celebrate – added to the allure.

Pindling's triumph was an enormous psychological fillip for men and women of colour, wherever they lived. None would have been more surprised by this turn of events than David Knox. He was under contract to the Bahamas Government to perform press liaison and public relations work. Like most expatriates working in the Bahamas at the time, he had a work permit and a fixed contract with a reasonable expectation that both would be extended under the white regime. The UBP were firm in their view that, to succeed economically, the Bahamas needed foreign expertise. Moreover, the importation of expatriates to perform key jobs ensured Caucasian dominance in a society in which colour gradations were all-important. Under the black government Knox's expectations, and prospects, changed dramatically. Pindling, in whipping up support at the hustings, had espoused the cause of 'Bahamianisation', promising to elevate the people in every area of life, and especially in the government service. It was strongly implied that expatriate functionaries of the old regime would no longer have security of tenure.

In true 1960s style, the times really were a 'changin'. Inevitably, Knox was a natural target for Pindling. Apart from his patrician airs, his Caucasian origins and imperialistic bearing, Knox happened to be South African born. He looked English, sounded English and even acted English, but Knox belonged not to the moist, rolling greenery of the Downs or the Moors, but the sun-scorched open spaces of the South African veldt. Even before the election, Pindling and his parliamentary colleagues liked to pick on Knox as symbolic of the white government's pro-foreign obsessions. His South African background provoked them to paroxysms of indignation. They wanted to know why someone they thought of as representative of a segregationist regime, was allowed to hold a well-paid post in a predominantly black country. It was a theme they pursued with almost nauseating relish. Their propaganda pilloried Knox as the embodiment of racist evil, for no better reason than that he happened to come from the land of apartheid. But as long as the whites ruled, Knox could afford to disregard the taunts and get on with his job. When power changed hands, Knox's contract in the Bahamas still had a couple of years to run. Admirably, he stayed on to face whatever came his way, a white spokesman for a black government, with all the burdens of his homeland on his back. It was easy to feel sorry for him. No-one was more aware than him of the absurdity of his position. It was to his credit that he continued to function at all because the temptation all around must have been to banish him into a side office, to serve out his time.

My associations with Knox were strictly professional. He was the man I, along with all reporters working on Nassau newspapers at the time, approached for official government information. If Cabinet ministers were unavailable, Knox was the conduit through which ministerial comments flowed. He was always competent in his job, and unflaggingly obliging in manner, even if he did sometimes create the impression that the press were a contagion to be endured rather than an important component of the Bahamas' democratic process. He was brisk, efficient and polite, even under duress: all the qualities which, presumably, the UBP had been seeking when he was appointed. While no-one questioned his commitment under the new regime, it was easy to imagine the growing untenability of his position.

In his early months in power, Pindling became increasingly triumphalist, continuing to decry the UBP and three centuries of bondage under the British. As a London-trained lawyer, he was the beneficiary of a university system which, even in the depressed 1950s when he was a student, offered generous concessions to Commonwealth citizens, often to the detriment of the indigenous British working class, yet political expediency demanded that he adopt an emphatically anti-British stance. It was a fashionable position to take at the time, as the mother country's grasp loosened on her former territories, and it was well-received among Nassau's oppressed Over-the-Hill communities. He was likened to Moses leading his children from the wilderness. Hosannas were sung in his honour. The people gloried in their deliverance. Pindling took on the aura of a maximum leader. The Bahamian masses began to revert to their tribal roots in proclaiming him Father of the Nation. The black-over-white message was being driven home with a vengeance.

Knox's discomfiture deepened with every day that passed. His natural *joie de vivre* gave way to solemnity and, probably, just a little despair. All those who knew him wondered how long it could last. Then came May, 1968, just a year and a half into what was to prove a quarter of a century of increasingly corrupt and irresponsible rule by Pindling and most of his cohorts. It was a month which was to change Knox's life — or what was left of it — forever. The extent to which Knox was responsible for his own fate will be for you to judge.

The scene moves from Nassau, the Bahamian capital where Knox had his office, to the southern island of Inagua, where a sparse population ekes out a meagre living by fishing and farming and, improbably, by scraping salt. Like many of the southern islands of the Bahamas, Inagua is still quite backward, offering its inhabitants little by way of social exhilaration or economic well-being. Apart from the vast salt pans which constitute its main industry — the production of coarse and fine salt for the big consumer markets of the western world — Inagua's only distinction is its magnificent flamingo flock, reputed to be the biggest in the Americas, a huge pink cloud which lifts off from the island's wetlands with an elegant whoosh that leaves onlookers transfixed. The contrast between Nassau life and that of distant Inagua could hardly be greater. The capital, even in the 1960s, was comparatively sophisticated and cosmopolitan, with its colourful resort hotels, elegant restaurants, raucous nightclubs and suave casinos. Nassau had always attracted a rich mixture of brigands and sophisticates, categories which frequently overlapped, and was noted as a playground not only for the idle rich, but also an interesting array of fugitives. The European gossip columns portrayed it as 'James Bond Land', where gangsters, high-rollers and royalty mixed almost on equal terms while the deprived natives looked on with the lassitude and resigned acceptance of perpetual underdogs. Islands like Inagua, on the other hand, were still relatively primitive. The only bright lights it ever saw were the crackling flashes of tropical summer storms. Its people were used to the hard but simple life of subsistence agriculture, handline fishing and working for Morton Salt Company.

Nassau, by contrast had traditionally provided a fascinating conjunction of almost obscene wealth and debilitating poverty. A narrow ridge divides the two lifestyles even more markedly today. Walk a few hundred yards from the jewellery stores of Bay Street in a southerly direction and you will find yourself traversing that narrow ridge and descending into what Bahamians call Over-the-Hill, the festering ghettoes of Bain Town and Grants Town, where some people still live in tiny concrete homes with no bathrooms, only pee buckets in corners and sewage piles on adjoining lots.

During 25 years of Pindling rule, those ghettoes saw little or no improvement, only an intensification of resentment, and a proliferation of guns and drugs, among people who felt left out of what everyone else seemed to be regarding as an economic boom. Pindling ultimately acquired a knighthood, a $3 million home well away from those heaving slums, and a coterie of prospering acolytes who continued to see him as the man to follow along the road to almost inconceivable wealth. However, the masses remained as they always had been — dirt poor and quiescent, but now deprived of their old down-home standards of decency and mutual respect, which had been supplanted by crushing envy and shattered dreams.

The Square Deal went banana-shaped while Moses amassed riches and his disciples became multi-millionaires. Even the almost total predictability of the situation could not soften the wrecking of dreams, or the sense of betrayal. Like so many very small men, Pindling wanted to play big and he did so at the expense of those who were relying on him. Behind his heavy shades, sharp suits and two-toned shoes, he took on the aura of the archetypal banana republic dictator, though within the context of a functioning democracy. While still under the watch of his colonial masters, Pindling stayed within the bounds of common decency. It was only much later, long after independence from Britain had been achieved, that the excesses of his regime became all too evident. In Inagua, though, little ever changed, and the island of the year 2000 was much the same as that of 1968, except that it had suffered the ravages of depopulation, as the young went off in search of lusher grazing. While Nassau buckled under the weight of a growing crime rate, the simple folk of Inagua continued to go to bed with their doors unlocked and windows wide open. Well outside the maelstrom of political change, Inaguans fell in with the new order but carried on life more or less as they always did, with quiet, unhurried doggedness in wresting a living from the land and sea around them.

Speak to islanders now and few recall the details of May, 1968, but the international press was clear enough in its appraisal of what went on there. Inagua was the isolated land, where exiles from another nation tried to live out their dream, and met disaster in the attempt. Their venture was to have a profound impact on David Knox, not only during the months that followed but for the entire four years remaining to him. It was a sad, heart-rending episode which again exposed the true nature of Papa Doc and those who sustained him. By 1968, the Duvalier Government had been in power for eleven years. Any pretence of good-intent, compassion or even everyday consideration for the poor people of Haiti had long since evaporated. The country doctor, who had made his reputation fighting crippling diseases among the poor, had transmogrified into the wicked dwarf of world politics. In his case, power had not only corrupted absolutely, but left him a distorted approximation of his former self. It's interesting that Katherine Dunham, a prominent dancer of the 1950s and 1960s who regarded Haiti as home, spoke of this inexplicable physical change at the time. It was as if Papa Doc had undergone some deep inner transformation. He was no longer even trying to maintain any pretence of humanitarianism. His people were suffering deeply while he underwent a Kafka-esque metamorphosis. The country doctor now inspired international revulsion.

What later became known as 'The May 20 Invasion' will go down in Haitian history as just one more false dawn, a badly-botched attempt at insurrection, in which an undetermined number died along with their shared dreams of better times ahead. It was, like The Bay of Pigs, ludicrously under-funded and ill-conceived, though much less significant in the eyes of the world than the doomed Cuban adventure. In retrospect, it now appears more of a gesture than military operation, but its objectives were honourable enough. The idea was simple and, given the very limited resources at their disposal, fairly ingenious. Somehow, Haitian exiles in Florida managed to acquire a World War II twin-engined B-25 bomber which, they thought, could be used to rain terror on the National Palace in Port-au-Prince, where the self-styled President-for-Life lived behind a security screen as tight as any in the Americas. With good reason, Duvalier felt under threat from the many external forces that wanted to remove him. Having thwarted one major plot in 1967, which had been engineered by ambitious army officers, his paranoia was deepening by the day. He distrusted the army and, indeed, practically all around him, except the thugs of the Tontons Macoute, who survived on his patronage and proved an effective counter to the national forces and the treacherous elements within. By raiding the National Palace, and landing an invasion force in the north of the country near Cap Haitien, the exiles believed they could provoke an uprising against Papa Doc and sweep him from power, exposing his vulnerability in the process and destroying forever the myth of his supposed immortality.

There were undoubted echoes of The Bay of Pigs in both the conception and execution of the plan, except that there was never any suggestion of American involvement, or even agreement, with what turned out to be a comic opera exercise which ended disastrously. The bombing raid over the palace, such as it was, was not seriously intended to rip apart the Duvalier fiefdom in one sweep. Its real purpose was to unsettle the President and his staff, and show the populace that salvation was at hand from their exiled compatriots. Combined with news from the north that an invasion force had landed, it was felt a general uprising might well erupt, and that Papa Doc would fall, to be expelled or worse. But the plot was bedevilled by a miscalculation of the public will, and of the depth of their fear. Papa Doc, in the eyes and minds of the people, was more than a mere man. He was a myth sustained by dark forces. A silver bullet through the brain of their tormentor might prove to be the only path to salvation, but who would ever get close enough to fire it? And who would ever dare? Agency reports of the time were short of detail, but the basic outline of events emerged over a period of days, and it became clear that, like The Bay of Pigs, this was an invasion gone badly wrong, with exiled troops caught in a trap from which there was no escape. As with the Cuban adventure seven years before, the 'invaders' did not get beyond the beach before being rounded up and dealt with by Haitian forces.

Treachery was blamed for the debacle, almost certainly combined with the incompetence and naiveté generally associated with military amateurs whose ambitions were unrealistic, given the power of Duvalier and the paucity of their resources. As with so much associated with Haitian resistance, the raid was as much a subject for condescension as admiration. Few were to cite it in future years as an example of military ingenuity. The air raid by that forlorn B-25 was almost laughably ineffective. The home-made bombs it unleashed on the palace bounced harmlessly off the front lawn without going off, and the plane was eventually forced down by Haiti's tiny air force into what was then known, predictably, as the Francois Duvalier International Airport just outside the city. It was an ignominious end to a foolhardy venture. For some years afterwards, the plane sat like a trophy on an apron at the airport, proof in Duvalier's eyes of his own invincibility, and the approval of whatever gods he worshipped. Knox became implicated in the invasion by two factors. Firstly, that the B-25 was said to have taken off from the airstip in Inagua, the nearest of the

Bahama islands to Haiti's shores. Secondly, that Knox chose a weekend in May, to go off to Jamaica, in search of solace in the arms of the Oriental women he favoured so much. Quintessential Englishman he might have seemed, but Knox was a man of exotic tastes, and yellow beauties with hidden realms of passion were a side dish he relished away from his job as the Bahamas Director of Information. This odd conjunction of events was to have almost unimaginable results, and I found myself deeply ensnared in the preliminaries, the main event and the aftermath. It was to prove both a fascinating and deeply disturbing experience.

For the entire summer of 1968, I worked on the David Knox story. In a land like the Bahamas, where politics is a national obsession, this unusual diversion was welcomed by the readership of *The Tribune*, the crusading daily where I worked primarily as a political reporter after leaving *The Nassau Guardian* in the spring of that year. For them, it had all the elements of a seriously good story: mystery, intrigue, illicit romance (though that had to remain as unpublished speculation at the time) and, when all became known, the macabre fascination of all things to do with Papa Doc. For some time, though, the Knox story was purely a mystery, a protracted inquiry into his whereabouts. When he failed to turn up for work on that fateful Monday morning, there was much speculation about where he'd gone and why. Not surprisingly, some surmised that the pressures of his job under Pindling might have got the better of him, and that he'd decided to cut his losses and go. His rather elegant wife Phillippa, who had the English upper-class hauteur one would expect in the spouse of a man with soaring social aspirations, was in Britain at the time. No-one knew for sure whether she was being kept abreast of his movements. When the government expressed official concern, its story was that he had gone to Jamaica privately for the weekend. No-one sought to elaborate on this version of events and it was widely accepted as true.

The search for Knox was concentrated on Jamaica, with consular officials there liaising with local police in an attempt to cast light on the mystery. After a few days, friends, relatives and colleagues of Knox began to show deep concern. It was unlike him not to appear for work because, whatever personal faults were later to emerge, professional irresponsibility was not among them. Like the English gentleman he purported to be, Knox was a stickler for keeping appointments, doing his duty and being seen to do the right thing. It was, therefore, a truly stunning surprise when, some days later, agency reports broke the news of Knox's presence in Haiti. Even more surprising was the disclosure that he was in the hands of the Tontons Macoute. And, more surprising still was the photograph released by Haitian officials showing Knox with his face swathed in bandages. But that was only the beginning.

Papa Doc's law enforcement agencies eventually charged him with spying 'against the Republic of Haiti' and being directly implicated in the May 20 invasion. The suggestion seemed to be that Knox was in Port-au-Prince, the Haitian capital, as a revolutionary co-ordinator, a link man in the grand plan for invasion formulated by the exiles. To all who knew him, it seemed improbable, even preposterous, but none could shake off the disturbing suspicion that there was probably much more to 'good old David', as they fondly called him, than they had ever imagined. Fired by Graham Greene's disclosures, enraptured by the special allure of Haiti, and gunning for a string of good stories, I tackled Knox's incarceration with gusto. Because the matter was now in the hands of British consular officials in Jamaica, who could be relied upon to be excessively circumspect about everything, there was plenty of room for speculation, all fed to me by Knox's friends and colleagues. There was also a steady trickle of official information from Port-au-Prince itself. Together, they made a potent mix. The seriousness of the situation was not fully appreciated at the time, and many of the words I wrote that summer deepened Knox's plight as he sat in his cell pondering the spectre of Fort Dimanche, where Papa Doc's prisoners were held, tortured and despatched with increasing rapidity as his paranoia intensified. It was only much later that I discovered how my stories in *The Tribune* put Knox's life is jeopardy.

Once news of Knox's whereabouts was released, I gave full rein to the speculation of those who knew him best. Some of this speculation was wholly fanciful, much of it based on what people thought they knew of Knox. What they thought they knew, and what they actually knew, turned out to be very different things. Knox was a man with at least two faces, probably more. To this day, 30 years after his death, he remains an enigmatic figure, a multi-layered man either deeper than the Marianas Trench or shallower than a Norfolk beach, depending on your viewpoint. Before his disappearance, there was much talk in Nassau about Knox's military credentials. It was widely felt he was in one of the Guards regiments. This was an impression Knox himself did nothing to dispel. There was, unquestionably, a military air about him and subtle asides from the man himself about his intelligence connections.

Knox is now long dead, and, therefore, unable to defend his corner, but those who recall the period well, believe that his own romantic turn of mind was as much to blame for his fate as anything else. He liked to give the impression that he was a member of MI5, the British intelligence agency, an additional flourish to the image of urbanity he chose to cultivate. This was to prove a crucial plank in the Haitian government's case against him. The fact that Knox was both an 'information director' and former spy was, for them, pretty conclusive proof that he was up to no good in Port-au-Prince. As 'a white South African' — as the Haitians insisted on calling him — at a time when his homeland was an international pariah state because of the evils of apartheid, Knox was viewed as a ghoulish figure by the extremely racially conscious black regime of Duvalier. A bizarre conjunction of circumstances had deepened his troubles. Journalist and publisher Paul Bower, who still lives in Nassau, reflected on the Knox saga when it was given prominent exposure in *The Tribune* in 2003. He was not only a close friend, but also Knox's landlord when he moved into an annexe at Bower's Cable Beach home while Phillippa was away in Madeira, which was eventually to be their retirement hideaway. During the months preceding Knox's departure to Jamaica, they socialised frequently and Bower was able to get a fairly vivid impression of his friend's character. Even today, he says: "He was an entertaining and colourful personality." Several months after Knox's arrest, Bower was to fall foul of the formidable Phillippa, who blamed him for 'leaking' Knox's supposed MI5 connections to the press. But Bower insists that Knox himself was the source of the information, which was known to all his Nassau friends. Bower told me: "I knew David Knox well. As a journalist and publisher, I was often in touch with him professionally, and on social occasions we would exchange views on current affairs, and anecdotes about our World War II experiences and subsequent careers. He was a great raconteur and had a self-deprecating sense of humour — always an endearing quality."

The MI5 link came from David Knox's anecdotes about his service as British Information Officer in British-controlled Cyprus in the fifties. At that time, the island was wracked by strife between Greek and Turkish Cypriots over 'Enosis', the proposed union with mainland Greece. Archbishop

Makarios, the Greek Cypriot patriarch, was vigorously pressing for this union, whipping up religious fervour to fever pitch in the process. Enosis, naturally, was bitterly opposed by the Turkish Cypriots and, of course, by Turkey — and a large consignment of British troops was in Cyprus trying to keep the peace while complicated negotiations went on between the two sides. David Knox's job, of course, was to be briefed by all the British elements involved — the Colonial Office, the Foreign Office, and the Military — and then to feed the press with the official line. Since the Military, encompassing Army, Navy and Air Force, was a major player, Military Intelligence — MI5 and MI6 — were inevitably involved. When David talked about it to friends and acquaintances in the Bahamas, he would say that he worked closely with MI6 — his exact phrase which I remember well. Not knowing the subtle difference between the two MI units, most listeners would remember MI5. This eventually reached *The Miami Herald*,' Bower concluded.

From *The Miami Herald*, the MI5 reference quickly implanted itself in the minds of all journalists covering the story, including myself. During the early stages of the story, when Knox was no more than a missing man, and the Haiti connection pure speculation, the MI5 element was undoubtedly the kind of spice we were looking for. Essentially, this was a story of intrigue, and what could be more intriguing than a missing MI5 man? Every day, before its horrendous significance in subsequent events was known, I happily hammered the MI5 reference into every story. It added a mysterious dimension to what were, at the time, basically mundane events, and gave Knox a patina of glamour that, in any other circumstance, he would doubtless have welcomed. However, I was later to regret doing so, as will become clear as this story progresses. For Dr Duvalier, poring over every press clipping in his study at the National Palace, the MI5 reference was confirmation of his darkest suspicion, that David Knox was a conspirator involved in a misguided plot to overthrow him. Knox was in deep, deep trouble.

CHAPTER 2

A CASE OF PARANOIA

The trial of David Knox offered many insights into a dark, impenetrable regime. It was a time when the notorious paranoia of Dr Duvalier was governing every presidential move. He saw enemies all around him and rarely strayed from the palace, a stark white edifice in central Port-au-Prince, which for decades has symbolised the height of Haitian authority. Papa Doc's reclusiveness added substantially to his mystique, which he used effectively to quell dissent and discourage incipient usurpers. It helped, too, when he bestowed upon himself divine powers, equating himself with God and drafting a special version of the Lord's Prayer in honour of himself. Faith cannot thrive off familiarity which, we all know, breeds contempt. Papa Doc made himself scarce, partly for self-protection, but more significantly to preserve his image of invincibility. His mystique became a powerful feature of his psychological armoury. Though in reality small in stature, Duvalier grew in the public consciousness the less the people saw of him. It was an effective ploy by an astute ruler to keep the masses in check. For Knox, Papa Doc was a phantom figure who now held his fate in his hands. If there is one strong impression to be gleaned from the three weeks I spent in Haiti to cover the Knox trial, it is that Papa Doc's presence could be felt in everything. In the courtroom itself, a converted gymnasium at the Dessalines Barracks, just a few yards from the palace, he was visible only in the most modest form, a black-and-white photograph stuck to the wall behind the heads of the five-man military court. But there was always a spectral element to Papa Doc, and one felt that he was presiding over the deliberations in spirit, if nothing else, with the senior military officers on the panel merely carrying out his will.

In early July, 1968, when Knox had been under arrest in Port-au-Prince for four weeks, his wife, Phillippa, collected his Hillman car from outside Paul Bower's Cable Beach apartment in Nassau, where her husband had been staying, and began a long stand-off with the press which generated much tension on both sides. There is no question that Mrs Knox felt, not entirely without justification, that the press had been at least partly responsible for her husband's predicament. If his own foolishness and vanity had precipitated his ordeal, it was the seemingly outlandish speculation of the press which had exacerbated an already dangerous situation. After all, the Duvalier regime had a reputation for acknowledging none of the standards expected of a western society. Its idiosyncratic approach to diplomacy was in line with the bloody-minded individualism it had shown since attaining independence in 1804. It was never an easy country to deal with, but under Duvalier it had become even more resistant to the sensibilities of its First World neighbours. In Knox, Papa Doc had stumbled upon a powerful symbol of western oppression, a South African seemingly engaged in conspiracies to undermine the world's first black republic. There was much mileage to be gained from this totally unexpected turn of events, and he could be relied upon to make the best of it.

When Knox's whereabouts became known, the Chief of the Bahamas Special Branch, Gregory Bentley, flew from Nassau to Port-au-Prince, to glean as much information as possible from the prisoner himself. It was the first contact Knox had with the outside world since being seized. Joining Bentley in Haiti was Charles Sanderson, a British diplomat based in Jamaica, who was to follow the whole sorry affair through to the end. Together, they tried to offer Knox whatever reassurance seemed appropriate, and form a link between the prisoner and his wife, whose absence in Madeira seemed to cause him concern. He wanted her back in Nassau, where she could follow events more closely. At Government House, where Sir Ralph Grey lived as the Queen's official Bahamas representative, there was a flurry of irritation and indignation, as the Knox affair threatened to disrupt the Governor's departure plans. At a time when he was winding down his official duties at the end of his tour of duty in Nassau, Sir Ralph was obliged to deal with the potentially toxic fall-out from Knox's indiscretions.

As Haiti's version of events began to unfold, it appeared to be no ordinary case of a weekend adventure gone wrong, but an act of folly with serious international implications. Had Knox, a senior Bahamas Government official, really been implicated in a raid on Haiti launched from Bahamian territory, then the ramifications were deeply troubling. After thirty-one days in custody, Knox had still not been charged, but all the unofficial information I was receiving from Haitian sources suggested that the connection with the May 20 invasion attempt was well-founded. There was little to be said that could possibly console Knox or his wife at this point. It was all bad news. From within Haiti itself, details began trickling out about the invasion and the sorry band of rebels behind it. As usual, the story bore most of the vaudevillian hallmarks of an anti-Duvalier insurrection attempt. There were tragi-comic elements to the story which left bemused observers wondering whether to laugh or cry. In the end, crying seemed the more appropriate reaction, especially when the heads of two invaders were paraded on pikes before the cowed populace of Port-au-Prince.

Associated Press reporter John Vinocur wrote in a front-page Tribune story on July 2, 1968, that a group of idealistic young men had tumbled out of the B-25 aircraft on that ill-fated venture. They fired a few shots but were captured within 36 hours, two of them making it to Port-au-Prince on stretchers, two more as gruesome trophies, their glassy-eyed heads gazing grey and bloodless at the assembled crowds. For Duvalier, the raiders themselves were considered little more than dupes, a rag-tag platoon of no-hopers who could muster only a few words of Creole and shuffled around uneasily in scuffed, non-military footwear when they were brought before the authorities. Much more significant for the President was that Oswald Brandt, a 78-year-old multi-millionaire of Jamaican origin, who had lived in Haiti for 55 years, was seen as the brains behind the plot. Brandt and his son Clifford, 44, were people of considerable financial influence at the time, businessmen who were major players in the impoverished country's commercial life. It was they, according to Haitian sources, who supplied $150,000 to New York and Montreal exiles for the express purpose of funding the raid. As they reclined in custody at the Dessalines Barracks, the Brandts were accompanied by Charles Plasimond, a manager they employed at one of their plants, and the Leger brothers, Georges and Jean-Claude, both lawyers representing major United States interests in Haiti. According to Vinocur, Papa Doc's demeanour at this point was one of barely contained anger. He was angry at the Brandts, angry at the United

States and Bahamas governments, which he blamed for allowing military training on Inagua, and angry at the impact the raid had on Haiti's already desperately poor tourism business. Almost overnight, the meagre trickle of visitors vanished, cutting off yet another revenue source for a country in need of every cent it could lay hands on.

Feelings in Port-au-Prince were running high and whatever Knox said to explain his presence in Haiti — the story emerging was that he paid a backstreet surgeon $60 to disfigure his face with a cosmetic scar — was likely to do little to lessen his problems. He was at the mercy of a regime known for merciless behaviour. There was no reassurance to be offered. As things stood in the high summer of 1968, he was a white man in a black dictator's jail, his suntan fading after prolonged incarceration. Brandt, too, was worryingly pallid, but his alabaster whiteness was due primarily to chronic illness. For Duvalier, though, their mere presence behind bars was heavily symbolic, a graphic demonstration of his own growing power. Throughout its troubled history, Haiti had been a cauldron of simmering racial resentment in which gradations of colour had always been vitally important. During their trials, he would show the world who was boss in his festering fiefdom. That was the most important thing.

The picture of Knox released by Haitian authorities was a far cry from the image his friends in the Bahamas remembered. In fact, when it appeared for the first time in *The Tribune* on July 5, 1968, it shocked those who knew him and worked with him. With thick white pads and bandages on the left side of his face and across part of his forehead, his shirt collar open and dishevelled, he looked like the victim of a drunken street brawl. This was in marked contrast to the familiar Knox image, which testified to his fastidious attention to sartorial detail. Meanwhile, diplomatic efforts were underway to find out exactly what was going on in Haiti, and what Duvalier's thinking was on Knox and his fellow prisoners. Sanderson began shuttling between Kingston and Port-au-Prince, meeting Haitian government officials, including Foreign Minister Rene Chalmers, with a view to gauging the official mood. In these early weeks, British diplomats didn't know what to make of Knox's situation. They found Haiti's accusations implausible, even laughable, but there was something even more absurd about the story Knox himself was telling, that he had paid for a scarring operation to give himself a more romantic, dashing image. Incredibly, given his fractious state at the time, Duvalier chose to reprieve the surviving young invaders whose raid on Haiti had come to such an ignominious end. It was an uncharacteristically compassionate act, but not without purpose. Later, it would be seen to fall into a carefully planned pattern, but none of this was evident at the time.

The act of clemency was at first interpreted as a hopeful sign for Knox, but this illusion was soon dispelled when Duvalier began explaining his actions. The President was eager to differentiate between the foot soldiers and their 'generals', as became clear when he began vilifying exiled, white-collar plotters in the United States. What he reviled, he said, were not the misguided, lower-rank functionaries in such adventures, but the 'grasping and lazy elite' who were intent on thwarting Haiti's progress. He decried these 'veritable leeches' as obstacles on the road to national recovery. These were clearly references to the Brandts and their ilk, in Duvalier's mind a small, grasping group of whites and mulattoes who were determined to block his 'democratic' revolution. Unfortunately for Knox, he was regarded as fitting comfortably into this self-serving milieu, so the President's published utterances brought him little comfort. Duvalier felt the Brandts were financing those in Miami and Manhattan, mostly Haitian professionals, who wanted power for themselves at the people's expense. Knox, he felt, was somehow tied into this international conspiracy, either because of an ideological commitment to overthrowing a black regime, or as a mercenary with special intelligence skills.

During his detention, Knox was kept in the barracks hospital. He told Sanderson he had no complaints about his treatment. For a gregarious man with a good mind, prolonged incarceration was dispiriting, but Knox kept up morale by sketching drawings on the hospital wall of the home he hoped to build one day on Madeira, the island he and Phillippa regarded as their ultimate haven. Throughout the long, hot days of a Haitian summer, he continued to wear the clothes he arrived in, including the chukka boots and fawn suit which were soon to become familiar to reporters at his trial. To kill time, he read books and chatted with those guards who were able to cobble together a few words of English. As if Knox's predicament were not bad enough, it worsened during those early days of July because of events in Grand Bahama, the northernmost island of the Bahamas, where the President's newly-appointed Consul was shot in the back with a revolver, in what appeared to be an anti-Duvalier gesture. The body of Joseph Dorce, 36, was found in the bush just a few yards from the Freeport apartment where the shooting took place. If Duvalier needed further evidence of a Bahamas-based conspiracy against his regime, this was it. Through his Washington Ambassador, Arthur Bonhomme, the President said the killing was part of a plot by 'an international terrorist force', dedicated to the overthrow of his government and intent upon spoiling relations between Haiti and the Bahamas. In fact, Dorce was one of three diplomats sent to the Bahamas by Haiti as 'watchdogs' with the express purpose of unearthing evidence of conspiracy in the islands. Haiti had told the United Nations Security Council that rebels were at work in the Bahamas and cited the May 20 invasion as hard evidence. Dorce and his two colleagues were part of Papa Doc's counter blast, but their presence was seen by anti-Duvalierists as provocative and it did not take long for them to act.

In New York, the Haitian Coalition, with offices overlooking the busy streets of Manhattan, was beaming radio reports into Haiti and the Bahamas, alerting the people of Duvalier's plans to undermine exile groups. According to Bonhomme, the Coalition had urged violent action against Dorce and his companions. For fifteen days, he said, the broadcasts had tried to spur Haitians in the Bahamas into taking matters into their own hands. At the time, Bonhomme told me: "You will find that violence is creeping into Haiti. Every time there has been violence, it has come from outside." As Dorce was being murdered in Grand Bahama, he said, another diplomatic official was attacked in a nightclub — evidence, he claimed, of co-ordinated international action against his country. "There is no question in my mind that these events are linked," said Bonhomme. "Dorce was a nice man, a church man, a peaceful man, and I believe this was why they attacked him. If he was the rough type of person, it would probably not have happened." Exiled anti-Duvalierists, he claimed, had become an international terrorist organisation, using the Bahamas and other island nations in the Caribbean as bases from which to launch attacks on Haiti. "However", he said, "all these incidents are being reported to the Security Council — the situation is still existing and still developing." Asked if Duvalier himself feared a revolution, Bonhomme said: "The President is a historian and even before he was elected, he knew because of his social programme, he was going to be attacked. But he has prepared himself by reorganising the army and militia. He is not afraid because, in Churchill's words, he knows that he can lose a battle but the big thing is to win the war. He is quite confident he can hold out against them." Bonhomme said it was important to remember that Duvalier was supported by the peasants, who formed the majority in Haiti. Meanwhile, Bahamian police put the two surviving Haitian Consuls under 24-hour guard. The men, Yvon Desrouleaux and Max Cave, were both with Mr Dorce shortly before he was shot.

As the manhunt for Dorce's killer got underway in the Bahamas, Knox was still languishing in prison awaiting his fate. By mid-July, the attorney who had been compiling the case against him was in a position to present a hefty dossier to one of Haiti's leading judges, Justice Roc Raymond, who would decide exactly what charges to put before the court. Meanwhile, in the Bahamas, disclosures began to appear in the press which suggested that Knox was not all that he seemed. Throughout, newspapers had been describing Knox as an ex-major in a Scottish regiment. It was certainly a suggestion Knox had done nothing to discourage among friends in Nassau, who were told he had been in the Scots Guards. But investigations by Bahamas police revealed a different story: that he was a former lieutenant in the far less fashionable Royal Natal Caribiniers, from which he was discharged in 1945 after service in North Africa and Italy, including a short secondment to the Royal Scots. It was the first suggestion that Knox — would-be creative writer — was probably a fantasist. In the immediate post-war era, Knox went to Britain, where he held a variety of subordinate jobs in commerce. Before long, however, he had entered the film industry, which was much more in line with his glamorous illusions of himself. He was not an actor, however, nor even a director. Instead, he worked with the Rank Organisation in the educational films department.

By 1955, Knox was sufficiently disillusioned with films to make his future elsewhere, and he travelled to Cyprus to become assistant manager in a food store. So, ten years after his war service ended, the urbane young South African was still a long way short of the kind of role in life he relished, though he still had no clear idea what that was. Then fate took a hand, and he was propelled along the path that was eventually to lead to a Haitian jail. When a state of emergency was declared in Cyprus, Knox obtained a position as a government information officer. Literate, well-spoken, and always well turned out, he was just the man for such a job, and he found himself in the thick of things, at a time when the Cyprus conflict commanded headlines around the world. He had discovered his forte. According to *The Daily Express*, Knox worked with the British Secretariat, helping to write and edit a newspaper giving the British Government's point of view. It was his first taste of the world of journalism, and the experience had a lasting effect, for newspapers were to play a significant role in his life from that point on, though he never worked as a journalist in the fullest sense of the word. In 1961, he moved to the Seychelles as Government Information Officer, and four years later, flew across the world to the Bahamas, where the white government of the Bay Street Boys saw him as the embodiment of their most cherished political and social ideals. He signed a three-year contract and settled into what was to prove an extremely congenial lifestyle in Nassau. During Phillippa's prolonged absences, he became the colony's arch-seducer. "He never lacked for female company," an associate disclosed. "His girlfriends covered a wide range."

On August 12, 1968, I found myself sitting in the makeshift courtroom in Port-au-Prince, the youngest among a quite large press corps of seasoned correspondents who had flown in from New York. There was the veteran Jeffrey Blyth of *The Daily Mail*, Ian Ball of *The Daily Telegraph*, Richard Wigg of *The Times*, John Bland of *Reuters*, John Vinocur of *Associated Press* and, if memory serves me correctly, Henry Lowrie of *The Daily Express*. There was a reporter from Haiti's own *Le Nouveau Monde*, Bill Cole of *The Nassau Guardian* and yours truly of *The Tribune*. We all sat round a press table in a room packed with soldiers, Tontons Macoute and members of the Haitian public, who were in a state of high excitement as the session convened. Getting there had been a trial in itself. I was in Britain on holiday when the date for the start of the case became known. I flew from London to Miami and then on to Port-au-Prince, where I was ushered across the arrivals hall at the inevitably named Francois Duvalier International Airport, into a battered cab which whisked me through the festering, congested, sun-hardened streets of the city. This was a hair-raising experience in itself, the driver seeming to choose the side of the road on which to drive, only when confronted by a vehicle coming the other way. At first, I thought this the result of sheer bad driving, but the truth was that the roads were so poorly surfaced that it was nigh impossible to pass another vehicle in the conventional fashion. Potholes deepened by summer rains posed a constant hazard and the lumbering 1950s saloons used as cabs in those days bounced over and around them, like balls in a bagatelle. Along the route into town, sleek Haitian women, hips swaying, bore huge loads on their heads as they picked their way past the roadside slums. Men sat and slouched outside hastily assembled shacks. There was woodsmoke everywhere, wisps spiralling skyward in the thick heat. I had always known that Haiti was a transplanted chunk of unreconstructed African culture, but it was during this journey into Port-au-Prince that it registered fully. Cockerels and chickens squawked across the cab's path as the driver fought with the steering wheel and honked the horn madly. On seeing me, beggars emerged from every nook and alleyway, gnarled hands outstretched. "Papa, papa, papa," they said over and over, as if every white man were a father figure, a provider. In Haiti, I discovered, pan-handling was an industry, though pitifully rewarded, and every tourist a target for the supplicants. "Give them nothing," said the driver with peculiar venom, probably out of self-interest, working out that anything received by the beggars would not go to him. At one point, when a beggar loomed close to his window, he wafted her away with one hand and she fell backwards, arm still outstretched as if she were no more than an effigy, a ragged approximation of life. In a land so deprived, only the hard and pitiless survived, it seemed.

In what may have been only a few minutes, we were in front of the National Palace, home of Papa Doc, its blinding whiteness reflecting bright sunlight from behind its perimeter fence. By any standard, this was an elegant building, and how strangely this balconied edifice, so ordered and symmetrical, contrasted with all around it. It every sense, it was like a gemstone set in dung, a truly palacial home in the midst of a heaving slum. And somewhere within, I thought, sat the brutal gnome. "The Palace," said the driver in simple, heavily accented English, "The President lives there." Considering its turbulent past, its history of comings and goings, the bloody happenings that must have occurred within, the fear it engendered, there was an odd serenity about it, as though it were the only constant in a city of unpredictability and chaos. "Is he at home?" I asked, knowing the answer, for Papa Doc never left home nowadays. "Ah, yes." said the driver. "The President never leaves the palace." Outside, a poster proclaimed "Francois Duvalier, President a Vie", the latest incarnation of Haitian democracy, the father of the nation installed for life. Beggars limped across the road, wretched souls hoping that some of the presidential gloss would rub off on them. Ah, such a painful sight, this wretchedness, this hopelessness, on sun-scorched streets where dislocated Africans loped in a state of perpetual disorientation. The cab had no air-conditioning. Few things worked properly in Haiti. The lights went out every night. Some attributed this to incompetence, others to pre-planning, giving the Tontons Macoute precious extra hours in which to perform their hideous work, whisking away the dissidents, the enemies of the revolution.

The heat was powerful, leaving the cab airless. My shirt was sodden, clinging to my back. Then the driver swung up a tree-lined road, climbing out of Port-au-Prince towards Petionville, on to the green slopes overlooking the city and finally drew up outside the hotel door. The air was cooler and fresher here, free of the urban odours, the stench of foul drains and the unwashed hordes. Bougainvillea hung in orange, blue and crimson cascades from a stone wall. A scarlet tropical bloom, huge like a tuba, loomed alarmingly from a clay pot. By Haitian standards, the hotel seemed modern and fairly big. The cool dampness of air-conditioning struck my face as I stumbled with my weekend bag into the lobby. How long would it keep working, I wondered. Uniformed busboys ran to my aid and escorted me through check-in and then to my room, which was light and spacious, disgracefully well-appointed for a land so poor. I formed the impression that I was one of probably only three or four guests in the place, two of the others being Catholic priests apparently on some humanitarian mission. From my balcony, I enjoyed a full vista of Port-au-Prince, the palace sitting incongruously amid the squalor, over which seemed to hang a thin veil of smoke. Cockerels crowed in the far hills. From here there was no hint of the chaos below, the hectic turmoil of city life, the desperate clamour for existence against the odds. There, in the distant barracks behind the palace, shielded by ochre walls, sat Knox. Alone, wretchedly vulnerable in alien hands. I poured myself iced grapefruit juice and sat watching evening shadows fall.

In the courtroom, I became an uneasy target for the Tonton Macoute's attention. Sinister men in dark blue suits, shades hiding their eyes, watched me unabashedly. When I braced myself to look at them, they didn't flinch, but stared back. It would have been easy to interpret this as intimidation, but curiosity was a likelier reason for their unwavering gaze. After all, a tall young white Englishman in a bow-tie was an uncommon sight in Port-au-Prince, where the masses were black, short and poorly attired. Only Papa

Doc wore a bow-tie. As the trial got underway, I discovered new reasons for their scrutiny. Several of my articles formed the backbone of the prosecution case. They referred, none too subtly, to Duvalier's 'gun toting thugs, the Tontons Macoute' and made disparaging references to the regime. When they were written a few months before, there was no way of knowing how significant they would become, and certainly no indication that they would be mulled over, analysed and torn apart by counsel in a foreign court. The Tontons, presumably, had been briefed to observe me, and more than once their observations became disconcertingly intense, with one assigned to taking photographs of me from close quarters, and from all angles. "What do you suppose they want?" I asked a colleague as the photographer moved close to my right ear for a profile shot. "Don't worry, John, they probably see you as the personification of British imperialism," said Richard Wigg of *The Times*. "A kind of artefact, a curiosity." The Tontons photographer didn't appreciate the humour in this remark. He was like a hippo, expressionless.

Knox was marched under armed guard from his prison room at the barracks hospital across the drill yard to the courtroom. Young soldiers flanked him as he proceeded, ramrod straight, towards the waiting crowd. He was dressed in the same beige suit he left Nassau in, some ten weeks before. In my first report from Port-au-Prince, I noted that he looked very tired 'and seemed to be staring into space as if in a trance.' He had lost a considerable amount of weight, but there was no sign of the new facial scars he was supposed to have acquired from a back-street surgeon. The five-man military panel was sworn in under the chairmanship of Jacques Laroche. Two members, Octave Cayard and Georges Danache, were heads of the Haitian Coast Guard and Air Force respectively. The prosecutor was Lieutenant Colonel Franck Romain, a particularly unpleasant character whose bull neck, reddened eyes and bellicose manner made him a formidable and frightening presence. His fat gut hung over his gunbelt, from which a revolver jutted menacingly large. To add to his intimidating sleaziness, he sucked surreptitiously at a cigarette which he cupped in his hand. This was not the Old Bailey, that's for sure, and Romain was a long way short of Hartley Shawcross.

Knox was offered the chance to select a lawyer, but this he declined to do, preferring instead to rely on his own persuasive powers. All he needed, he said, was an interpreter to translate Creole into English so that he could follow the case being made against him. In his opening statement, Romain drew a damning picture of Knox, and specifically in relating some of the asinine things he said and did during his first few hours in Haiti. There were messages, for instance, mentioning that he had moved into a hotel 'within machine-gun distance' of the National Palace, just the kind of thing a romantic with a wry sense of humour might say to a close friend back home. In the context of his present predicament, however, the comment took on serious implications, bolstering his image as a conspirator and, in Haitian minds at least, linking him with the invasion plot. The pro-government newspaper, *Le Nouveau Monde*, reinforced whatever allegations were to be made in court with claims that Knox 'played a certain role, and not a small one, in the preparations' for the invasion. As Romain moved into his stride, Duvalier asked for transcripts of the trial to be sent daily to his study at the National Palace. He intended to be kept fully informed. Meanwhile, Knox replied 'not guilty' eight times as Romain listed the charges against him, including five of espionage, another of offering a bribe to a police officer, yet another of having his face scarred illegally, and one of sending coded messages from his hotel in Port-au-Prince.

The gist of the prosecution case was that Knox met the invaders in Inagua before their raid on Haiti and arrived in Port-au-Prince to act as a liaison man for any ensuing insurrection. From the beginning, it seemed ridiculously improbable — the timeline was wrong, for a start — but there was enough in the prosecution's claims to keep their case alive, especially as the court was operating under the Napoleonic Code, with the burden of proof on the defence. Knox sat behind an improvised dock — a card table — to hear the evidence against him, betraying little emotion and gazing forward non-committally for long periods with his chin perched on a pyramid of fingers. He remained impressively impassive throughout as Romain's address to the tribunal mushroomed quickly into a tirade. Knox, he said, would soon know how Haiti treated those 'who play the role of James Bond badly.' The defendant, he added, was 'like a frightened animal'.

In a First World court, Romain's demeanour would be construed as supercharged with malice, but here it seemed not only acceptable but apparently expected. There was no pretence of balance. Though Romain was strictly a military man, he was sufficiently skilled in advocacy to make Knox look worse than he was ever likely to be in reality. Comparisons were drawn with Kim Philby, the British traitor who spied for Russia, and frequent references were made to his South African origins, though it had been made clear repeatedly that Knox was ideologically opposed to his birthplace and was now a British citizen. Romain, I was to learn much later, was rated unpleasant even by the standards applied to other Duvalier henchmen, none of whom were allowed into the inner circle because of their compassion and empathy for others. Duvalier favoured those who shared his own remarkable capacity for malevolence, and especially if their foul thoughts bore racial connotations. Romain epitomised the regime's darkest aspects. Even nearly two centuries after Haiti's escape from French clutches, it was impossible to over-estimate the influence of race on national politics. Pigmentation remained a defining factor in the man, whatever his rank, and blackness became the theme colour, the brand, of Duvalierism.

The President even changed the national flag from its customary red and dark blue to red and black, to reflect the mood and intent of his regime. This was now, emphatically, a black nation and all other hues were peripheral to its guiding doctrine which — theoretically, at least — was to empower the masses and undermine the traditionally lighter-skinned elites. From the start of proceedings, it was clear that Knox would emerge from this experience as either an idealistically inspired revolutionary — which his Nassau friends scoffed at as an impossibility — or a preposterous fantasist with a deep streak of vanity. The first could lead to the death penalty, the second to universal mockery, neither of which would sit well with a proud man, who, at bottom, was a likeable loser, someone who fell short of his own aspirations but desperately wanted to do better.

His friend, Paul Bower, believed Knox's predicament could have been the result of a late charge for glory, as though he felt his military life in the Royal Natal Caribiniers had not quite come up to scratch. Having been gazetted as captain during the North Africa campaign in World War II, Knox was part of the whirlwind drives against the Italians in Abyssinia, Somalia and Eritrea. His regiment eventually joined up with the British Eighth Army, and he was seconded to the Royal Scots, a development which probably led to the later myth that he was in the Scots Guards. Bower said: "Like many others of his generation, David Knox viewed the war as a chance to win glory — but glory, alas, eluded him. No VC, no MC or lesser decoration came his way. But the desire for glory, of some sort, persisted, and this desire, amid others more mundane, played a key role in his extraordinary late-life adventure in Haiti." It was just as well for Knox that the tribunal was not privy to other information which was later to emerge.

When the Bahamas Deputy Police Commissioner, Stanley Moir, went with Knox's wife, Phillippa to pick up his belongings from his apartment, they found in his jacket pocket a book on survival. "Clearly, David Knox was planning some dangerous enterprise when he left on 'vacation', ostensibly for Jamaica, but in fact for Haiti," said Bower. "Also in his apartment was a framed cartoon with the motto 'Glory is fleeting, but obscurity is forever' – a joke which, in his case, became meaningful." Bower added: "Knox did not find the glory he sought, but he certainly avoided obscurity. No-one who met him will now ever forget his trim, moustachioed military persona, with his impeccable 'U' accent and all the aura of a Guards Officer." In court, the 'U' accent and Guards Officer aura did nothing to help Knox's cause. In fact, they were the equivalent of a matador's cape to the bullish Romain, who snorted with indignation every time he made a new disclosure about the man in the dock. If I were the personification of British imperialism in the eyes of the Tontons Macoute, Knox must have appeared even more so, with his clipped tones and clipped moustache.

In the early stages of the trial, Knox seemed subdued, answering questions quietly and sometimes almost inaudibly. But he became more animated when it was suggested he used deceitful means to obtain a visa to enter Haiti. When Romain hinted he was South African, Knox was firm in declaring he did not need a visa because of his status as a British citizen. An agreement existed between London and Port-au-Prince, he said, but he had been led by Haitian consular officials in Nassau to believe he needed an entry visa. Ignoring his remarks, Romain told the court: "Haiti would not enter into a visa agreement with South Africa – a country which treats Africans in such a way and exploits them and keeps them in the state they are in now." Knox countered: "It is quite incorrect to describe me as South African. I am a British subject and I hold a British passport. I can prove British citizenship. I don't carry documents to say I am not a South African. I have no documents to say I am not a Russian. If I was born in China of British parents would that have made me Chinese?" His objections were over-ruled by the tribunal, as they were moments later when he protested over photographers being allowed to take pictures in court.

"This is a democracy," countered Laroche, "There are photographers here and they can do as they wish."

As the case dragged on, *Le Nouveau Monde* provided its own asides, claiming Knox's fancy for duplicity and his South African background explained why he was attracted to 'the idea of participating in a plot to overthrow the only black republic in the Americas.' The newspaper further contended that Knox would, meanwhile, do all in his power to create the impression that he was 'the victim of circumstance and a series of unhappy coincidences'. For me, personally, things were heating up, especially as it became clear that the alleged MI5 connection was to play such a major role in the Haitian case against Knox. On the indictment, each count was prefaced by the MI5 reference, meaning that the Haitian legal authorities were placing great store by the suspected British intelligence link. Evidence for their claims was to be found, for the most part, in my news clippings, all of which were to be read in court, in laboured English, by the translator John Pickering, a man who appeared to be perpetually fearful of those in power. He walked as though his bowel movements could not be relied upon, all too aware, one assumes, of the immense responsibilities laid upon him. As he stumbled through my hastily-written prose, holding up pages of *The Tribune* for the court's perusal, Pickering seemed to emphasise every reference to MI5 and Knox's supposed intelligence connections. He also seemed to dwell upon every disparaging reference to the Tontons Macoute, being sure to include my byline every time. As my discomfiture grew, so did the Tontons Macoute's interest in me. More pictures were taken as we adjourned to the verandah outside the court. They seemed to be particularly interested in profile shots. "Tell them to piss off," said one English colleague, confident that the Duvalierist thugs knew no English. "Rather not," I replied, favouring discretion over recklessness in a land where the reckless generally died, up against a prison wall. Back in court, Pickering produced yet another of my articles. It was a blistering condemnation of the Duvalier regime, with frequent references to the 'evil little tyrant' and his 'sinister thugs'. An old New York correspondent, veteran of a thousand trials, leaned towards me over the press table. "Take a tip from an old hand, my boy," he said. "Be on this evening's flight out of Haiti." He meant it, but I was foolish. I did not catch the flight. I felt an obligation to stay with Knox to the end, whatever that end turned out to be.

CHAPTER 3
TRIED AS A SPY

The opening exchanges did not go well for Knox. Evidence was produced by the prosecution suggesting that he did, indeed, visit Inagua before the May 20 invasion and that he was a key link man in the operation. Referring specifically to the espionage charges, Romain reminded the court, with no small measure of satisfaction, that the Haitian Manual of Military Justice permitted 'death for spies', a remark which turned the prisoner's long face what a pop song current at the time described as a whiter shade of pale. He closed his eyes and swallowed hard. If there were any doubts about the seriousness of his plight up to that point, they were instantly dispelled by Romain's disturbing aside. Worse still, a young Haitian, Raymond Toussaint, testified that he recognised Knox from the Inagua training camp during the run-up to the invasion. Toussaint was one of ten invaders captured by Haitian forces and subsequently released in an act of clemency by Duvalier. His evidence provided the crucial link between Knox and the Inagua preparations and added credence to the prosecution's contention that Knox was far more than the sad Walter Mitty character he was pretending to be. Romain's aggressive, provocative manner in court was in marked contrast to the diplomatic manoeuvres going on behind the scenes in Washington and Kingston, the headquarters of the British Foreign Service's Caribbean operation. Haiti's US Ambassador, Arthur Bonhomme, persisted in disseminating the official line that Knox was part of an international conspiracy against the Port-au-Prince government. The British Ambassador, Dalton Murray, a dapper little envoy of the old school, peddled a contrary view, that Knox was no more than a preposterous fantasist, who wanted to add a touch of glamour to his lack-lustre life as a government functionary and got into trouble doing so. The really interesting thing about the Knox case is that, even after all these years, no-one can be really sure exactly where the truth lies.

By the time the Knox Trial got into its stride, no fewer than seventeen foreign newsmen were in the courtroom, a fact which pleased Duvalier and his chief spokesman, Gerard de Catalogne. They wanted exposure for a trial they billed as 'a showpiece for the world', and were happy that the story was getting prominent play in American and European newspapers. Haiti's own newspapers kept a wary eye on the press corps' performance, the evening newspaper *Le Nouvelliste* condemning Associated Press reporter, John Vinocur for writing stories it considered unflattering to Haiti, but praising *Daily Express* photographer, Harry Benson for the quality of his pictures. Technologically, Haiti was ill-equipped for the transmission of such huge quanities of copy. The telex office in Port-au-Prince was packed daily with fretful and disgruntled correspondents, who were obliged to wait their turn, as colleagues pecked away at the telex keyboards. One reporter became particularly unpopular because his quality broadsheet newspaper demanded highly detailed accounts, which meant he commandeered one of the two machines available for long periods. As deadlines loomed, he was pressured mercilessly. "For Christ's sake, are you writing a bloody novel?" he was asked. Proceedings went slowly in the early days. There were frequent adjournments, including a day-long break for the feast of the Assumption of the Virgin Mary, and reporters found themselves having to convince their news editors that it was worth staying around. With expenses claims growing, some papers withdrew early on, lessening demand on the telex machines. There was a frisson of excitement on day four when Knox admitted giving a false name to a Port-au-Prince taxi-driver on his arrival in the city. This, in the eyes of the Haitian authorities, deepened the intrigue surrounding him, and helped to confirm their view that he was involved in a conspiracy of some kind. He also admitted writing the false name, Peter Johnson, on a doctor's registration card while in the driver's presence. Fortunately for Knox, this falsification of his identity was not pursued when he found himself in police hands. Knox's explanation for using the name Johnson was plausible to western ears, but seemed to carry little weight with the tribunal. He said he resented the driver's 'cross-examination' of him as soon as he entered his cab. "He wanted to know my name, where I came from and other questions. But I resent being cross-examined by a taxi-driver and as far as I know there is no law which compels me to answer questions put to me by a taxi-driver. For that reason I did not answer his questions correctly." Explaining why he continued the deception in the doctor's office, he said: "Perhaps I did it only because the driver was standing next to me." Witness Captain Henry Boucard said that, during police interrogation, Knox offered a $500 bribe to an officer 'to drop the matter' but this was turned down. Knox subsequently changed his plea on this count and admitted making the offer to Police Chief, Frederic Arty. The tribunal rejected the changed plea because he refused to admit the espionage charges.

Five days into the trial, I wrote a commmentary alongside my daily news report, referring to Knox's demeanour in light of the formidable odds stacked against him. It appeared on The Tribune's front page of August 17, 1968. 'David Knox may have gained only one thing from the first four days of his trial here — respect. For the slender, sunken-eyed figure in his slightly creased suit and suede chukka boots has remained calm and dignified while under relentless verbal fire. It is doubtful if he has gained anything else from this courtroom charade. His points of argument, conveyed in his inimitable brand of upper-class English, have been systematically demolished by the khaki-clad legal eagles of President Francois Duvalier's armed forces. Knox is, despite being born in South Africa, the almost theatrical personification of the notorious English stiff upper lip. And never was an upper lip stiffer than Knox's since Monday, when Duvalier's lawmen began the gigantic task of converting the Bahamas official — apparently a dreamer with a penchant for peculiar places — into not just a poor man's James Bond, but a sophisticated snooper like Kim Philby." I added that it seemed the Haitian authorities had "put two and two together and somehow got 104 in this bizarre affair", but that the face-scarring operation, the use of a false name, and the foolish note to his wife were probably the only three solid pieces of evidence they had against him. This, I suggested, added up not to espionage, but the fact that Knox was "a basically insecure figure showing off".

At the time of his arrest, Knox was swathed in bandages. He was 'excited and afraid' when police called at the Park Hotel to arrest him, said the proprietor, Marcel Assad. Having been away from the hotel for twelve hours, staff wanted to know what had happened to him. Knox told them he had been hurt in a fall. Assad, 65, told the court that Knox registered at his hotel as D J Knox, saying he was of British nationality. He said he arrived in the company of cab-driver, Tolem Joseph and chose an air-conditioned room. "When he came, he was in sound health," said Assad. Knox spent the night at the hotel and the next day went out with the same driver. "When he came back after twelve hours, we observed he had bandages on his face," he said. Assad said staff were whispering that perhaps he had been hurt in a brawl, but Knox went straight to bed and said nothing. In the afternoon, he added, a police car arrived heavily loaded with soldiers. Assad, acting on police orders, went to fetch Knox from his room, but there was no answer when he knocked on the door. "Then I opened the door and when the client saw me, he rose and went to sit on the bed. I told him that a police officer was asking for him and wanted to speak to him." Knox replied: "What do the police want?" Assad said they probably wanted to know about the bandages on his face. "I saw he was deeply moved and got the impression he was afraid. I told him the policeman was a gentleman and would probably need information on what happened to you." As Knox left the hotel with his hand luggage, Assad told him not to worry, and that he would be protected in Haiti. Before setting off on his ill-advised venture, Knox had apparently called the Haitian Vice-Consul in Nassau, Jean Massena, to ask if Haiti was a safe place to visit, in light of recent political upheaval. Massena said it was, though this proved to be in conflict with the official line, which suggested that President Duvalier and the nation's institutions had been 'menaced' by foreign elements. As it turned out, Knox picked the worst possible time to acquire his cosmetic scars, which had been cut into his face by a surgeon whose own fate was to lie in the balance because of his involvement in the escapade.

After my first week in Haiti, I became aware, through semi-official sources, of the presidential paranoia that was driving Port-au-Prince foreign and domestic policy at that time. I even wrote, with remarkable prescience as it turned out, that Knox would be used as part of a Haitian propaganda campaign to win approval around the world. I also discovered how desperate Haiti was to counter the damaging images put about by exiled dissidents and, more importantly so far as Papa Doc was concerned, the distinguished novelist Graham Greene, whose book The Comedians had so vilified his regime. Greene's condemnation of Duvalier, his militia the Tontons Macoute, and the culture of terror they had promoted since Papa Doc's rise to power in 1957, had deeply hurt Haiti's interests so far as the President was concerned. He felt that Greene was a stooge of imperial forces dedicated to damaging, and possibly disabling, the Haitian Government. He even tried to belittle Greene's name by telling Haitian newspapers that his novel was 'no more than the work of a journalist' and therefore not to be taken seriously. But his words rang hollow and did nothing to endear him to working newsmen, who relished the opportunity to besmirch the dictator's image even more. Desperate for foreign aid, and especially American approval, Duvalier wanted to engage in a public relations exercise to restore whatever good name Haiti might have enjoyed in the past. The survival of his economy depended on it. But Haitians, even educated Haitians like Duvalier, have been described as having a pre-Enlightenment mindset, a value system rooted in the 14th Century, and he was, therefore, ill-equipped to accommodate western expectations.

This credibility chasm was to manifest itself in many ways over the years of Duvalier's rule, but especially in relation to his treatment of opponents. A good example was his decision to leave the corpse of a dissident sitting in an armchair outside the arrivals hall at Francois Duvalier International Airport. The few tourists Haiti attracted in those days were treated to the unappetising sight of a bloated, fly-blown cadaver as they passed through the immigration check to find a taxi. For Duvalier, the spectacle was symbolic of his strength. For the tourists, it was an horrific demonstration of his savagery and barbarism. Duvalier seemed unable to comprehend this difference in approach. In at least one sense, however, Duvalier scored as a ruler. He offered a certain constancy that most of his predecessors lacked. Though Haiti had been an independent nation since 1804, the country had never enjoyed a sustained period of stability or prosperity. It had traditionally tottered from one dictatorial regime to another, a pattern broken only by a couple of periods of American occupation. The world's first black republic was seen internationally as a basket-case, a dysfunctional state in which violence and corruption were indispensable components of governance. Duvalier's regime had done little or nothing to change things, but it did possess two characteristics most Haitian regimes lacked — resilience and durability. These were now being cited by Duvalier as the mainstays of his presidency, buttressing his own commitment to retaining power, whatever the forces ranged against him. However, he was forever obliged to confront his personal demons, one of which was a conviction that the white world was against him. While he needed Washington's financial aid, he was also convinced that the Central Intelligence Agency (CIA) was somehow implicated in underhand schemes to unseat him. In the eyes of Duvalier and his henchmen, Greene, Knox and the militant exiles in New York were merely dupes of the CIA, whose overlords wanted most of all to discredit the world's first negro republic. The May 20 invasion was, Haitian sources claimed, part of this evil scheme. I was told: "When that plane flew over Port-au-Prince and tried to bomb the palace, Duvalier's ministers almost went crazy at the thought that an attempt had been made on his life."

Massena appeared in court with his left arm in a sling, having been injured in a judo fall. In his grey suit, this dapper, articulate figure looked every bit the 'very important witness' Romain had promised earlier in the trial. With accountancy and legal training behind him, Massena was well-qualified to have represented his country overseas, and it was while in Nassau as a consul that he first met Knox, he said. Knox wanted a visa to add Haiti to the many Caribbean territories he had visited over the years. "He led me to believe he had lived in Africa and had had the opportunity to see many countries in the Antilles, except Haiti," he told the tribunal. During their conversation, Knox expressed a desire to start a business enterprise in Haiti, though he was unspecific about its nature, other than to say it might involve tourism. Massena said at no time did Knox present himself as a Bahamas Government official, simply as a tourist with a vague interest in pursuing business opportunities. Interestingly, Knox was said to have reddened his hair and moustache at this time, and Massena admitted the defendant had called him to ask if it was safe to travel to Haiti because of recent political disturbances. He told him tourists were coming and going in Haiti all the time and that the security situation was satisfactory. The red hair allegation was denied by Knox, but for Haitian authorities the evidence added another plank to their conspiracy platform. The morning newspaper, *Le Nouveau Monde*, weighed in with theories of its own, describing Knox as an agent provocateur, who had been travelling with false papers, as part of an extensive plot to discredit the Duvalier regime. If Knox were totally innocent of the charges laid against him, he must by now have felt overwhelmed by the scale of the conspiracy outlined by the prosecution and the Haitian press. The May 20 invasion was not, in their eyes, a localised incursion by ill-advised adventurers, but a carefully planned military operation with enormous international ramifications.

Knox was now being burdened with the full weight of Haitian history, as *Le Nouveau Monde* accused him of being part of a scheme to undermine the Haitian political system to such an extent that the United States would be justified in occupying Haiti once again. "The author of this attempt tried to create an atmosphere of panic to persuade the Department of State to renew the ignominy of July 27, 1915, when the American occupation of Haiti started," the paper said. "It is normal for agents provocateur to be anonymous sort of people," it added insultingly. The long American occupation of Haiti, which extended right into the 1930s, and has been characterised by many Haitian intellectuals as a brutal era in which red-neck whites systematically humiliated peasants in the western world's first free black society, has always been cited as a grim period in the nation's turbulent past. It has also been blamed for many of Haiti's current problems. For nearly 20 years, Haiti's sovereignty, so bloodily seized in the struggle with the French, had been undermined by outsiders whose only objective was to exploit the country's resources and undermine the dignity of its people. That was the crux of the anti-US propaganda of the day. It was not entirely unwarranted, but it's unlikely that Knox had any such thing in mind when he set off on his ill-starred venture in Port-au-Prince.

In court, Knox's foolish letter to his wife was dissected by Romain with the help of the hapless interpreter, John Pickering. Knox had been uplifted briefly by the press corps whistling 'Happy birthday to you' on his 45th birthday as he marched into court, a spontaneous act of goodwill which brought an appreciative smile. But the letter soon turned the smile to a frown as its implications became clear. Knox told his wife he had been given the chance to extend his air ticket from Jamaica to Haiti for no extra charge, though his presence was 'politically unwise at this juncture'. He also referred to a taxi accident in Jamaica which he used to explain away the scars on his face. The letter then put her mind at rest by saying he had been 'patched up' and had been examined physically from head to foot. "The taxi company is a fly-by-night organisation and without even going to a lawyer I can see there is no point in trying to sue them. In any event there is nothing wrong with me apart from a few cuts." In the letter, he said Haiti reminded him of the Seychelles, where he had worked previously. The papaya, mangrove and breadfruit trees near the hotel made him feel at home. "Three shots rang out today and the madame informed me with a gallic shrug that someone must have walked close to the palace. The shots are by way of warning to keep the others on the far side of the road." He referred to Haitians as the best-looking people he had ever seen and added: "Frankly, I could live here." He said he appreciated Haitian art which, though primitive, was not crude 'as it is in Africa.' In some respects, the letter's contents indicated not the thought processes of a plotter, but the preoccupations of a thoroughly romantic man who felt strangely comfortable in the hemisphere's most enigmatic land.

For Knox, who disliked the formalities of the civil service life, his sojourn in Papa Doc's fiefdom was more in line with what he desperately wanted to be: a writer, an adventurer, a devil-may-care itinerant with a colourful and captivating turn of phrase. The thought of returning to his office in Nassau, where tedious official engagements awaited him, was irritating and unpalatable. The predictability of government life was never really to his taste. Far better to be holed up mysteriously in the land of darkness.

Journalism has taught me never to under-estimate the power of naivete, even if that naivete is contrived. Many times I have played the fool to penetrate the guard of awkward and obstructive sources, and while I have walked away with the information I required, they have been none the wiser. In Haiti, naivete helped me to secure one of the interviews of my life. And it left my more seasoned colleagues from big news organisations in New York spitting blood and paper-clips as they marvelled at my apparent audacity. In fact, I was only twenty-four at the time of the Knox trial and what happened was more the product of sheer guilelessness than cheek. Bill Cole of *The Nassau Guardian* and I were by far the youngest of the foreign press pack, and were treated as such by the British and American correspondents who congregated for the trial, most of whom dated back to the pre-war era, when they bashed out prose on battered Underwoods and sucked untipped cigarettes for intellectual sustenance. Somehow, working as a cabal, they managed to keep us away from the telex machines, assuming priority on the basis of their seniority and pulling every imaginable ploy to delay our transmissions in favour of their own. "We're five hours behind time-wise, old man," one insisted on reminding us. "London's desperate for this stuff. Can't get the bloody newsdesk off my back. Surely your readers can wait for your deathless prose."

In the evenings, after proceedings had ended for the day, we gathered at the Oloffson Hotel, the gingerbread structure made famous by *The Comedians* and always a favoured haunt of visiting journalists. It stood on a hillside overlooking Port-au-Prince and I recall even now, nearly forty years later, its quaint bar and open verandah, which was enveloped by scented tropical flora. In many ways, the Oloffson was symbolic of a slightly seedy, down-at-heel but strangely bewitching expatriate lifestyle. There were echoes of Casablanca: one expected Ingrid Bergmann, sucking hard on a Gaulois, to emerge from a back room, claim a high stool and cross her elegant legs. The hotel appeared to be chronically under-occupied, though the arrival of the press pack had clearly boosted business for at least a week or so, so a hint of restrained euphoria hung in the air. It was reminiscent of the good times, the Paul Magloire days when Truman Capote was in town, the days before Duvalier had planted his curse on an already blighted land. The consensus round the bar was that no-one, but no-one, would be allowed access to President Duvalier. The May 20 invasion had deepened his pananoia so markedly that he would not even appear on his palace balcony anymore, let alone venture on to the streets or allow foreigners through his tight security cordon. The old hacks, particularly, were pessimistic. "No use trying. He's too preoccupied with staying alive, poor old bugger," said one reporter, "Anyway, he hates the foreign press, absolutely loathes us. He blames us for half his troubles. He thinks our portrayal of his wickedness keeps the foreign aid away. He doesn't see himself as owing us any favours." As the Scotch whiskies went down apace, the mood became increasingly maudlin. But for Cole and me, the booze merely reinforced whatever chutzpah we possessed, convincing us that there was nothing to be lost in asking.

The following day, the pair of us were at the door of Gerard de Catalogne, the oddly ashen figure who edited *Le Nouveau Monde* and was the President's closest white confidante. The encounter was to yield remarkable results. De Catalogne was not a lovable character. For a start, he was a striking incongruity in Port-au-Prince, a white French scholar who had somehow insinuated his way into Duvalier's close circle. He came over as a professional sycophant, a man built to lap at presidential boots and do his master's bidding. In truth, he was Duvalier's adviser and translator, a perceived expert in the English language and, it seemed, a trusted retainer with an unerring sense of what best served his and the President's personal interests. As editor of *Le Nouveau Monde*, he was Haiti's number one apologist for whatever excesses Duvalier and his henchmen chose to inflict on the Haitian people. "We would like to see the President," we told him, secure in the belief that we would be turned down, but alert to the possibility that miracles can happen. His fat face registered a mixture of irritation and surprise. "Mmmmm," he said, "The President doesn't make himself available to visiting journalists, but I will certainly forward your request." Then de Catalogne's lumbering, baggy-suited figure turned away, prompting both of us to remark on his similarity to Alfred Hitchcock, the film producer. We felt we had done our duty, but were convinced nothing would come of it. We strolled off to court, where Knox's fate was hanging by a thread.

The following morning, the phone rang at the Castelhaiti Hotel, where Cole and I had been banished as lowest of the low. It was up the hill from the Oloffson, which had been commandeered by our senior colleagues, and a less beguiling place all round, so under-utilised that we appeared to be its only guests. "This is de Catalogne," said the languid, gallic voice at the other end, "I would like you to call at my office." Cole and I were ecstatic, believing our request was about to be approved. But our naivete was on display again when one of us, I forget who, let drop to the assembled foreign press corps that it was likely we had been granted an audience by Papa Doc. They insisted on being part of it, of course, and nothing we did could deter them. They put their case to de Catalogne, and he eventually agreed that they should be part of the proceedings. It was all of us, or none of us. So our initiative benefited the pack, depriving us of our exclusivity. Journalism's lessons are usually learned the hard way.

I was very conscious, walking through the palace gates, that a little bit of history was in the making. Like him or loathe him, I was about to meet one of the most fascinating people on earth, an unfathomable ghoul whose tiny frame offered little clue to the deep vaults of evil within. By any standard, Haiti's presidential residence is an impressive building. It dominates central Port-au-Prince with its impossibly white walls, like a jewel glinting amid the dross. We were led up the steps by wary Tontons Macoute militiamen. Army sentries eyed us with suspicion as we were escorted into the hall, and then up a staircase towards Duvalier's study. Inside, the palace was noticeably threadbare. There was little of apparent value, which was unsurprising, if one considers that successive Haitian presidents have viewed their tenure as opportunities for personal enrichment rather than a means of promoting the national interest. Genuine statesmanship has rarely featured in the history of Haitian governance. Many of the country's leaders fled for their lives, having taken their chances during short presidential reigns to enhance their foreign bank accounts.

The Duvaliers were to perpetuate that dishonourable tradition with greater alacrity than most. It was, therefore, inconceivable that much of value would be allowed to stand around the palace for long. Anything that was redeemable as hard cash would have been sold off years ago. Duvalier's inner guards were twitchy as we stood outside the President's study door. One Tonton watched us through heavy shades. An army officer was ramrod straight, one hand on his gun butt, as we were ushered into the tyrant's presence. There was a solemn hush as we shuffled into a room dominated by a massive mahogany desk. Behind the desk, myopically vulnerable in appearance, was a frail figure with a disproportionately large head. Heavy spectacles sat over a flared nose and gigantic lips. We were face-to-face with Papa Doc. As we were offered seats, a senior member of the press corps – a well-spoken British correspondent with an old-school penchant for protocol – stood to offer our collective appreciation. He thanked the President for his time, his consideration, his willingness to speak to us and practically everything else he could think of, all in the impeccable English of a privately-educated gentleman. There was an awkward silence as he sat down. Then Duvalier's soft voice asked: "And who will translate for the President of Haiti?" If protocol had been at least partly observed, it did not extend far enough for Papa Doc, who was now quietly insisting that the interview be conducted in French. There was a collective clearing of throats all round, with the eyes of reporters darting back and forth. The British are notoriously unschooled in foreign tongues, and there was no-one from the London press willing to chance his arm as an interpreter. My own extremely limited schoolroom French – *ferme la porte, sur le table, parlez-vous Francais, bonjour monsieur, joie de vivre* – flashed before my eyes as notebooks were scanned and rustled awkwardly. "Marquis, aren't you French by descent?" whispered one wag, desperate to break the deadlock. "Yes, as of 1680," I said, "But the family has forgotten the language after three centuries of exile."

An American, a lank-haired agency correspondent with saturnine looks, then stood and offered his services, much to the relief of all. For the best part of an hour, he was our link man in a rambling press conference with the President. In many ways, it was among the most enlightening hours of my life. In terms of disclosure, the exchange was unremarkable. There were occasional platitudes, routine courtesies, a few minor news points to hang on to, but for the most part this was not a momentous encounter from a journalistic viewpoint. Duvalier was, however, a revelation in himself, and that for me was the enthralling aspect of this singular experience. Throughout the chat – and it was conducted largely along informal lines – this strange little man was in expansive mood, laughing frequently, answering questions directly and, after the initial awkwardness, appearing to be quite enjoying the occasion. Two things about his physical presence were instantly noticeable, his signature specs and his unusually large hands, which wafted before him like palm fronds. In some respects, Papa Doc was almost avuncular in manner. The compassionate country doctor of old was presumably still there, though by now buried under a welter of myth and mystery. To retain power, he had cultivated a spectral dimension, encouraging his people to believe that he was much more than merely a man. Sartorially, he was likened to Baron Samedi, a mythical symbol of death, and Papa Doc did nothing to discourage such an association, realising that perception is often more powerful than reality. The presidential father-figure was one aspect of his persona, but there was a good deal more to him than that.

As I sat there, watching his every gesture, I reminded myself that this physically slight figure had personally supervised the execution of nineteen Army officers only a few months before, and had routinely consulted the severed heads of his opponents, in an effort to tap into their intelligence. He was influenced deeply by the witchcraft rites of Africa, the bloodstained voodoo drums, the biting off of chickens' heads, the calling up of sinister spirits. This was no ordinary man, but one whose psyche had been fashioned by Africa, a distant voyage away. To the average western white, he was the embodiment of an alien and barely comprehensible culture. Blackness for Duvalier was the foundation of his political philosophy. In a country like Haiti, where race and social standing were entwined like tree roots, and where gradations of colour were defining motifs, his blackness was crucial to any understanding of the man and his presidency. There was, undeniably, a powerful pride in his Haitian heritage, an eagerness to underscore his country's unique place in negro history. There was, too, an attempt at international understanding, a recognition that Haiti could not exist alone but was part of a much bigger Latin American picture. Interestingly, his desk bore photographs of the Pope, President Lyndon Johnson, Martin Luther King and Chiang-Kai Shek. In their different ways, each was potently symbolic; the Pope as head of Haiti's very large Roman Catholic community, President Johnson as the great provider (US aid was crucial to Haiti's survival), Martin Luther King as the liberator of black Americans and Chiang-Kai Shek as a committed anti-communist. One assumes all were Duvalier heroes. Together, they certainly offered at least an approximation of his political, philosophical and religious outlook.

Above all else, Papa Doc wanted to be known as a symbol of Right-Wing resistance to communist ambitions. Apart from expressing confidence in the Bahamas Premier, Lynden Pindling, and his efforts to bring the activities of armed Haitian exiles under control, Duvalier said little of note, except to reiterate what he had said many times before: that the so-called 'rebels' were no threat to him, and that the Haitian people were behind him all the way. The President was a strange mixture of vulnerability and indestructibility, the former manifest in his paranoia, the latter at least partly mythical. But on this day, he was a model of measured calm. He reminded us that he had survived eight armed invasions in eleven years. The rebels, he said, were wasting their time. "I do not think their threats are to be taken very seriously," he said. The government was strong, he added, and used to such happenings, as were the Haitian people and their leader. By this time, Papa Doc's brutal excesses were well-known, yet he tried hard to maintain an illusion of affinity with his people. Whatever outsiders thought — and especially imperialist intellectuals like Graham Greene — he and his countrymen were in this together, barricaded against a hostile and mischievous world. Accepting that most raids originated in the United States, he said: 'I don't like interference in the internal affairs of Haiti.'

All the time, when it came to relations with Uncle Sam, he was forced to steer a precarious course between resigned acceptance and outright disapproval of Washington's strategy towards his beleaguered little nation. Though keen to maintain Haiti's political independence, he was forced into accepting the economic imperatives of a backward Third World country in the Americas. Like it or not, Duvalier needed United States approval. The nation's survival rested upon it. During our interview, he betrayed none of this, but it was implicit in everything he said. Duvalier also explained his decision to free the May 20 invaders, saying he hoped it would serve as an example to leaders of the free world, and especially America with its racial and political problems.

Of Haiti itself, and specifically its overwhelming social difficulties, Duvalier said relatively little. But what he did say indicated a predictable buoyancy, with boasts about the number of schools constructed, increased per capita income, and improvements in housing and personal possessions. He wanted the world to believe that Haiti was not as bad as American analysts had suggested, and that this supposedly moribund land was now in a state of resurgence. The plight of David Knox, sitting in his cell only a few hundred yards away, was clearly not a priority for the President as he wrestled with his country's economic woes. The case was touched upon only briefly, but he made it clear that the matter was strictly for the military tribunal and nothing to do with him, though he revealed that the prisoner's fate was ultimately his to decide. His knowledge of the proceedings extended only to the press reports, which he was reading every day, he said. The fact that Knox was the Bahamas Director of Information did not affect the President's relations with Mr Pindling or the new Bahamas Government. "I extend once more my feelings of deepest respect to Mr Pindling and his enlightened leadership of the Bahama Islands," he said, adding that he hoped the country would enjoy the greatest prosperity because "for the first time a coloured man has been elected by a majority of the Bahamian people as their responsible leader."

When the President called a halt to the meeting, we stood in line to shake hands and receive three Duvalier books, one of them a tribute to Martin Luther King. The most interesting by far, though, was his 'little red book' of political thoughts, signed in my presence with a flourish and, interestingly, the kind of final dissecting slash which graphologists regard as evidence of suicidal tendencies. The volume was his answer to Chairman Mao's book of the same name. It remains one of my most treasured mementoes of a long career in journalism. Before we left, I noted something which probably gave a greater insight into the nature of Papa Doc and his cruel regime than a million press conferences would have conveyed. Behind the vase of blood-red roses on his desk was a pending tray, in which lay a heavy revolver. The gentle, amused affability was but one facet of this complex character. Another was his obsessive paranoia, ever-present if well-disguised. As we left the palace, a twinkling electric sign across the road spelled out the reality of Haitian democracy. 'Francois Duvalier, President a Vie,' it said. President-for-Life. No argument, no dissent. A beggar with only half an arm and half a leg scuttled like a land crab across my path. This was Haiti uncensored.

Knox, meanwhile, was faced with the task of unburdening himself of the MI5 'connection' which was so much a part of the prosecution case. This was a particularly troubling period for me because the interpreter, John Pickering, laboured through my prose in heavily accented English, dwelling on my scathing references to the Duvalier regime. He quoted from one *Tribune* article which attributed information to Nassau journalist Paul Bower, who first disclosed the possibility that Knox was under arrest in Haiti and floated theories about his being linked with the May 20 invasion. There is no doubt that Bower's speculation at the time was entirely innocent, but it had now taken on an unsettling significance as Knox fought for his life. The prosecutor, Romain, made much of the intelligence connection, producing a *Miami Herald* story by Latin America editor, Don Bohning referring to Knox's stay in Cyprus during the Enosis troubles and his work for the British Government.

As the case against Knox gathered momentum, The Tribune's editor-publisher, Sir Etienne Dupuch, felt moved to dampen down the MI5 speculation and sent a cable directly to President Duvalier. He accepted that the MI5 reference had been carried in *The Tribune* and that the source had been a close friend of Knox. But he said he was now satisfied the information was untrue and that Knox had never been associated with any British intelligence organisation. To undo the damage further, I volunteered to appear before the tribunal as a witness, but this was considered unwise by Knox's British advisers, who suggested the less said the better. It was left to Knox himself to counter the charges. In any other country, Romain's emotionalism would have been considered good grounds for appeal, but the tribunal members seemed unfazed by his flagrant verbal abuse of Knox, who showed admirable restraint in the face of the prosecutor's outrageously provocative behaviour. At one point, Knox claimed he was beaten with a baton while in police custody. Romain took this as an affront to Haiti, giving the impression that physical abuse was alien to the government's way of doing things. Compared to the excesses of the Tontons Macoute, a mere baton beating was minor fare, but Romain was claiming the moral high ground. "We are soldiers of a small nation, but we are men of honour," he said.

Throughout proceedings, Knox's principal problem was to repel the 'intelligence' claims and the false allegation that he was a South African citizen. His wife, Phillippa, sent documents to Haiti which she found among his belongings in Nassau. These appeared to confirm his British status and his dislike of South Africa's apartheid regime. Among them was a statement written by Knox in August, 1965, which was attached to his application form for the Bahamas post. It said he left South Africa "because I could not live under a government whose policies offended my personal views on multi-racialism." The statement added that he had given up a promising career in the country of his birth because of his strongly-held views.

For some days, the Knox case had made news in the London papers, but on August 21, 1968, something happened which shifted the international spotlight. Soviet tanks moved into Wenceslas Square in Prague to crush the liberalisation programme of Czech leader, Alexander Dubcek. It was the first major challenge to Soviet authority since the Hungarian uprising twelve years before, and it was to have far-reaching consequences. Dubcek was arrested and for a time was thought to be dead. His 'Prague Spring' move towards loosening the Soviets' authoritarian stranglehold on his country was to become a defining event of the late 1960s, along with the Civil Rights Movement in the United States, the assassinations of Martin Luther King and Robert Kennedy, and the first successful Moon landing the following year. Knox, a pathetic romantic in a sad predicament, was now no more than a minor diversion amid the great events of the day. As a result, all the 'big-time' correspondents flew off, ordered by their newsdesks to redeploy, and I was left in Port-au-Prince with Bill Cole and a small group of local reporters. The world's press had diverted its gaze, but the climax of the Knox story was still to come.

In Nassau, fears grew that Knox would die before a Haitian firing squad. Though the evidence against him was extremely weak and purely circumstantial, it seemed he was up against far more than a court of law and the vagaries of the Napoleonic Code. The main dynamic of the prosecution case was prejudice, a prejudice so deeply buried in the Haitian psyche that no amount of mitigating evidence could or would make any impression. Romain was the embodiment of this prejudice, a man whose anti-white feelings were almost palpable. Knox's plight was worsened by two factors: the apparent disappearance of the back-street surgeon, Dr Samedi, who gave him his facial scars, and the refusal by the Haitian Foreign Ministry of permission for British diplomat, Charles Sanderson to appear as a witness. This meant that the tribunal would not be granted incontrovertible proof of Knox's status as a British subject, so Romain would be allowed to continue his abuse of the defendant's supposed South African sympathies. As photographs of Knox appeared in *The Tribune* showing him looking ten years older than when he left Nassau three months earlier, his wife was moved to speak out on his behalf, again ridiculing the MI5 allegations and berating the press for perpetuating them in print. "David's career is now completely ruined," she told The Tribune's social reporter, Nancy Savage. "Our home may be gone, our future, all because of this. But what I can't understand is why the British press are still persisting with the MI5 thing. True, they have denied it over and over again, but they have played into the hands of the Haitians. The story could literally cause David's death." She and her husband had planned to go to Madeira after Knox had finished his contract in Nassau and take a long holiday. "That was before this whole mess came up. If that MI5 story had not been brought up, it would merely have been a case of diplomatic negotiations to free David and our future would have been all right. Now the Portuguese authorities may not wish us to live in Madeira and we will have no home at all." Then she added, dramatically: "It is a foregone conclusion what Haiti will do. It will be the death sentence. I don't think they will kill him, but I am prepared for it. David is the victim of a set of circumstances. It was very foolish of him to go at this time and you can't really blame the Haitians for being suspicious of him." However, it was clear from her *Tribune* interview that Mrs Knox never received the letters her husband was supposed to have sent from Haiti. The one referring to the 'machine gun distance' between his hotel and the palace was found unfinished in his hotel room. "It was just a way of speaking," she said, "I could say I was within balustrade jumping distance of Buckingham Palace. It doesn't mean anything, but this was meat and drink to the Haitians. I have heard so much rubbish about this that I am beginning to discount everything I hear. At first I was appalled and frightened. Now I am mad. The horrible part is that I can't fight back." Then she said: "It's all so silly. David isn't interested in Haitian politics. He isn't interested in anybody's politics." With reference to suspected beatings of her husband, Mrs Knox was vague but fearful. "I don't like to think about it. I hope to God it's not true." She said she was worried about his health because she knew he was not eating and under great stress. "He must have been through hell. I'm worried about food and the sanitary conditions, but I understand he has a room to himself. He must be physically very uncomfortable." For weeks following Knox's incarceration, she had maintained a dignified if inexplicable silence. But she claimed both she and British Government officials were concerned that loose words might cut across any diplomatic efforts on his behalf. For the best part of a year, Knox and his wife had lived virtually separate lives while she searched for accommodation in Madeira. "But there is no rift between us," she said. She told *The Tribune* that she couldn't stand the climate in either the Bahamas or the Seychelles, where Knox had been information officer in the past. Madeira was to be their final bolt-hole, a fragrant mid-Atlantic hideaway where they could follow peaceful and unhurried lives.

As the trial moved steadily forward, it became clear that the Haitians were well-briefed on rebel activities in the Bahamas. It appeared that the guerrilla network was well-established and reasonably well-organised. At Burrows Cay, off eastern Grand Bahama, part-time soldiers had been preparing for action, using the bush as a rifle range. Duvalier had learned to despise the efforts of those amateur combatants who sought to depose him, but they lacked nothing in resolution and commitment. In fact, their failure was probably in their idealism, which seemed to exceed their strategic expertise as freedom fighters.

In court, Knox appealed to the tribunal's humanity and compassion, a forlorn hope in a country where life was considered dispensable, and where compassion was nigh non-existent. He said that for 'an act of harmless folly' he had spent nearly three months in prison, almost certainly lost his job, and rendered unlikely the possibility of future employment. His remarks came during a 90-minute statement in which he admitted obtaining facial scars through 'cosmetic surgery', which he sought for personal and private reasons. His attempts to enlist the diplomat Sanderson as a witness, have The Tribune's denials of his MI5 connections admitted as evidence, and bring Dr Samedi into court to support his version of events were all unsuccessful. Knox was also denied a chance to interview the man who had allegedly seen him at a rebel training camp. So, by the eleventh day of hearings, Knox was effectively alone, caught up in a legal process he barely understood in a country whose thought processes were totally alien to those of developed nations. He was at the tribunal's mercy.

To friends and associates back in Nassau, Knox's evidence about facial scarring seemed incomprehensible. It was difficult for them to square the urbane David of their acquaintance with the sad character in the dock, who was admitting a penchant for strange fetishes which involved cosmetic scarring of his face. At one point, he admitted that he was too embarrassed to broach the scarring operation with any Nassau surgeon. Knox confessed to offering the Haitian police chief, Frederic Arty, a hundred dollars following his arrest because "my mind was in a panic and I seized on anything which I thought would get me out of this nightmare." Again, he referred to being manacled and beaten with a baton during interrogation. "I wish to state here with emphasis that I do not consider that I was interrogated in circumstances of torture. It would be untruthful for me to say that. I consider, however, that I was interviewed in circumstances of interrogation, but I am not complaining about this. For all I know, this may be standard practice." Knox added: "I have no complaint about the treatment I received at the hands of the police. I make the point of mentioning these facts, because I would like the court to see, in proper perspective, the circumstances in which I made many of the statements, which Colonel Arty said in his testimony were unconnected and conflicting. There I was in the hands of the police for the first time in my life, kept under an armed guard and apart from being deprived of my sleep, I could not sleep anyway, being taken out and interrogated nightly. And in those circumstances, Mr President, I could not produce reasoned and logical answers."

While under arrest, Knox wrote to his wife, asking her not to send money, which he referred to as 'do-ray-me', a slang term he claimed was in common use in Europe. The Haitians had interpreted this as code. Some days later, he claimed, he was taken to the military hospital to have stitches removed from his face. "By this time the diet of restaurant food I was receiving stopped and I was being fed on crushed maize and boiled rice and water. I ate one meal in three days." Knox said on June 16 his diet suddenly reverted to better food, and six days later, he was called to the police chief's office, where he saw former Haitian Vice-Consul in Nassau, Jean Massena. "During the period of interrogation, I had constantly asked to see the British Consul, which request was refused. I then asked police if they would get in touch with Mr Massena who would vouch for me. So I was very pleased when I saw him. I was most surprised, however, when Mr Massena asserted that until I had entered his office, he had never seen me. He did not know my name and he did not know my post. He told the Chief of Police he knew everyone working in the Bahamas Government and that if I had joined the Bahamas Government, I must have done so while he was on leave a month ago. I was most surprised because I have already said I knew him well. I had seen him at several public functions and I was under the impression I had had a drink with him in a group of people. He denied this, so I accept that. But had our roles been reversed and had someone asked me if I knew Mr Massena, I would have said immediately I know him very well."

On June 28, Knox said, he was transferred from police headquarters to the National Penitentiary. He also underwent a four-day interrogation by a Justice of the Peace. On July 12, he was taken to the Palace of Justice, where he was interviewed by a judge in chambers. On both occasions, he signed depositions. Earlier, Knox covered events leading up to his trip to Haiti and admitted he had not told friends and colleagues of his intention, for fear that they would try to veto the idea. As he was in his last year with the Bahamas Government, he thought he would probably never see this part of the world again. So he tried to visit places he wanted to see in the Caribbean region. "Early in May, I decided to do this," he said. "I am one of perhaps thirty Englishmen of my rank or above under contract to the Bahamas Government. I had seen Mr Massena on many occasions at official functions. I had seen him at a nightclub in town and I knew perfectly well who he was. It never occurred to me for a second that he did not know who I was." About May 25, he said he became aware of what happened in Haiti on May 20, so phoned Massena to ask if it was safe for him to travel. "He assured me everything was calm and told me that many tourists were going to Haiti and I had nothing to worry about. Meanwhile, I had not told my friends that I was proposing to do this at this time. I thought they would have vetoed the idea and I did not want to postpone my visit because I was already committed for my next long weekend, and thereafter

I was to start a new job in the government which I expected would not permit me to get away."

He explained 'cosmetic surgery' as something which happened every day in the United States and Europe. "People have the shapes of their noses changed and they have their faces lifted and pay thousands of dollars for this. The operation that I wanted was much more superficial. I wanted a couple of small cuts made on my face. Because of the nature of the operation, I was embarrassed to ask a doctor in my home town – the town where I was working – to do this. On the aeroplane going to Haiti, I turned over in my mind the possibility of finding a doctor in Haiti who would do this. Then I half-dismissed the idea. I thought it would be difficult in the time I had and my thoughts at the time I landed were that if I found a doctor who would do this I would have it done and if necessary I would cut short my stay and go home." Knox said he arranged for a taxi-driver to organise an appointment for the operation. This led to his meeting Dr Bontemps, who refused to scar his face. Earlier, he had told the driver he was prepared to pay no more than $50 for the operation. In his brief meeting with Bontemps, the doctor asked 'what I had got' but Knox replied: "It is not something I have got, it is something I want. I told him the reason for my visit and as he said in this court he refused to undertake this. He pointed to his certificate and said it was against his professional ethics." Afterwards, the driver took him to the smaller, less impressive establishment of Dr Samedi, who performed the operation after giving Knox two injections.

Realising the scars would make him conspicuous, Knox decided to leave the country and to tell friends he had been injured in a car accident in Jamaica. He accepted this was 'an elaborate and clumsy lie.' It was while he was waiting at the hotel for a plane home that the police called. Right up until the time he went to the police chief's office, Knox claimed he thought police were concerned about his welfare as a result of seeing the bandages on his face. Knox admitted telling Arty he had fallen down while drunk, but had no complaint to make as it was a minor matter. Minutes later, Dr Bontemps walked in and Knox then realised why he was being detained. He explained to Arty what he had done to his face. Later, the driver and Dr Samedi were brought in. After asking to see Arty alone, Knox admitted offering him a hundred dollars to drop the matter. Knox said he was later stripped down to his trousers, shirt, and boots without laces or socks while his possessions were examined. He was given a bed, chair and food that was "edible but not very appetising."

In my *Tribune* report of August 27, 1968, Knox was quoted as saying the scarring was an 'adornment', adding: "I confess to an idiosyncrasy and a vanity, but I have never thought of resembling any specific person." This was in answer to Romain's questioning. "Did you wish them to look like war wounds, a gangster or hired killer, or a spy?" he asked. Knox replied: "I'm afraid I had never really thought about that aspect of it." As Knox's courtroom ordeal continued, the newspaper *Le Nouveau Monde* continued to snipe from the sidelines. A front-page article by Haitian congressman, Antoine Herard described the defendant as 'Knox the Fox' and said his demeanour was 'distant, phlegmatic and cold.' Unable to resist more racist slurs, he added: "He is basically a native of the land of apartheid. One can see without difficulty his repressed rage at being judged by negroes." More comparisons were drawn with Kim Philby, the British traitor, who was depicted as Knox's inspiration. "In any case, he chose the wrong field of operations as regards the free Republic of Haiti, accustomed since 1804 to looking the white man in the face. We have no need to feel in his presence any sense of fear, respect or even terror."

As a committed non-racist, Knox must have been hurt by this constant harping on the black-white theme. Yet it was no more than a reflection of Haiti's inner contortions. It was a land whose nationhood was wrought from the fires of ethnic conflict. In his final plea to the tribunal, Romain returned to the racial theme again, hammering his table and shouting excitedly that Haiti was not a colony or protectorate. "He should be condemned and the verdict and sentence he deserves is the death penalty," he yelled. If Knox felt uneasy at this point, he didn't show it. He gazed fixedly ahead, his eyes wide open, betraying nothing. From the courtyard outside wafted discordant music from a military brass band performing its daily drill. Romain, sucking at a cigarette and adjusting his gunbelt, claimed Knox's own statement had amounted to a confession. After more questioning by the chairman, Jacques Laroche, the prosecution rested its case. Knox was now left to the vagaries of Haitian justice, such that it was.

CHAPTER 4

DEATH SENTENCE

Having heard my own stories cited as prosecution evidence against Knox, the sentencing phase of his trial was something I did not relish. Having known him in his professional capacity for a couple of years, and liked him at a superficial level, I also felt something of a personal involvement in his fate. The tribunal's verdict, though expected, was no less shocking when it came. Laroche announced that Knox had been found guilty of all six charges against him, five of spying and one of endangering the external security of Haiti. He would, in accordance with Haitian law, be put to death by firing squad. At this precise moment, I recall Knox looking straight across the courtroom at me. I could not decide whether it was an accusing glare or an expression of fear. Certainly, he seemed slightly stunned. Suddenly, having shrunk inside his suit since his arrest three months before, he looked incredibly delicate and vulnerable, a man at the mercy of an alien culture, with no expectation of the basic decencies. Knox, standing erect with his hands by his side, was immediately handcuffed from behind by armed guards and pushed down into the chair behind the bridge table, which had served as the dock for the duration of the three-week trial. There was an unseemly scrum as Haiti's veil slipped. Suddenly, he was surrounded by soldiers. Laroche said he would be taken to a place of execution in Port-au-Prince and be put to death at the convenience of authorities responsible for the process. There was something disturbingly unedifying about the whole thing. Having conducted what passed for a trial, certainly in the eyes of its own authorities, Haiti now felt justified in going ahead as it pleased, in disposing of Knox. The crowd in the sweltering courtroom was in a state of excited agitation. Announcement of the sentence brought forth a collective gasp. As Knox stared fixedly through hollow eyes, an untidy melee developed around him, the soldiers and onlookers babbling crazily in Creole.

The courtroom charade conducted by Romain would, in fact, have been amusing had the implications not been so serious. In his final address, he claimed Knox was sent to Haiti five days after the May 20 invasion, to lay plans for another raid aimed at destroying the National Palace and killing President Duvalier. The prosecutor offered not a single shred of evidence to support this contention, but he pursued it with passion, saying Knox was 'in collusion' with the raid organisers. The racist Knox, he said, was involved in a plot to destroy the palace 'whose ruins were to bury our chief and his family.' Claiming that Knox had taken a hotel room near the palace to witness the culmination of the plot, Romain said: "The one we have before us will soon, I am sure, learn to his fate what this people keeps in store for all those who dare tramp upon its liberty." Referring to Knox's bid to bribe the police chief, Romain said: "He does not believe there is such a thing as an honest negro", then added menacingly: "Accused, you have made a mistake." Romain said people like Knox were the plague of humanity, sowing discord in the world and arming brothers against brothers. He described his forebears as 'smugglers of gold and adventurers of diamonds' who got rich in places 'where our race brothers are used as common cattle.' Knox, he said, was like the author, Graham Greene — 'another intelligence agent with racist thoughts.' Then, referring to Haitian refugees sent back to Haiti from the Bahamas, Romain said: "Knox has not been mistreated. He has not had the fate of our compatriots arrested in Nassau who come back to us with marks on their feet and marks made by the manacles of their captivity. He has never had the fate of those who come back in the holds of ships as in bygone times, in the times of the slave trade. He was well accommodated, well-fed and his every wish was satisfied."

In his final plea to the tribunal, Knox himself had admitted acting "extremely foolishly", adding: "I can understand why my actions should have been regarded with suspicion, but the fact remains that these were acts of folly." He said the facial scars were the result of 'a strange vanity, an obsession' which led to him being caught up in a web of circumstance. Admitting he was now ashamed of his actions, Knox said: "It was an act of great foolishness, but it was not a criminal act. I have committed no crime against the Republic of Haiti, only against myself." His supposed connections with MI5 were, he said, "myths and fairy tales" with no supporting evidence except two newspaper articles and a piece of writing about British intelligence. He said one article in *The Tribune* had been disclaimed by its publisher.

Knox said again that it was unfortunate he could not confront his accuser, Raymond Toussaint, who claimed to have seen him at a rebel training camp in the Bahamas. Toussaint, he said, had nothing to lose and everything to gain by offering such information because it would 'lighten his load' with the Haitian authorities. Describing Toussaint as a traitor to his country, Knox said if precise allegations regarding his alleged visits to rebel bases had been produced, he would have been able to rebut them with affidavits. But this had not been done. His speech ended thus: "I know that I will get a fair hearing from this court and pray that the Almighty will guide you in your deliberations." Romain, still barely able to control his indignation, ended his final tirade by saying: "I denounce David John Knox as a member of the international mafia." Interestingly, this was the first mention made of the Mob and its possible involvement in the plot. Once again, Romain offered no evidence and was not challenged to explain himself.

Once the death penalty had been handed down, Britain began diplomatic efforts to save Knox's life. British Ambassador, Dalton Murray, who flew into Port-au-Prince from Kingston for the end of the trial, said he was in contact with London to decide their next move, and President Duvalier had already promised to review the proceedings. He was hoping for a meeting to convey the British Government's views. Knox, back in his cell, was now left to contemplate the appalling situation in which he found himself. For me, there were many mixed feelings. Guilt, perhaps, at having written so extensively about Knox's supposed MI5 connections, when they were to have such serious ramifications. Pity, at seeing this once proud and noble figure humiliated by the odious Romain. Anger that Haiti had found him guilty, having failed to construct anything resembling an adequate case against him. Regret, that I was preparing to fly out of Haiti to leave Knox to his fate.

A week earlier, I had travelled to Francois Duvalier International Airport to see off my Nassau colleague, Bill Cole. His newspaper had decided proceedings were moving too slowly and pulled him out of Haiti, leaving me as the only foreign reporter in Port-au-Prince. Considering I continued to be under the constant watch of the Tontons Macoute, this was not a happy time for me. I remember standing outside the airport fence and watching the Pan Am jet lift off, sweeping northwards against a backdrop of mountains. I continued to watch it until it was no more than a speck in the evening sky. Then I turned and walked back to my cab, a down-at-heel American limo with wired-down bonnet. The driver, MP, so called because he had once been a driver for American occupying forces, and specifically the military police, looked at me with solemn eyes. He was a man who had known hard times, but somehow he maintained a trace of good humour in this hellish land. He finally managed a smile. "Back to the hotel," I said. The car bumped over pitted roads, through the malodorous confusion of downtown Port-au-Prince, then up the slope to Petionville. There the air was fresher, and sometimes even fragrant from cascades of flowers. It was where Haiti's elite lived, far above the wretched hordes. From my hotel room now, I contemplated once more the city vista, the palace and the looming hulk of the Dessalines Barracks being consumed by dusk. Somewhere down there, I thought, sits poor old Knox, awaiting death. Sad, so sad.

CHAPTER 5

A TORTURED LAND

Children born amid trauma often live traumatic lives. The same is true of nations, and Haiti's birth was more difficult than most. Perhaps therein lies the key to its predicament. Before the first voyage of Columbus in 1492, the island, later to become known as Hispaniola, was home to bronze-skinned Arawak-Carib tribesmen of a race spread throughout the Americas. They lived simple lives as hunters and gatherers amid spectacular beauty in a land of deep green valleys and towering hills. When Columbus first stepped ashore in the New World at San Salvador in the Bahamas, a group of similar folk was on the shoreline to greet him. They were Lucayans, a peace-loving tribe driven north by the more hostile Caribs. When the explorer saw what San Salvador had to offer — namely, nothing — he took their advice and sailed south, to a mountainous land their forefathers had once called home. Like all the Bahama Islands, San Salvador was and is little more than a scrub-covered rock. It had virtually no soil, no rivers, hardly a tree worthy of the name. For a man on a mission to unearth new wealth for his sponsors, it represented poor reward for a perilous voyage on a seemingly endless ocean. Despite the obvious difficulties of communication, Columbus managed to convey to the Lucayans his intentions, to find a precious yellow metal that would represent riches in Europe. They pointed south, beyond the end of the Bahamas chain, where he would find a large island of impressive vistas and soaring peaks. So he and his disgruntled crew moved on, picking their way through the Bahamas' shallow seas, stopping occasionally to feast off whatever creatures they could find on the scattered reefs, until they reached the sixty-mile stretch of ocean that would lead to Hispaniola. Even from far out, the island appeared more promising than the Bahamas, a necklace of honey-coloured rocks now left slumbering in his wake. From the horizon its mountains loomed high against vast Caribbean skies, its forested slopes evidence of the kind of abundant fertility the Bahamas lacked. The explorer sensed he had found what he had come for, and so it proved, for Hispaniola was to become the most prosperous colonial outpost in the New World, a treasure that would be coveted and fought over by all the great European powers.

Today, Columbus's voyage is viewed by some Caribbean people with mixed feelings. The great explorer was, they say, also the great exploiter, harbinger of a colonial era many would like to forget. His voyage of discovery, they contend, opened up enormous new opportunities for his Spanish sponsors, but also heralded the doom of an entire way of life, as lived by the Indian tribes, and spawned a long era of systematic and brutal exploitation, not only of the Indians themselves, but the thousands of Africans who would later be brought to the Americas as slaves. Until the arrival of the Genoese adventurer, the Caribbean islands were home to sparsely-clad tribes who lived in tight communities, their existence sustained by the natural bounty of land and sea. On land, they speared birds, wild hogs and alligators. At sea, and from shallow canoes, they harvested snapper, jacks and grouper, prized produce of warm tropical waters. The dominant tribal group, the Caribs, were comparatively aggressive, but the painted men who greeted Columbus showed nought but goodwill to the strangers from distant lands who staggered ashore. When one of Columbus's three-ship flotilla hit offshore rocks, the tribesmen helped to rescue the crewmen and their possessions, dragging boxes of provisions up the beach. It was a gesture of natural friendliness which proved to be ill-rewarded. From that day forth, their very existence was under threat.

The Bahamian Lucayans, who had fled north from the Caribs around 900 AD, probably chose to stay on their barren rocks because there was nothing there that anyone else could possibly want. For the best part of 600 years, they lived blamelessly on the sunny archipelago, using simple dug-out canoes to fish, and relaxing between labours in hammocks, the one lasting contribution they made to mankind. In directing Columbus towards the mineral riches of the south, they put their own existence in peril, too, for the Spanish marauders who were to follow in the explorer's path saw them only as free labour for the plantations and the mines.

Within a few years of Columbus's landing, the Lucayans had been coerced into slave labour in Hispaniola, a period of sustained wickedness during which they were whipped and beaten into extinction by their Spanish masters. Before that, however, they were coerced into Christianity, too, the Spanish brandishing crosses as well as swords as they annexed the islands, dragooning the natives into the faith, ravishing their women, starving those who showed resistance, and working the men to death in the frenetic search for mineral wealth. Gratuitous murder was commonplace and defectors were rounded up by bloodhounds. In less than two decades, some 400,000 people were eliminated in what remains a searing indictment of early colonialism. It was the tragic decline of the Indians which ultimately sparked the African slave trade.

The Caribs and Lucayans were unused to the fatiguing demands of mines and fields and succumbed in droves to overwork and ill-treatment. As Hispaniola yielded up its natural wealth, more labour was needed to work in the searing tropical heat and cruel humidity. The Dominican priest, Las Casas, appalled at the looming extinction of the entire Indian population within a generation, came up with a solution: the mass transportation of tougher negro stock from Africa. The Spanish King, Charles V, responded with authorisation of the first consignment (some 15,000 people) to Hispaniola, in 1517, and effectively launched a trade that was to have a resounding impact on humanity for more than three hundred years, and whose reverberations are still being felt today. In so doing, he also laid the framework for Haiti's current plight.

Franck Romain, Knox's tormentor in court, was unable to contain the bitterness he felt because, like so many of his kind, he sensed deeply the indignity heaped upon his people in the past. Race distinction came to define Haiti, the strained relationships between black and white fired by the excesses of a callous plantocracy. The Europeans' exploitation of slave labour bred a resentment that has never died. Once the bountiful nature of Hispaniola was well-known, it was inevitable that it would become a coveted prize among other colonial powers. The original Spanish settlement in southern Hispaniola attracted the French to the isle of Tortuga, off the northern coast, and the ubiquitous English on their voyages of acquisition. For three decades, the superpowers of their day wrestled for ascendancy, with the British colony of Jamaica eventually drawn into the mix, as raiding parties plundered the two islands.

In 1695, Spain and France reached an accommodation. The Treaty of Ryswick laid down the matrix for modern Hispaniola, with France being granted the western third of this turbulent isle, Spain taking the other two-thirds. To this day, Haiti's native Creole is based on French, while the Dominican Republic is a Spanish-speaking nation. The border is a clear indication of their respective fortunes: from the air, the ravaged, degraded landscape of once-beautiful Haiti is in stark contrast to the relatively fertile slopes of the Dominican hills. While the Spanish territory has established a future for itself, Haiti has staggered from crisis to crisis, a long line of exploitative dictatorships interspersed by periods of foreign occupation and military rule. Papa Doc was but one of those dictators. Unlike most, however, he learned to retain power in a country where it could never be taken for granted. He and his son, Jean-Claude, were to hang on for nearly thirty years. Many, if not most, of today's Haitian blacks are thought to have originated in west Africa, and specifically the area of coast stretching from Guinea to the Congo. This was but one of the territories from which the slave traders herded blacks, in their thousands, into congested sailing ships for hellish voyages to the New World. When Haitians today talk of their origins, it is Guinea and the Congo to which they most frequently refer, and they appear to draw sustenance from the cultural connection.

Towards the end of the 18th century, slavers traversed the entire sub-Saharan region of Africa for strong, black labour to fuel the burgeoning economy of Hispaniola and other Caribbean territories. From Haiti came a short, deeply black breed whose incipient volatility was ultimately to fashion their future. It was to earn them comparatively early release from the white man's yoke, but also propelled them into two centuries of butchery and chaos. The indignity, humiliation and degradation suffered by the slaves are beyond question. The brutal aspects of the trade are not in doubt. From the dark interior of Africa, the blacks were chained together in columns and marched often long distances to the sea. Many died en route, diseased or exhausted. They were probably the fortunate ones. Aboard ship, they were shackled in horrific conditions in the holds, swilling around in their own vomit and excrement as the vessels fought the Atlantic waves. The fear and anxiety among these poor people were unimaginable, tethered as they were in rolling, filthy hulks which were alien to their lives in every respect. They knew nothing of the sea, or the ships that plied between the continents, for theirs was a landbound existence, lived on the hot open plains and in the dripping wet jungles of Africa. They were also from a strong tribal tradition, a social system based on mutual support and close family units. Suddenly, brutally, they were wrenched from their roots and sent on perilous voyages over hostile seas. Parents and children were parted, siblings split asunder, grandparents abandoned, as they became mere chattels in pitiless transactions. On the high seas, they perished in droves, either through disease, ill-treatment or suffocation.

The originators of the horror are to this day the subjects of protracted debate. Propaganda has intruded into the argument and two distinct schools of thought now dominate: those who believe the traders, motivated by avarice, hunted down the blacks, decimating the tribal system in the process, and those who say slaves were always part of the African tradition, the spoils of tribal wars, and that chieftains connived in the mass transportation of their people for gain. The pro-slavery propagandists said the slaves were delivered from purgatory, the constant butchery and bloodletting among native people all the way down the Congo coast and round the Cape of Good Hope to Mozambique. Africans were portrayed as little more than savages, mutually antagonistic, uncontrolled and cannibalistic. By hauling them into stinking ships and transporting them to the Caribbean for a life of unremitting labour, the traders were, they said, saving them from the horrendous reality of their own continent. At the time, communications being what they were, their arguments went unchallenged in the debating chambers of civilised nations. It was several decades before consciences were so challenged that the trade was halted, but by then irreparable harm had been done. The slaves and their forebears never forgave their tormentors.

Today, that resentment resonates in many Caribbean territories, but nowhere with such intensity as in Haiti, which has never recovered from its early traumas. The traders themselves were engaged in a high-risk occupation. Although, for the most part, they were untroubled by conscience, they lived in constant fear of insurrection aboard ship. With often recalcitrant crews, and holds full of vibrant humanity anxious to be somewhere else, theirs was not a stress-free life. Hard, uncompromising leadership was required, with a whip to hand if necessary. At times, brutalising of the 'cargo' was considered imperative to keep order. In desperation, slaves would free themselves from their shackles and attack the crew. Reprisals for such acts were swift and conclusive: a lashing, a beating, and probably even summary dismemberment right in front of their fellow blacks. The trade had a dehumanising effect on all, with the ships' crews seeing the slaves as something beneath human form. At the American and Caribbean ports, as the survivors were pulled from the holds to be paraded for prospective buyers, they were herded and inspected like cattle. Buyers would examine their eyes and teeth to determine age, feel the density of muscle in assessing work potential, and even draw off semen to test for fertility. The degradation begun in Africa, when they were lashed into line, continued at the New World ports, where the buying and bartering would go on apace, with no reference to the slaves' feelings or welfare.

In Haiti, this imported labour became the key component in what was to become the strongest colonial economy in the world. Coffee, sugar, cacao, tobacco, cotton, sisal and other tropical produce were harvested in abundance for the European markets, and the island was eyed enviously from afar by those who had no share in the riches. It became by far the brightest gem among France's overseas possessions. But its prosperity depended, almost entirely, on the sacrifices of the slaves, who were fed and housed like livestock, and regarded as such. If harshness and hard work were the slaves' entire portion, it would be bad enough, but torture was also common, not just as punishment, but as recreation for perverted masters. Inserting explosives into a slave's rectum before blowing him or her apart was a recognised form of fun for bored slavers. So was roasting on a spit and dipping heads into hot cane sugar. A grim fatalism developed among the Africans. Many considered life was no longer worth living. As on the open seas, when many leapt overboard to escape the pain, the slaves began to see suicide as a form of freedom, and a way of penalising cruel masters. A dead slave could mean the loss of a valuable possession. By killing themselves, slaves were also effectively robbing their masters. Thus, the colony established by the French in the western third of Hispaniola was a place of high tension and unparalleled terror from the start. The annihilation of the Indian tribes, originally numbering a million or so people in all, was but a prelude to the horrors to come during a slave era when the oppressed and their oppressors would eventually collide in conflict of a most horrifying kind.

Today (2006), Haiti is seen as a dangerous but insignificant slum. It carries little weight in world affairs and is viewed by its Caribbean neighbours as an embarrassment, a post-colonial failure. Apparently incapable of governing itself, it staggers from calamity to crisis, its people seemingly condemned for eternity to lives of poverty, brutality and intimidation. But in the 18th and early 19th centuries, when freedom was wrought from colonial subjugation, its significance was considerable. The transformation of Haiti, from an extremely prosperous but harshly-controlled French colony, into the world's first independent black nation, was actually a powerfully important development, in an age when the Old and New Worlds were undergoing a succession of radical convulsions. It is no exaggeration to say that Haiti's revolution was the first major blow to colonialism by negroes, and the first assertion of black rights in the Americas. Its subsequent failure socially, politically and economically has tended to cloud its importance as a major component in an emerging new order, but thinking blacks still recognise it as a symbol of negro revolution, the country which led the way to freedom.

One man's vision, intellect and leadership skills enabled the slaves to seize power from their masters, even though he was dead by the time Haiti was able to officially declare its nationhood. He was Toussaint Louverture and his story has, with considerable justification, served as inspiration for all blacks who embraced the ideals of liberation. To say Toussaint was a remarkable man is an understatement. What he achieved forced whites to change all their preconceptions of blacks, and to re-examine their own notions of military and intellectual superiority. For Toussaint defeated the three great colonial powers of their day — France, Britain and Spain — in creating the first negro republic in a land which, because of its bountiful natural wealth, was the equivalent of an oil-rich state today. His astonishing achievement shocked the European powers and the United States to the core, for it did more to dispel beliefs about Caucasian supremacy than any other event before or since.

The most remarkable aspect of Toussaint's achievement was not that he had undermined France's hold on Saint-Domingue, as the colony was known at the time, but the manner in which he did it. The beginnings of Haiti's revolution dated back to 1791, when a Jamaican upstart called Boukman first encouraged slaves to burn their masters' homes, but it was the fifty-year-old Toussaint, a lifelong slave who worked as a carriage-driver, who was to give the movement its shape and purpose. While Boukman's original uprising shook the French, and drove them to summon help from the motherland, it was regarded primarily as a show of force by savages, which would quickly subside once subjected to the clinical attention of a properly organised European army. Toussaint's involvement dispelled all such notions, for what he did was to meet the French on their own terms. Recognising that sustained success against a formidable Old World power was achievable only with proper organisation and a meticulously devised strategy, Toussaint created a powerful army from the plantation hands at his disposal, and proceeded to weaken a social order which had decreed certain men subservient, on the basis of race and colour alone. By any reckoning, Toussaint was one of the great military leaders of the 18th and 19th centuries, a man of humble birth who answered history's call to create a new nation from the flames and fury of an insurrection.

At the time, France had deep troubles of its own. When Boukman's uprising set Saint-Domingue aflame, it was itself a revolutionary nation whose leaders were cutting a swathe through the old order. French aristocrats were being guillotined in their hundreds as the new republic cast its past on the pyre and created a new order based on liberty, equality and fraternity. The slaves of Saint-Domingue were soon to discover, however, that the newly-minted equality and liberty of France did not extend to them. Once the commercial ramifications were known, the freedom which was nominally theirs was no longer considered part of the French revolutionary ideal. Committed as they were to overturning the rank injustices and excesses of the French monarchy and its perfumed entourage, the revolutionaries in Paris were not about to dismantle the system of oppression, which made the country's finest Caribbean possession the formidable revenue-earner it had proved to be.

The blacks, ultimately excluded from the process, were primed to stage a revolution of their own. And, in its way, it would prove as significant as its counterpart in Paris, with unimaginable repercussions. For Papa Doc, Toussaint Louverture and his right-hand man, Jean-Jacques Dessalines, who was later to become Emperor of the new nation, were to prove a lasting influence. As a scholar with a keen sense of history, Duvalier absorbed the lessons of Haiti's past with the passion of a disciple. Toussaint and Dessalines were to become role models, Toussaint for his ingenious rise from carriage-driver to national leader, Dessalines for his no-nonsense handling of the French plantocracy in the aftermath of Toussaint's death. Duvalier drew inspiration from both, sharing their deep patriotism, and intent on reinforcing their legacy. Like him, Toussaint and Dessalines were not notably impressive men in the purely physical sense. They were not hugely charismatic figures with captivating personalities. In fact, the only images available of both men show them to be fairly nondescript, though their overpowering sense of destiny was undisputed. Of the two, Dessalines probably prevailed in Duvalier's estimation because he, unlike Toussaint, did not allow himself to fall into a white man's trap. It was Toussaint's misguided trust, his belief that the French would act honourably, that led him to his miserable death in a mountain dungeon. For Dessalines, that was as much evidence as he needed of French treachery. He was to exact revenge in the most brutal and heartless fashion.

Up to middle age, Toussaint had shown little inclination to become a revolutionary. He was intelligent, undoubtedly, and learned to read at an early age, but beyond that there were few signs of the effective radical he was to become. However, Boukman's revolt awakened in him an implacable desire to raise his fellow blacks to a place of dignity in their own land. Failure to recognise his unique qualities was to prove an enormous strategic mistake by the French. As a carriage-driver, Toussaint had toiled for long, hot days on the plantations of his masters, with no hope of respite. Although he was to become an accomplished horseman, an ability that would serve him well when he was called upon to assume military leadership, there was little else about him to suggest the distinguished man of action he became. But, with the flickerings of revolution during the last decade of the 18th Century, his intellectual and physical energy was released, and he assumed command as though born to the job.

To assess Toussaint's achievement, it is necessary to consider the context in which he gained ascendancy. Remember, this was only two decades after the American Revolution, in which the former British colonies ejected their erstwhile rulers. It was also only a few years after the French Revolution, in which the brotherhood of man was again proclaimed aloud, as a fundamental doctrine of true nationhood. The Americans and the French were in the early stages of building new societies based on equality and freedom for all; for all, that is, except the negroes who toiled in the fields to bolster the white man's prosperity. That both Americans and French left blacks out of the equation is not surprising, for both considered negroes less than men, but it was an attitude that stirred the embers of discontent and laid the base for the inferno that was to follow. Whatever was good for Caucasian stock was not necessarily considered applicable to blacks, who were expected to endure their servitude with good grace. In fact, slave masters regarded negroes as essentially child-like, touchingly grateful for their lot, having been freed from the tumultuous continent on which their culture had taken root.

In the year of the French Revolution, 1789, the essayist and thinker, Henry Adams summed up the hierarchical system in Haiti in a single insightful paragraph: "Paris swarmed with Creole families who drew their incomes from the island, among whom were many whose political influence was great; while, in the island itself, society enjoyed semi-Parisian ease and elegance, the natural product of an exaggerated slave system combined with the manners, ideas and amusements of a French proprietary caste." At this time fewer than 50,000 French whites supervised working blacks who outnumbered them ten-fold. Slaves were still being imported from Africa because the reproduction rate of the black population in Haiti was relatively low. Thus, at the end of the 18th Century, the African language, along with African traditions and African religion, continued to predominate. Through their exertions under the whips of cruel slave-masters, the island continued to produce cacao, cotton, sisal and indigo in unparalleled quantities, making it by far the most productive colony in the world. Because their attitudes were so entrenched, it never occurred to French revolutionaries to assume that blacks might one day wish to aspire to the ideals which had moved them to throw off their own oppressors.

While Americans and French relished the fruits of political upheaval, the early paroxysms of a bright new age, they remained dangerously unaware of the ferment taking place beneath their feet. Toussaint's rise was the torch that lit the flame of rebellion in Haiti, a man who was later to be called the 'Black Spartacus' after the mighty slave who had challenged the rulers of the Roman Empire. His influence was to be felt down the generations, with echoes in the great Civil Rights campaigns of the 20th Century. People like Martin Luther King, Marcus Garvey and even Malcolm X acknowledged their debt to the unimposing Haitian, who rose from the drudgery of the plantation to become one of the great military strategists. In them he established an abiding belief that, whatever the pretensions of white rulers, blacks had the potential to raise themselves to take on the best and win. The spirit of Toussaint was very much alive during the Civil Rights marches of the 1960s, as it had been a century earlier, when slavery was finally brought to an end in America and the British Empire.

Like the portrait whose accuracy no-one can vouch for, Toussaint's early life is also shrouded in mystery. The Trinidadian historian C L R James, whose book *The Black Jacobins* remains one of the most complete records of Haiti's turbulent past, claimed he was born in northern Haiti in 1843, the grandson of an African chieftain. In spite of his inauspicious beginnings, he learned to read, developing an interest in Caesar's military writings. Thus, the man who was to become the black Spartacus, gained his early inspiration from the great empire, whose demise 1,400 years before had left behind lessons aplenty for those aspiring to power. He also absorbed the fundamental lessons of a great military strategist. This knowledge was to serve him well when his nation most needed it. Haiti today retains its close spiritual ties to Africa, even though 3,000 miles of ocean separate them.

Although Catholicism, imported by the French and Spanish, remains the dominant religion, voodoo continues to command a crucial place in the Haitian soul. Toussaint was a voodoo adept, as was his distant successor Duvalier, who was to seize control of Haiti one and a half centuries on. Today, voodoo drums continue to beat out their mysterious rhythms high in the Haitian hills, adherents of the faith possessed by the spirits, writhing and gyrating in response to the blood rites of an unfathomable past. These rituals, a belief system pre-dating the intrusion of Europeans on black culture, were undoubtedly a feature in bringing the Haitian slave revolt to fruition. However dire the reality of their lives, the slaves harkened back to a deeper and more congenial past, and this gave them their strength to cast off their shackles and take their destiny into their own hands. Toussaint became the embodiment of their ideals, and the man who laid the foundation for freedom, but most historians credit the Jamaican Boukman with lighting the first spark, in what was to become a terrifying conflagration.

During the dark hours of August 15, 1791, Boukman summoned up the spirits of Africa to overthrow the planters, and within weeks, the slaves had mobilised in what was to become a twelve-year campaign for liberation.

In the very first operation by the furious blacks, an estimated one thousand French died, as their properties were torched. Initially, radicals in France acknowledged the illogicality of denying negroes the freedom they had fought for in their own revolution, but pragmatism prevailed, as it became clear that slavery was essential for the continuing success of Saint-Domingue's economy. Indeed, cynics even today suggest that moves in Britain towards the end of the 18th Century to abolish slavery were inspired more by commercial considerations than altruism towards the slaves. Saint-Domingue was so prosperous, so productive, that it was creating an economic imbalance in Europe. Abolition of slavery would, it was reasoned, under-mine the island's economy and make its success unsustainable.

Within three years of the Haitian Revolution, the slave trade was abolished in the British Empire, though slavery itself would continue for another thirty years. In America, slavery would endure for thirty more years beyond that, extinguished only by one of the most savage civil wars in history. That Haiti's convulsions were the trigger is beyond doubt. The success of Toussaint Louverture in defusing the colonial might of France, forced a rethink among Europeans on all issues relating to the military and intellectual potential of blacks. When Toussaint began his mission against the colonial French, he was, in fact, acting in support of the new French Republic. He believed the planters were defying the principles of the new regime, and was determined to enforce the revolutionary objectives in France's most valued possession. The original impetus was not, therefore, the creation of an independent nation, but a colony at one with the zeitgeist in Paris. However, events were to prove that, despite a French National Assembly directive in 1794, ordering the end of slavery, the whites were ultimately more concerned with the impact the revolt would have on the western world.

Over the next few years, Britain and Spain would become embroiled in Haiti's affairs to their considerable cost. The rise of Napoleon Bonaparte, meanwhile, reinforced the racist doctrines of the plantocracy. As the island became the focus of so much European avarice and ambition, so it also became a cauldron of racial antagonism. The bloodbath which followed left an indelible stain on Haiti. It has never managed to live down the appalling examples set by the antagonists in this unfolding drama. It's as though a pattern was laid during these half a dozen years of turmoil, and Haiti is seemingly bound by it even today. Toussaint's triumph had parallels with the English Civil War of the 1640s. Like the English Royalists, the French faced the challenge of the slave revolt with the deep-seated conviction of their own superiority. There was an abiding belief not only in the natural supremacy of the Caucasian over negro, but also in the negroes' inbuilt, insuperable deficiencies. Toussaint was like the proletarian stock of the English parliamentary forces: though not born and bred for leadership, he adapted to it with ease. His instinctive rapport with his men, his inspirational presence in the field, was not unlike that of Oliver Cromwell, the rustic yeoman, at the Battle of Naseby. When he was around, defeat seemed inconceivable.

After the initial ructions of 1791, Saint-Domingue slid into a state of uncertainty. France's hold on its Caribbean jewel was no longer as firm as it had been, and England — forever alert to colonising opportunities — saw its chance to achieve new territory and consolidate its position in the Caribbean. In 1793, fearing the spread of revolutionary fervour in its other Caribbean possessions, and notably Jamaica, King George III sent a formidable force — some 27,000 troops — to Saint-Domingue, in an attempt to quell the uprising and further its own commercial interests, at the expense of its enemy, France. The venture was to prove one of the costliest mistakes in British military history, a debacle unprecedented in the annals of warfare up to that time. The English Redcoats were shocked not only by the ability of the slave army, but also by the impact of Saint-Domingue's tropical climate, which imposed appalling hardships. Within the next two decades, Napoleon would learn much from the folly of marching into the icy wastes of Russia, where his army was decimated by the extremes of cold. In Saint-Domingue, the English and French had to contend with the extremes of heat and humidity which, in their own way, were just as destructive. Saint-Domingue's draining climate, with its heavy summer air and frequent thunderstorms, provided ideal breeding conditions for mosquito-borne diseases. The English, immobilised by the suffocating heat, succumbed in their thousands to yellow fever, malaria and other tropical afflictions. Eventually, demoralised, they were forced to surrender to Toussaint, the first time any European force had capitulated to a negro military commander.

It was the end of England's ambitions in Hispaniola, and the prelude to Napoleon Bonaparte's ill-fated attempt to regain control in a colony which now had the bit between its teeth. Napoleon, whose imperial ambitions in Egypt and the East had come to nought, now saw the Americas as the future. Virulently racist, utterly assured of the inferiority of the black races, Bonaparte set out to rectify what he saw as the aberration of negro military success in Saint-Domingue. As the winter of 1801 closed in, he dispatched a task force to re-establish French control and, in defiance of his country's own revolutionary principles, to reimpose slavery on his black subjects. By the time the French expedition set sail, Toussaint was entrenched as Governor-for-Life of the colony, calling all the shots in a land which he felt was now more or less in line with the revolutionary ideals of Paris. It was a posture the French could not countenance. The objectives of this mission included the capture and detention of Louverture and a brutal reassertion of French interests. However, Napoleon had under-estimated the determination and commitment of the rebels. Whatever force he attempted to exert in the colony, its liberated citizens were determined to ensure there was no going back. To revert now to slavery was an unthinkable notion. As the French expedition closed in on the island, Toussaint ordered the coastal settlements to be torched, creating an orange glow in the Caribbean sky which would be seen from neigh-bouring Cuba and Jamaica. The acrid smoke hung over a wide area as Saint-Domingue burned.

The original French expedition was under the command of Napoleon's brother-in-law, Victor Leclerc, and included veteran warriors led by some of France's best generals. The 21,000-strong contingent was later to be reinforced until the total commitment of men topped 50,000. But even these were not sufficient to break the spirit of the blacks. At the fort of La Crete-a-Pierrot, in which 1,600 blacks held off repeated assaults by 16,000 French troops, the turning point was reached. By the time warfare and disease had taken their toll, only 1,200 of France's seemingly formidable force were still standing. However, before France's final humiliation, it was guilty of behaviour which confirmed in the black mind the perfidy of the French, and set the seal on negro attitudes to whites to this day.

In June, 1802, Toussaint allowed himself to be lured into negotiations with the French and, in the process, was taken captive and transported to France aboard a frigate. There he was thrown into a dungeon on the Swiss frontier. For five months he pleaded for his release, but finally succumbed to the insufferable cold and debilitating hunger, dying of pneumonia in his dank cell on April 7, 1803. In disposing of Louverture, the French thought they had cut the head from Haiti's revolutionary movement. In fact, they had reinforced the rebels' resolve, and provided the cue for a leader who was to complete the task Toussaint had so capably executed for so long. This was Jean-Jacques Dessalines, a fearsome illiterate who possessed none of Toussaint's conciliatory traits, but who had been close enough to him throughout the campaign of liberation to learn from both his strengths and weaknesses. Infuriated by France's treachery in allowing Toussaint to die in such appalling circumstances, fired by the justice of the slaves' cause, Dessalines was implacable in his resolve to eliminate the French from Haitian soil. He achieved his aim with a ruthlessness which has known few parallels. He ordered his men to butcher the French in a merciless campaign of retribution. Eventually, Napoleon, by now preoccupied by developments in Europe, abandoned the island to its fate. His New World venture was over, an early failure which would resonate a decade on, when his European ambitions would also stagger to an ignominious end.

Toussaint did not live to see Haiti's emergence as an independent nation on January 1, 1804, but his cause was celebrated among European liberals and intellectuals for the rest of the 19th Century. His prediction at the time of his betrayal, that the roots of revolt were too deep to be eliminated, proved to be true. Today, his name above all symbolises the triumph of the Haitian Revolution. Had more men of Toussaint's quality emerged in the aftermath, it's possible that Haiti's course would have proved smoother. Instead, the spirit of the less reasonable Dessalines was to lay the format of the new Haitian Republic. His methods, and his fate, were to find echoes down the years, culminating in the reign of Duvalier and the terrors which continue to prevail today. Dessalines' hatred for whites was all too evident in his first act as Haiti's ruler. He tore the white strip from the French tricolour and used the remaining red and blue as the basis of the new national flag. Apart from the Duvalier years, when Papa Doc replaced the blue with black, in a further assertion of negro dominance, these have remained the Haitian national colours to this day.

At the height of the American Civil War (1863), when the Union and Confederacy were settling their own differences over slavery, a book appeared which ensured due recognition of Toussaint's role in the political development of the western world. *Toussaint L'Ouverture, A Biography and Autobiography*, by J R Beard (1800-1876), published by James Redpath of Boston, is considered a standard work on the statesman and military leader. Beard, a churchman, was a fervent abolitionist and wrote the book as 'some aid to the sacred course of freedom' and 'in the removal of the prejudices on which servitude mainly depends.' Referring to 'unjust' reviews of the Haitian Revolution in French publications, Beard wrote: "The blacks have no authors; their cause, consequently, has not been pleaded. In the authorities we possess on the subject, either French or Mulatto interests, for the most part, predominate." M Saint Remy, editor of Louverture's memoirs, wrote: "What Toussaint, Christophe, Dessalines did — plantation hands and yet able warriors and statesmen, all of them — some Sambo, Wash or Jeff, still toiling in the rice fields or among the sugar canes, or howing his cotton row in the Southern States, may be meditating today and destined to begin tomorrow." At a time when the American consciousness over racial inequality was at its height, Beard's book proved a powerful persuader. It added energy to the abolitionist cause and undermined the bigotry of the south. Louverture's legacy is best captured in the tribute by the English poet, William Wordsworth, who, writing in the *London Morning Post* on February 2, 1803, acknowledged his contribution to the cause of freedom. "There is not a breathing of the common wind that will forget thee; thou hast great allies; thy friends are exultation, agonies and love, and man's unconquerable mind."

Thus, Dessalines made plain his desire to eliminate white influence in the country's affairs forthwith and named the new nation Haiti (or Hayti), meaning 'mountainous land' in the old Arawak Indian tongue. Though the indigenous Indians had occupied Hispaniola for centuries past, their extermination was so complete that the name Haiti is one of the few legacies they left behind. Within a few decades, it was as if they had never been there. If the ex-slaves thought expulsion of the French would bring a new era of harmony to their troubled territory, they were wrong. In fact, Dessalines' rise to power, and the manner of his fall, established a pattern for Haitian governance which was to be replicated, repeatedly, down the years and set the tone for the troubling events of 2004, the 200th anniversary year which was to prove so traumatic for the country. Without United States intervention, it was conceivable that President Jean-Bertrand

Aristide — the country's first democratically elected leader — would have suffered a similar fate as Dessalines, and deepened the political fissures which continue to bedevil Haiti today. So, two centuries after its birth, Haiti still found itself struggling to attain maturity, its people divided, with bloodletting on the streets. Worse still, experts were offering no hope of improvement. Though modern Haitian intellectuals might feel reluctant to concede the point, the country's recent turmoil has its roots in the savage era of Dessalines. During the relatively short period he was in charge, Dessalines displayed dimensions of ruthlessness unmatched even by the more egregiously cruel elements of the French plantocracy. In fact, his brand of despotic rule was so unbending, so authoritarian, that his reign as Emperor of Haiti was to bring unprecedented depths of misery, which ultimately propelled the country into a new spasm of despair. Race again was at the heart of the Haitian problem.

The post-revolutionary period brought little by way of fraternity or equality to the people, and liberty was always under siege while the old enmities persisted. Under the French, mulattoes were favoured over blacks for no better reason than that they had French blood in them. In turn, the mulattoes were less attuned to Haitian revolutionary fervour and tended to favour their European heritage over the African blackness in their souls. In fact, many mulattoes flatly refused to acknowledge any blood links with blacks at all. They harboured the illusion that they were, in fact, pedigree stock with clear genetic title. Thus, when the French had gone, these two mutually hostile elements of Haitian society were left to work out their differences. It proved to be a long, agonising process which, in truth, continues today. Dessalines' brutality was naturally directed towards whites and mulattoes, but it did not cease there. The negroes, too, found themselves under the irrational Emperor's lash, and it was not long before the perceived joys of independent nationhood gave way to painful disillusionment.

In circumstances remarkably similar to Duvalier's plight in the 1960s, Dessalines became surrounded by plotters. Like Duvalier, he did not always know who they were. The consequences were to prove disastrous. By the latter half of 1806, Dessalines' revolution had itself become the victim of rebellion, disenchantment with his rule finally exploding into open combat in the south under Mecerou. Wild-eyed with indignation, Dessalines cried "I want my horse to tread in blood all the way to Tiburon" as he sought to track down his enemies. On the evening of October 16, Dessalines and his troops, furiously intent on quelling the uprising, found themselves almost within sight of Pont-Rouge on the outer limits of Port-au-Prince. Early the following morning, Dessalines progressed tentatively towards the city with a small entourage of officers, having been assured there were no signs of revolt within its walls. Rebel guards were dressed in uniforms of the Emperor's own men to lure him into their trap. When faced by an order to halt, Dessalines shouted: "Soldiers, don't you recognise me? I am your Emperor!" Then, realising he was confronted by hostile troops, he grabbed a sword from his saddle and flayed at a barrage of menacing bayonets. A fusilier fired at him and missed, but a second shot struck him and Dessalines finally fell from his horse, after being pierced in the head with a sabre and stabbed three times in the chest by a dagger. As he lay dead at the feet of his assassins, Dessalines was mutilated in the most horrific way. His fingers, covered in decorative rings, were cut off and his remains so savaged that he was barely recognisable by the time a group of grenadiers hauled him away on a litter made from rifles.

The butchered corpse was taken into Port-au-Prince and tossed into the Government Square. Wild pigs began scuffling over the flesh. Then what was left of Dessalines was taken to the cemetery, where two soldiers buried him without ceremony. Dessalines, officially designated Jacques the First, was Governor-General and Emperor of Haiti for less than two years. As a follower of Toussaint, and sworn foe of the colonial French, he rose to become Colonel and Brigadier-General in the Revolutionary Army. His ability made him a natural successor to his mentor, but he fell foul of burgeoning notions of his own invincibility and paid the price. He would not be the last Haitian leader to allow power to go to his head, nor would he be the last to suffer at the hands of his own people. In fact, the errors of Dessalines were to become part of the weft and weave of Haiti's destiny. So many of his successors fell victim to his appalling example. And today, it seems, the lessons of history still go unheeded in this unhappy land. After Toussaint's forced departure, Dessalines had tried, though briefly, to unite Haiti's warring castes, the black and the yellow elements of its turbulent society. Having fought successfully against both the English and French, he cherished a vision of the races coming together as one family once the taint of colonialism had been eliminated. However, his idealism was short-lived and his vision proved misguided. His death heralded not unity, but division.

Haiti, the troubled child of the free world, was to suffer for the brutal nature of its conception and is suffering still. The despotism of Dessalines, the bitter racial feelings implied in the composition of the Haitian flag, and the savagery of his brief reign as Emperor were a poor base on which to build a nation. Two centuries of corruption, carnage, intimidation and presidential mismanagement have done nothing to strengthen that base, so Haiti can justifiably be said to be worse off in 2005 than it was in 1804. At least, the age of Dessalines began with hope. Following the overthrow of Aristide in 2004, all hope appeared to have gone. Today, Haitians still have a predilection for overturning presidents and butchering each other in struggles for power. The racial issue is just as marked, with blacks and mulattoes mutually hostile forces, locked in battles for ascendancy in a land now denuded of whatever riches it possessed. In a ravaged landscape, the poor remain poor, with no security except that sporadically imposed by outside forces. Meanwhile, the corrupt continue to prosper while the peasants die in the streets.

During the many years I have worked in the Bahamas, which has been a promised land for fleeing Haitians for more than four decades, I have come to know several refugees from the northern areas of Gonaives, Cap Haitien and Port-de-Paix and liked them all. Though it is the peasantry who find their way to Bahamian shores, rather than the cultured Haitian middle-class, there is no denying the deep sense of national pride these people possess in spite of the relentlessness of their plight. Of all those nations which suffer the consequences of harsh climates, crazy politics and poor government, Haiti remains the one with least apparent hope. Yet its people retain an unquenchable desire for peace, even though they seem temperamentally incapable of achieving it. One Haitian I see regularly shrugs whenever I mention his country's woes. "They people crazy," said he, screwing his finger against his head. "They don't know what they want. First one thing, then another. Crazy, crazy..." He was obviously pleased to be out of it, a Haitian refugee in a foreign land.

With such a past, it is easy to see how Haiti's pain found expression through the execrable Franck Romain in the trial of David Knox. Romain felt his blackness intensely when confronted by the South African born

Caucasian. Knox, through his 'act of harmless folly', had presented Duvalier and his henchmen with a hate figure of a type Dessalines himself would have recognised. In a sense, Knox allowed himself to become a symbol upon whom Haiti, through Romain, could vent its fury. The traditional bloodletting of this ravaged land left him with little room for optimism. Few who found themselves in a Haitian cell for offences against this paranaoid state emerged alive. As he was dragged away by his guards, I reflected on how isolated and defenceless he was in such a place, which owed allegiance to no-one, accepted none of the norms of civilised society, and saw in whites, and specifically South African whites, all the worst reminders of a savage past.

CHAPTER 6
DISCIPLE OF DESSALINES

Though I am deep brown by Caucasian standards, and especially under the full glare of the tropical sun, I have never felt more white than in Haiti, where blackness predominates to an extent equalled only in the most impenetrable tribal regions of Africa. The average Haitian, especially of the peasant class, is liquorice black with finely sculpted facial features, high cheekbones and flashing eyes. In the three centuries since their forebears were sold into bondage, there has been remarkably little dilution of their blood. The Haitian masses are still very much the products of their ethnic origins, following their tribal rites in what is, essentially, a piece of unreconstructed Africa. Apart from Creole, a rough patois based on French, the colonisers appear to have left little impression upon them. Unlike the natives of British Caribbean colonies, Haitians were bequeathed no governmental structure on which to build. Having wrenched control of the island from a nation which was itself in the throes of revolutionary change, and was living under the uncompromising rule of a rampaging emperor, they had no example to follow, other than the bloody excesses of Toussaint and Dessalines.

From the day of its birth, Haiti has been a nation of deracinated people whose deep sense of social dislocation has influenced them in everything. Part of them always seemed to be looking east, where remnants of their torn-up roots still lie buried in African soil. When I was there, it was the 'other world' aspect of Haitian society which left the deepest impression. The Knox trial was, in truth, a charade put on for western consumption, a coarse attempt at due process in a land where justice had little meaning. The niceties of the Napoleonic Code, under which men are assumed to be guilty until proven otherwise, were acknowledged in the hope that

America would take notice, but legal rights were not, in fact, high on Duvalier's agenda. Since the days of Toussaint and Dessalines, it was force, not justice, that dictated the destiny of Haitian governments. The people expected nothing of the courts, or the National Palace, but a ruthless disregard for their interests. If they could survive without interference, or intimidation, they were as near to contentment as they would ever be.

As Bill Cole and I walked the streets of Port-au-Prince, we were besieged by beggars crying 'Papa, Papa', their hands extended to take whatever we offered. Passing them a limp, filthy gourde note was unwise, for once your largesse was known, yet more beggars would emerge from the alleyways to hound you. Once, we found ourselves engulfed by a cataract of beseeching humanity, a hundred hands extended. The faces were, without exception, desperate to the point of hysteria. Disturbing numbers of them were crippled, some hobbling on crudely-constructed crutches, others scuttling along on their backsides, crablike. Others were without hands, or arms. Some were blind. 'Papa, Papa!' was the insistent cry as scaly stumps were thrust at us like batons. And always, the dilemma of instinctive magnanimity towards our tormented fellow men, or studied indifference to save ourselves from total immersion. Oddly, these scenes were never really threatening. Each of us carried in our back pockets more than the average Haitian's annual wage, yet the crowd never quite touched us. Well-dressed foreign whites must have seemed to them like demigods, potential sources of unimaginable wealth, yet harming us was clearly not an option. When a Tontons Macoute arrived we saw why. The beggars scattered under a tirade of Creole expletives.

Duvalier, for all his faults, ran a society in which there was a sense of order. Visiting foreigners, even working journalists, were protected by the thugs in blue. From behind his shades, the Tontons expressed nothing by way of greeting or acknowledgment, just the blank countenance of an enforcer at work. When he had climbed into his car and thundered off, the beggars were back again, strung out behind us like a comet's tail. In the cavernous dining room of our hotel, high above Port-au-Prince, Cole and I were the only guests for supper. Immaculately attired waiters lined the room observing our every move. I recall being presented with an artichoke for the first time in my life and not knowing what to do with it. This odd, spiky piece of vegetation appeared to be as inaccessible as a porcupine. "How do I eat it?" I asked Cole. "Don't know," he said. We were not from a section of English society in which artichokes were part of the daily diet. Both were returned untouched, an act of reckless ingratitude in a land so poor. A waiter descended upon us with swift efficiency, whisking them away. And all the time, in a distant dark corner, a pianist played mournfully. All for us, I thought, their only guests.

Apart from the Knox trial itself, and the unforgettable encounter with Papa Doc, I recall in detail only four vignettes from everyday Haitian life. One was a cockfight, where a scrum of men tossed tattered gourde notes onto a pile. As the men scuffled and jostled to place their bets, I recall the proud cock owners preparing their birds for the fray, and a scattering of indifferent women breast-feeding babies in the background. Then the contest itself, a frenzy of torn feathers as the cocks leapt high to trap their assailant's head between their horny spurs. And soon the blood began to pour forth, both cocks with eyes pecked shut grabbing and tearing and spurring to a state of exhaustion. At the end, as one bird flopped down, its ragged wings hanging limp, the winner was hoisted aloft by its master, its head an unsightly blob of blood, its comb in shreds. Then, out of respect or affection, I'm not sure which, the owner took the entire head in his mouth and sucked away the gore with a stomach-churning slurp. He spat the blood on the ground as the beat-up bird shook its swollen head in appreciation. I wanted to retch, but somehow held on. This was Haiti, with sights to unsettle even the hardiest of souls.

At a waterside restaurant one night, the press corps gained an insight into another aspect of Haitian life, in its way just as harsh and distasteful as the cockfight. It was a nightclub-cum-brothel and, when the meal was over and the whisky had done its work, a line of women was produced for our delectation. It was as degrading a spectacle, in all respects, as those quayside slave sales of two centuries before, when humanity was traded like livestock. The women, eight or nine of them, a mixture of Dominican mulattoes and deep black Haitians, stood in line to be appraised. One or two of the journalists made their choices, then bought them drinks and sat with them, the girls solicitous in their attentions, stroking the men's ears, smoothing their hair. The aim was to arouse them sufficiently for the men to want sexual intercourse. Then, for ten dollars, they would take the girls to a block of rooms where favours were offered up on slender beds bearing slim mattresses. One reporter had a Dominican called Julia, a short but stunningly attractive creature with smooth, toffee-coloured skin. When she left, clutching her ten dollar note, the same reporter was pestered by a tall, slender Haitian, who had been passed over in the first round of selection. She offered herself to him for five dollars, a bargain-basement deal, and he took her off to the same room, where he did what he had to do in less than five minutes. "I don't think I've ever had two women in ten minutes before," he said afterwards, a sated smile bisecting his face. In the atmosphere of the evening, with coloured lights strung out alongside the club, creating spangled reflections in the Caribbean Sea, and with the solemn beat of Haitian music, not to mention copious supplies of rum, such carousing seemed natural enough. It was no more, no less, than scenes played out in ports all over the world, and especially in the Far East, but it had an added poignancy here, where human life, human dignity, was considered so valueless.

At simple street stalls, craftsmen offered splendid mahogany heads at ridiculously low prices. There was also an array of voodoo drums and vivid pictures painted on wood. All the time, the desperation showed, with bartering no more than an exercise in cutting prices to the bone. Anything, but anything, was acceptable to people so deprived. They saw their lovingly created work change hands for cents. I bought several heads which were later confiscated by Bahamian customs as 'potentially hazardous' to local flora. "They will have to be burned," they said. So whatever deal I managed to extract from the vendors in Haiti proved a bad one for me. Losing the heads was especially irritating because I knew the customs men, far from consigning them to the flames, would sell them on to traders, who would then profit from huge mark-ups from American tourists in Nassau, where dishonesty was a way of life for many.

One night, I went with Cole to the Oloffson Hotel, the gingerbread watering hole in Petionville where foreign correspondents traditionally stayed. It was here, in *The Comedians* by Graham Greene, that a couple made love in the swimming pool. I remember sitting, notebook open, on the verandah under twinkling lamps as cicadas buzzed in the trees all around, interviewing someone with interesting things to say about the regime. As the Barbancourt rum went down, I recall feeling ridiculously happy in this strange, exotic place. The contact's words were being recorded in what I imagined to be my pristine Pitman's shorthand. At the end of a splendid evening, Cole and I staggered off into the darkness to find our hotel, which hovered somewhere on the hill above. I never saw the notebook again, and recalled little of what I had been told. We ascended the slopes buoyant with Barbancourt, its sugary power dispelling cares with ease. Below us, Port-au-Prince, its scattered lights shimmering in heat haze. My abiding impression of Haiti in 1968 was that, in spite of the regime, it was a magical place where high art, soulful music and a natural *joie de vivre* somehow prevailed amid so much misery. Quite how the Haitian people achieved this, I do not know. And over everything loomed the spectral presence of Papa Doc, President-for-Life, whose infrequent excursions from the palace were for the purpose of spreading largesse among the street folk, tossing coins from his car as his people fought and scrambled in the dust. 'Papa, Papa!' — the same plaintive cry Cole and I had heard when we found ourselves surrounded by beggars. It was Duvalier's way of forging the bond between himself and the poor blacks who, he knew, constituted the real Haiti. If they could be kept in a state of moderately satisfied compliance, his power would never be in doubt. But then lessons of the past told him that the masses, once inflamed, could be transformed into a destructive force. Dessalines had learnt that lesson too late and to his cost. Duvalier was determined that no such fate would befall him.

On Inagua, the southernmost of the Bahama Islands, from which the May 20, 1968 air raid was launched on the Presidential Palace, the name Duvalier has a sinister resonance. It was here, just sixty miles across the straits from Haiti, that two brothers called Duvalier brought tumult and death during the 1930s. Today, some Bahamians will tell you that Papa Doc was a Bahamian, and his name somehow became entwined with those of George and Willis Duvalier, incorrigible troublemakers who have become part of Inagua folklore for reasons that do them little credit. While North America and Europe were submerged in a crushing economic depression, the Duvalier brothers incited labour unrest of their own at Inagua's salt company, the foundation of the local economy. Until the arrival of George and Willis on the island, the name Duvalier had been carried with dignity by a totally blameless family of Bahamians since the 19th Century. While it's likely that their origins were in the French territories south of the Bahamas, by the 1930s they had become fully integrated into Bahamian society and were happily engaged in Inagua's simple fishing, farming and salt-raking pursuits. George and Willis, lean, fit young men, were noted rabble-rousers who developed a gripe against an islander called Munroe. They said he was feeding mischievous information to the salt company directors about certain local folk, creating unease in the community. In fact, they said, Munroe was a company spy. The unpleasantness created by the brothers' presence on the island erupted into serious disturbances in 1936. During a full-scale riot — something unheard of in those parts — Munroe was shot dead. The Duvalier brothers were hanged for his murder.

For Mrs Inez Farquharson, who was 88 when I interviewed her in December, 2002, these troublesome events were especially memorable. In that year, she gave birth to one of her eight children, Etienne Louis Farquharson, who was named after Louis Duvalier, a good friend of Mrs Farquharson's husband, Theo. Louis Duvalier, by all accounts a likeable man, was an uncle of the infamous Duvalier brothers, who brought such unhappiness to the peaceful island on which he had been born in the 1880s. He died aged 50 in the year before the riot, so was spared the gruesome fate of his delinquent nephews, whose executions in Nassau were considered well-deserved. Mrs Farquharson told me: "Those boys were little devils. They shot Mr Munroe in the street because they thought he was a 'traitor' who was telling tales about people to the company. I knew their grandmother very well. She was a lovely lady. The whole business upset her very much. They had been visiting her when all that happened. It caused such a disturbance in Inagua." The grandmother, Eliza Duvalier, was a respected figure in Inagua and was best-known for the tiny candy and bread shop she ran from her home. As Louis and his brother Sam had left the island many years before, she also became the last known Duvalier link with Inagua. Twenty-one years after George and Willis Duvalier were executed, their family name sprang to the fore again with the rise to power of Dr Francois Duvalier in neighbouring Haiti.

Speculation about Papa Doc's family links with Inagua persisted throughout his 14-year reign, and rumbled on during the 15-year regime of his podgy son, Jean-Claude. Today, the few Duvaliers left in Nassau, the Bahamian capital, are not eager to claim affinity with Papa Doc or the executed brothers, but the familial connection is claimed, unequivocally, by an engaging singer-composer called Maureen Duvalier, who was 79 when I interviewed her in Nassau in early October, 2005. Ms Duvalier, who as Bahama Mama is a well-known entertainer in the Bahamas, claims to be Papa Doc's niece and last met him in 1961 when she found herself in Port-au-Prince aboard a cruise ship. Her uncle invited her to the National Palace, and there they chatted for some time, the dictator then having been in power for four years. "I remember little about it except that I had to go through lots of gates, all of which were locked behind me as I passed through," she said. Contrary to official accounts of Duvalier's origins, she claims he was born in Inagua and was taken to Haiti as a boy. Later, she said, his mother moved to Nassau and he visited her there frequently, in the days before he entered college to study medicine. Ms Duvalier recalls him as 'a very nice person', a description she also applied to his wife Simone, who she met in Miami. When he qualified he was "like a good doctor — he was a very gentle man." She recalled that he rode around the Haitian countryside on a donkey, treating the poor for nothing. It was during this time, she said, that he gained the people's trust. These pro bono medical missions were to lay the base for his political career. "It's why they had such confidence in him," she said. So how did the quiet, caring medic become the tyrannical monster? "I would not venture to say why he changed," said Ms Duvalier. "People are like that. They can be one way one minute and ten minutes later they are something else. That's because they have another thing going on in their head." Since finding God in 1992, she said, she would have liked to sit down with him and teach him the meaning of love for people. "I wish he were alive so that I could talk to him. I was shocked by what he became." Ms Duvalier said Papa Doc's mother died in Nassau in 1930. By then, he was a philosophical young man making his way in an uncertain world. But the Bahamas, it seemed, had played a significant part in his young life. And the dreaded brothers, George and Willis Duvalier, were his cousins, she said. So perhaps there was a murderous strain in the Duvalier genes all along.

At the time of my interview with Mrs Farquharson, I wrote an article in *The Tribune*, Nassau's daily newspaper, referring to the first flood of refugees in the 1960s, and drawing a contrast between life in Haiti and its neighbouring island of Inagua, one a land in turmoil, the other a serene refuge. With the limb-lopping Tontons making life impossible, the Bahamas offered new hope for fleeing Haitians, I wrote. Some of these haunted souls made their landfall in Inagua, the closest Bahamian territory to their tragic homeland. For many years, there had been seaborne trade between the two countries, but the refugees were an 'import' the Bahamas did not want, and the problem of illegal immigrants has been with us ever since. Mrs Farquharson, though, remembers happier days, when little sloops plied under their ragged sails between Inagua and Haiti, carrying nothing more than provisions, including day-to-day household items and local produce. "My daddy had a schooner that used to trade between Haiti and here," she said. "In those days we depended more on Haiti for our food and other provisions than we did on Nassau. My father went to Haiti every month and came back with rice, sugar, onions, fruit and other foods. When I was a little girl, all my school shoes came from Haiti and I still have relatives living there. My son, Carlton, a pastor, still goes there from time to time as a missionary."

Nowadays, some trade from Haiti is more sinister. Apart from immigrants, sloops today carry marijuana and cocaine as Haiti establishes itself as the drug clearing house of the Caribbean. But they bypass Inagua en route for Nassau, where the network arranges onward shipment of human and drug cargoes to Florida. Although the Royal Bahamas Defence Force uses Inagua as a base for interdiction activities in an attempt to stifle this illegal traffic, everyday life there is much as it has always been. Urgency is alien to Inagua's inhabitants. Slow pace and no pace best describe its measured progress in the modern world. Since Mrs Farquharson's girlhood, Inagua's population has dropped from 6,000 to only 1,200 as islanders have sought their fortunes elsewhere. Some now live in Nassau, some have made their lives in the US. Those who stayed behind still rely on simple pleasures, and Mrs Farquharson – born in Mathew Town, the island 'capital' – would not choose to live anywhere else.

With the Duvalier regime in Haiti now long gone, and the murderous Duvalier brothers of the 1930s a fading memory, the connections between Inagua and the Duvalier name become increasingly tenuous as time moves on. While Haiti still suffers from the Duvalier legacy, ensuring constant political upheaval and civil disorder, Inagua enjoys timeless serenity. People still go to bed with their doors unlocked, and serious crime is a rarity. It is incredible that two places so close geographically should be so different socially, one in restless turmoil, the other as tranquil as a wetland pond.

While the people of Haiti still fear the noises of the night, Inagua's good folk sleep soundly, with quietness all around. The hanging of George and Willis Duvalier left Inagua in trauma, and their surname carries sinister overtones even today. It was inevitable, therefore, that when Papa Doc rose to power in 1957, and subsequently became an internationally-known figure, that the family connections would arise again. The tyrant's notoriety somehow became entwined with the brothers' infamy, especially when Papa Doc manifested his partiality for homicide on a large scale. Was killing, a Duvalier family trait? It was the question some observers began asking, as they speculated that the dictator's origins lay in the southern Bahamas and that his family traversed the channel between the isles sometime before, or maybe, even after his birth. The notion is not entirely fanciful, and Ms Duvalier's recollections tend to support it. She even said Papa Doc's father owned sailing boats which plied the waters between Haiti and the southern Bahamas.

On a clear day, it is possible to see the mountains of Haiti from Inagua, and during the early years of the early 20th Century, there was — as Mrs Farquharson pointed out — a lively seaborne trade between the two. Small sailing craft carried fruit, charcoal and other goods to Inagua, returning with coarse salt from Inagua's salt ponds. The shuttling back and forth of small boats inevitably led to relationships between the people, and a degree of intermingling. However, since the Duvaliers' departure, it's surprising how few French-sounding names took root in Inagua. Today, scanning the island telephone book, the names are largely of known Bahamian slave plantation origin: Lightbourne, McIntosh, Major, Hanna, Cartwright, Burrows and Burnside. Only Deleveaux, which is well-known throughout the southern Bahamas, hints at Frenchness, but there are not even any Josephs, the most common of Haitian surnames.

That Duvaliers had associations with Inagua over many years is beyond doubt. That Inagua Duvaliers spread to other parts of the Bahamas is also unchallenged because a few still live in Nassau. However, Papa Doc's origins are thought by Haitian historians to lie not in the Bahamas, but one of the French territories to the south, Martinique, where his father was born. There was little in the Martinique Duvaliers' background to suggest that they would spawn such a monster. So far as is known, they were as blameless as the Inagua branch of the family before the arrival of George and Willis. Papa Doc was probably as much the creation of circumstance as genetics. He was able to discern early on how power was achieved and retained in a country where the racial, social and economic ferment was so pungent and toxic. Whatever his faults, his pragmatism was beyond question.

At the time of Jean-Bertrand Aristide's departure from Port-au-Prince in 2004, when the United States military was implicated in his removal, a Nassau attorney, Eliezer Regnier, articulated feelings about the nature of Haitian politics which would have found approval among the ravaged country's political analysts. "What Haiti needs," he said, "is a benevolent dictator, someone strong enough to maintain control, but with the country's interests at heart." Incredibly, his call coincided with a growing demand for the return of Jean-Claude Duvalier, son of Papa Doc, whose self-indulgent reign was now being seen, in retrospect, as a golden era. As I wrote of the Duvaliers in *The Tribune*, Nassau's leading daily newspaper, in May, 2005: "In their day, there was a sinister but real sense of order in this traditionally chaotic country. Today, the chaos is almost total, with few redeeming features. Haiti is among the world's true tragedies, a perilous place where bullets fly day and night." Regnier, a Bahamian citizen of Haitian background, bases his legal practice largely on the Haitian refugees who have sought to make the Bahamas their home over the last forty years. He appears frequently before the Nassau courts to represent the woebegone souls whose desperation has driven them into unlawful acts, usually breaches of the immigration laws, which the Bahamas Government uses to stem the tide of Haiti's fleeing hordes. Regnier's remarks, made after witnessing the mayhem in Haiti following the ousting of Aristide, including the slaughter of peasants by the heavy-handed police force, were significant because they encapsulated what many now feel: that democracy is an unrealistic proposition for a country where politics has been reduced to an unseemly scrum among factions whose objectives have nothing to do with elevating Haiti or its people.

At the time of Duvalier's birth, April 14, 1907, the situation was little different. Those who built stores alongside Port-au-Prince's rutted streets invariably incorporated cast-iron doors into their design, protection against revolutionaries who pillaged at will as they took full advantage of Haiti's chronic instability. It was a time when the peasant's lot was every bit as abject and unpredictable as it is today, with political power changing hands every year, one dictator succeeding another in a long procession of insurrections. Francois Duvalier, according to the official account, was born a few blocks from downtown Port-au-Prince, though the mystique which was later to become such a feature of his regime was apparent even then. Duvalier was always a deeply mysterious figure, and he seemed intent on keeping it that way. As a child, he was delicate and introspective. His studious nature singled him out as slightly odd. Though physically unimposing, there was always something chillingly enigmatic about him which left others wary.

In Europe, the upper classes were enjoying a golden age of prosperity and tranquillity, the great colonial powers were at their height, and nothing seemed capable of undermining a status quo in which class and wealth were clearly delineated. Within a decade, of course, the gilded age would prove illusory: the whole of Europe would be consumed by the worst war in history, and the great dynastic rulers of Russia would be swept away by the Bolshevik Revolution. The savaging of Europe, and the obliteration of an entire generation of young men in the trenches of northern France, and on the beaches of Gallipoli, were to spawn additional tensions among the continent's leading powers, and lay the base for a brutal reprise two decades later.

In Haiti, however, all this seemed distant from its own current troubles. A century after independence, it was still a land in turmoil, unable to forge a political structure for itself. Chaos was still the defining element of everyday life. Duvalier was born into a lower middle-class family, his father Duval, a teacher and mother Uritia, a bakery worker. As a small boy, he witnessed first-hand the abject, hopeless reality of his homeland. Port-au-Prince itself was a malodorous slum, its streets a network of pitted thoroughfares along which peasants drove their donkey carts. Open drains, heaving sewage and the foul slurry washed into the streets by tropical rainbursts, were repellant features of the capital as its people struggled from day to day to survive against formidable odds. Theirs was a country without a plan or the means of formulating one. In the first eight years of Duvalier's life, no fewer than six presidents came and went, some removed under pressure, at least two eliminated altogether.

As now, Haiti was hell on earth. In 1912, the year the Titanic sank with massive loss of life in the north Atlantic, Haiti itself seemed to be sinking under the weight of presidential mismanagement. In this latest political convulsion, the National Palace was blown to fragments in a plot reminiscent of the 1605 attempt at insurrection by the English Catholics against King James I. Where Guy Fawkes and his fellow plotters failed, the enemies of President Cincinattus Leconte succeeded, demolishing the palace and killing the national leader in a single devastating act of treason. A year later, President Tancrede Auguste also succumbed to conspiracy, dying horrifically from poisoning. By this time, the old European powers were convinced that Haiti would warrant all their most pessimistic predictions: that a black-ruled republic could not succeed, but was destined to be riven by corruption, greed and a reckless hunger for power. Insidiously, they began to exert economic power in a land adrift in a slop-pail of its own making.

During his formative years, Duvalier was to be influenced not only by the seemingly incessant unrest in Haiti's political life, but also the racial dynamics of Haitian society. Like many Caribbean territories, Haiti was obsessed with gradations of colour, and Duvalier, emphatically black, grew up with all the complexes associated with true, full-blooded negroes of the day. As in the Bahamas and Jamaica, true blacks were inconvenient reminders of a bitter past. These were undiluted slave stock, and their colour was to commit them in the public consciousness to the lower orders, the peasant classes. For a clever boy like Duvalier, being black was not only a reminder of what the mulattoes would consider his genetic inferiority, it was also an obstacle to progress in an extremely race-concious society. Little wonder then that negritude – the glorification of blackness and the African heritage – would become a dominant theme in his thinking.

Duvalier was alert to African consciousness from an early age, and familiar with the voodoo rituals which were to so influence his life. But he was also alert to Haiti's Frenchness, and the strange affinity it shared with colonies and ex-colonies to the north and south, the Louisiana settlements on the north American mainland (sold by Napoleon to the United States in 1803 in the Louisiana Purchase) and Martinique, his father's birth-place, which shared with Louisiana and Haiti the unique patois of French derivation known as Creole. In fact, there were differences: Haiti's native tongue borrowed something from English and Spanish, too, but the tongue's main thrust was the same. French was its dominant strain, and Duvalier proved as adept in this as in the weird rites of African witchcraft. Both were to prove vital attributes in his climb to power. Though French occupation left Haiti with a strong Roman Catholic tradition, it is voodoo that exercises the strongest grip on its people. The Haitians' obsession with the super-natural springs directly from their African past, and it permeates every aspect of their lives. Though African superstitions exist in various forms in different parts of the Caribbean region, no country is so immersed in witchcraft rites as Haiti.

In the Bahamas, where *obeah* is still widely practised, especially in the remoter outer islands, Haitian people are still treated with suspicion, and a certain wariness, because of their supposed mystical powers. While *obeah* is viewed as a comparatively mild form of witchcraft, voodoo is seen in the Bahamas as an anti-Christ abomination, and a prime cause of Haiti's continuing misfortune. Devout Bahamian Christians are convinced that Haiti's woes are a manifestation of God's vengeance. At the time of Duvalier's birth, voodoo was but one feature of Haiti's African past. In many other respects, this was a transplanted society whose mores and traditions had survived the impact of colonialism almost without alteration. In spite of the imposition of Christianity, and specifically Catholicism, the people went about their lives much as they would have centuries before, in Guinea or the Congo. Rural communities were collections of simply constructed homes with distinct echoes of Africa. Thatched, wooden-framed, mud-daubed with earthen floors, these huts were shelter from intense tropical rainfall and shade from the pitiless sun. Polygamy was commonplace, and the men free-ranging hunters, so women were the foundation of Haitian society, the home-makers charged with child-rearing and the day-to-day business of ensuring sustenance and survival. At night, the hills above Port-au-Prince rumbled with the beat of voodoo drums as *houngans*, the voodoo adepts, conducted arcane rituals among the glassy-eyed worshippers by the light of open fires. If voodoo offered the people a spiritual refuge from the brutish nature of their lives, it also provided much of life's colour. Haiti's primitive art is rooted in voodoo, with its vivid imagery. Haiti's native music and dance, too, are inspired by the glory of the pagan gods.

The impact of the supernatural on the Haitian people is significant in any study of the Duvaliers, for it was superstition, mysticism and the fears they induced which sustained them for so long as they pillaged and plundered the country. As recently as the early summer of 2005, I was offered an insight into the power of Haitian voodoo. On the Bahamian island of Abaco, local people were growing uneasy over what they saw as an unacceptable level of 'creolisation' of their society, the result of four decades of illegal Haitian immigration, beginning during the early years of the Duvaliers. In spite of this growing unease, Bahamians were reluctant to speak out in defence of their culture. Then a lone crusader against the Haitian onslaught called Jeffery Cooper told me why. Mr Cooper, a black Abaconian entrepreneur, had taken it upon himself to dismantle Haitian shacks which had been built without permission on Crown land in the bush. Several times during this mission, he had received veiled threats from Haitian settlers, all of which hinted darkly at 'fixing' of one kind or another. He said his fellow Bahamians were frightened to speak out against Haitians because they feared being cursed by *houngans*, whose hostility would translate into an eternal blight on their lives. His view was not far-fetched: in relatively sophisticated Nassau, opposing factions in a taxi union dispute conducted *obeah* rituals to bring misfortune down upon the heads of their rivals. Upturned, open Bibles were sure signs of these extraordinary ceremonies, which prospective rivals countered with the sprinkling of turpentine.

The influence of witchcraft can never be discounted in the Caribbean islands. But Haiti has always been seen as the hub of such sorcery, a sinister land of malevolent spirits. Based, as it is, on blood rites and animal sacrifice, voodoo is so much a part of the heart and soul of Haiti, so inextricably linked with the land and its creatures, that it has never been subjugated by Catholicism, for all of the latter's insistent demands and strictures. Instead of Catholicism accommodating voodoo, Haitians have absorbed the Christian saints into their own mystical practices. The *houngan*, who is called upon to cure sickness or counter misfortune, has always been a more powerful figure than the Catholic priest, for the Haitian imagination is beset by a thousand demons, all of them redolent of a vibrant history in another place. Catholicism, for them, will always be a European belief system not entirely appropriate to themselves. This resistance to 'white' religion (an attitude evident in the Haitians' cautious approach to the later blandishments of the Anglicans) is the product of black consciousness, which is still a significant dynamic in Haitian society and politics today.

This pride in negritude, to which Duvalier was committed throughout his years in power, is not entirely convincing. Generations of enslavement induced powerful feelings of self-loathing. Even today, marrying spouses of lighter hue is considered an upward step in the social order. Duvalier himself was to follow this course, marrying a mango-skinned beauty who could be relied upon to lighten the complexion of his off-spring. It was a significant step towards social acceptance. This obsession with pigmentation is rife throughout the Caribbean. When Lynden Pindling led the blacks to power in the Bahamas, Haiti's close neighbour, in 1967, he was immediately identified as a soul brother by Duvalier, partly because he had led a revolution of a kind — the whites had ruled the Bahamas for 300 years before being deposed at the polls — but also because he was so emphatically black. Like Duvalier, the ambitious Pindling had also married a bright-skinned Out Island woman while two of his senior Cabinet colleagues had married British whites. Though Pindling, like Duvalier, championed blackness at every turn, he shared this strange compulsion to marry lighter than himself, and saw his statuesque spouse, Marguerite, as a trophy wife on the route to the top. Duvalier recognised in Pindling many shared traits, but it was the up-ending of an entrenched racial and social order which really attracted his admiration. Though the Bahamas 'revolution' came more than 160 years after Haiti's painful birth, it was rooted in firmer and deeper soil. Britain, whatever its faults as a colonial power, left its territories with some sense of order, a legal and governmental framework in which to work. Today, 30 years after independence, the Bahamas is a solid democracy which has made impressive strides. Haiti remains mired in chaos and confusion. In both, however, colour continues to define and delineate people's lives, the blacks still beset by the insecurities of their past, the whites unsure of a future which no longer belongs to them.

The old Jesuit maxim — give us the boy for the first seven years, and we will give you the man — had a resonance in the life of Francois Duvalier, for it's beyond dispute that those early years laid a template in his soul. The mystery of his boyhood was not explored during the long years of Duvalier rule — indeed, research into his early life was actively discouraged — but all accounts suggest that the young Francois was intelligent enough, and sensitive enough, to absorb the influences all around. If taciturnity was his predominant characteristic, it was accompanied by a dogged inquisitiveness, a longing to learn, and did not denote in any sense a degree of stupidity. If the looming conflagration in Europe was far off in geographical terms, it exerted pressures on Haitian life in subtle ways. As the Edwardian idyll in Britain dimmed into the shadows of an approaching war, so European enmities intensified. Haiti, as it had a century before, became a New World focus for this growing animus, for German influence was burgeoning in Port-au-Prince, a development which unsettled the United States and its European friends. If colonialism had offered easy pickings in Haiti for the European powers during the 18th Century, it was political instability which made it such a tempting prize by the time the twentieth was properly into its stride.

In the first eight years of Duvalier's life, the legacy of Dessalines was all too apparent. Power changed hands so often, and in circumstances of such savagery, that the streets of Port-au-Prince became, almost literally, rivers of gore. The blowing up of Leconte in 1912 was the most egregious act of terror in an age of terror, but it was run close by the horrific fate of President Guillaume Sam, whose march on Port-au-Prince to claim power coincided with increased American interest in Haiti's future, and an alarming influx of German loans. Sam, like most of his predecessors, was a short-term incumbent as president. And, as with Dessalines, his demise was brutal. Suspected of enticing the US into an involvement in Haiti's affairs, Sam found himself under threat and took refuge in the French Embassy, a manoeuvre which might have ensured his safety in a more rational land. However, mob law had sound precedents in Haiti's century of independence, and diplomatic immunity counted for nought. His enemies kicked their way into the embassy and found him cowering in a bathroom. He was carried bodily into the embassy compound and impaled on the surrounding fence. Then the mob tore him to shreds, an act of barbarism comparable to the slaughter of Dessalines in 1806.

All this happened in 1914, as the European superpowers were embroiling themselves in cataclysmic events which were to last four appalling years. Sam's murder, continuing revolutionary activitity in the north, and the growing fear of German influence in a land disturbingly close to the American mainland were enough to trigger a nineteen-year occupation of Haiti by US marines. So for much of his boyhood, adolescence and early manhood, Duvalier was living in an occupied land, Haitian sovereignty having been emphatically crushed by a country which placed its own strategic interests above Haiti's hard-earned rights to self-determination. For the young

Duvalier, the indignity of it all was to leave deep psychological wounds. That Haiti should find itself, one hundred and nine years after Dessalines, effectively under white man's rule again was a situation he found hard to countenance. It also impressed upon him the need for Haiti to preserve itself from interference by any means, and for the black masses to break the oligarchical nature of Haiti's governance once and for all. The humiliation of occupation was deepened by the painful realisation that Haiti's development as a nation had been callously obstructed by United States intransigence.

For half a century after Dessalines' triumph, Washington had refused to recognise the negro republic, choosing instead to depict its birth as an aberration, a hideous distortion of nature. Right up until the American Civil War, when slavery was abolished and black men began their long struggle for equality in the so-called land of the free, the United States persisted in ignoring its black neighbour, hoping it would crumble back into colonialism. As the second free nation of the New World, its revolution coming less than thirty years after the American colonies had shaken off the British, Haitians expected fraternal feelings from their fellow revolutionaries. However, they didn't come. Instead, the Americans viewed Haiti as a threat, an example that restless blacks might be tempted to follow. Modern Haitians point to that half a century of ostracism as the root cause of their continuing plight. A country whose birth had been bloody, painful and traumatic was abandoned and ignored in its formative years.

Duvalier, though still a child, was now witnessing the Americans at their most paternalistic: they had sent warships and marines to pacify, placate and discipline this recalcitrant child to the south. For nearly two decades, Washington ruled Port-au-Prince, often uncompromisingly. As the young Duvalier roamed the city streets, the American presence was everywhere. Had the US been there merely as peacekeepers, maintaining law and order until Haiti was able to regain its equilibrium, the humiliation would not have been so keenly felt. But the marines exerted their influence in every sphere of Haitian life except the courts, the schools and postal services. In every meaningful sense, this was a takeover. As Washington established its grip, Haiti's disorderly past was best symbolised by the National Palace itself, which had been reduced to a ruin by the lethal attack on President Leconte. This was the second time Haiti's presidential seat had been destroyed, the first having been sacked and razed in 1869.

However, when Duvalier was only eleven years old, construction of the present palace was completed and it has somehow survived every upheaval since then, a triple-domed edifice which sits behind an iron fence under heavy armed guard. By any standard, the National Palace is a handsome structure, modelled to some extent on the White House in Washington, and it represents a sense of constancy and consistency in an otherwise chaotic city. As he watched its rise, did Duvalier ever dream of occupying it one day as patriarch of a two-generation dynasty? Maybe not. The slightly-built boy, with his retiring ways, was hardly material for the harsh, uncompromising world of Haitian politics. Haiti was traditionally a country where sheer force was the decider. There was nothing in Duvalier, in his early years, to suggest he would become a tyrant among tyrants, a slight figure who would make big men quake. To his schoolfriends, he was a bespectacled bookworm who shunned confrontation, a retiring 'hole in the corner' figure who preferred his own company.

As one would expect from such a turbulent land, Haiti did not accept the US presence uncomplainingly. In the early years of occupation, rebel groups affronted by Haiti's apparent loss of sovereignty began underground movements against the invaders. The US, bedding in for the long haul, reacted with sometimes brutal efficiency. Leaders like Charlemagne Peralte, a mulish but imposing figure who had once been a regional commander, was summarily despatched after failing to react positively to imprisonment. In early 1918, he and his brother, Saul were sentenced to five years hard labour, but subsequently escaped to mount a peasant uprising against the occupying forces. An armed squad tracked him to his mountain hideaway and shot him as he sat with compatriots at their campfire. The attempt at insurrection did not last long, but the images it left in the young mind of Francois Duvalier, now in early puberty, are not hard to imagine. As so often in the past, Port-au-Prince became a killing ground, its homes set ablaze as marines tried to fight off the marauders. Duvalier would have seen the by now familiar sight of corpses in the city's pitted streets, and smelt the pungent odour of smoke, an inevitable by-product of civil unrest which hung like gauze in the alleys and byways. Meanwhile, Peralte's body was pinioned to a door at the police base in Cap Haitien, a gruesome trophy for the US marines, and a reminder to troublemakers of what awaited them if peace was not allowed to reign.

It seems unimaginable to those reared in quieter lands that anyone could pursue anything resembling a useful education in such a place. But Duvalier, a silent loner in old-fashioned clothes, was nothing if not diligent, and set out to establish himself as a professional man by studying hard. Contemporaries viewed him as strange, diffident and reflective. Those who were more perceptive detected from early on a quiet but quite unnerving resolution, a defiant air. At the Lycee Alexandre Petion, the secondary school in the Bel Air district where he was to acquire his early political influences, Duvalier was exposed to two teachers who were later to make important contributions to Haiti's development. One was Dumarsis Estime, champion of the black middle-class, who was to be in the forefront of the organisation to end the US occupation. The other was Dr Jean Price Mars, who gained prominence as a writer of seminal works on Haiti's ethnic past. Both were, in their different ways, commanding figures for anyone with young Francois's intellectual aspirations. Educationally, Duvalier was exposed to a trait common throughout the Caribbean, a reverence for medicine and law. These professions offered in public estimation both respectability and security, plus tangible evidence of advancement from the much-reviled slave state, as represented by manual labour. There was also a reverence for literature, because Haitian intellectuals were astute enough to realise that only through the written word would Haiti's true nature be defined. Duvalier was not immune to these influences. He gained entrance to medical college against all odds in an attempt to achieve the respectability he craved, and wrote articles for the newspaper *Action Nationale* to give vent to his views on how Haiti should develop.

In his twenties, Duvalier's growing sympathy for the nationalist cause was tempered by the indignity thrust upon his father, Duval, who lost his job as a primary school teacher for no better reason than that he was from Martinique, and thus considered foreign. It was an injustice, later rectified, which must have cut deeply into the young Duvalier. At a time when his nationalistic views were taking root, his Haitian identity was under challenge. In the context of Haitian politics, there is no doubt that the young Duvalier was initially quite radical. While national identity was important to him, it was of no higher priority than the plight of the poor. In his newspaper articles, written in an uncompromising polemical style, he railed against Haiti's elite in intemperate terms. Implicit in all he wrote was the recognition that blackness was synonymous with the oppressed, that mulattoes were still the dominant force in Haitian political and economic life, even more than a century after the death of his hero, Dessalines.

While Duvalier studied medicine, under a scheme to help clever but under-privileged children devised by the US occupiers, his contemporaries were orchestrating opposition to the foreign takeover. Young Haitian intellectuals could not imagine national development against the backdrop of foreign dominance and began making their views known through positive action. Student strikes focused on the untenability, and unacceptability, of the US takeover and began pressing for a troop withdrawal. Though Duvalier viewed these developments from the sidelines, he was by no means a dispassionate bystander. Removal of America's heel, he felt, was essential if Haiti were to achieve its destiny. There is no question that the students' action began to impress upon the Americans the need for a rethink, and Duvalier's sympathy for the cause was total.

In 1930, when Duvalier was twenty-three, the eight-year reign of President Louis Borno came to an end, primarily the result of the strike action and the Americans' growing realisation that the Haitian occupation was unsustainable in the long-term. The Forbes Commission was established to consider all questions relating to Haiti's future and President Herbert Hoover offered Haitians hope by recommending a five-year development plan leading to withdrawal. It would be all too easy to condemn the United States for placing its own strategic interests above Haiti's existence as an independent nation, but the occupation, while offending Haitian sensibilities, did bring results. Despite minor revolts and student strikes, Haiti benefited from a nineteen-year respite from the madness of the status quo, and inherited some tangible benefits.

The presidents who occupied the National Palace during the American occupation may have been mere figureheads, Washington's puppets, but they enjoyed tenure for much longer than most of their predecessors. In addition, the Americans invested millions of dollars in creating an infrastructure on which Haiti could build for the future. They constructed roads, installed utilities and repaired docks. Under their watch, Port-au-Prince achieved a level of order and efficiency it had never known. In 1934, they were ready to go, and President Franklin Delano Roosevelt was to become the first serving president to visit Haiti when he conducted the formal departure ceremonies at Cap Haitien, handing over control to President Stenio Vincent, who was soon to preside over the more familiar pattern of Haitian political life, one of confusion and disorder, violence and blood-letting. The Americans had barely disappeared over the horizon when furious Haitians, in an irrational frenzy, began undoing their good works, ripping up structures the US had funded, tearing down power lines, and even raiding school buildings the Americans had constructed, in an effort to get the country's education system up to an acceptable standard. This self-defeating orgy left Haiti facing more years of hopelessness and despair — and convinced even its most ardent supporters that, temperamentally, the Haitian people were probably incapable of extending their many talents into the realm of governance.

The American withdrawal coincided with Duvalier's qualification as a professional man. He received his diploma and began his internship at the Hospice St Francis, in Port-au-Prince. In every sense, it was a new beginning for the outwardly sensitive, retiring, deep-thinking medic. With his newly-earned professional status, he had acquired the respectability he craved, and struck a telling blow for negritude. Of the fifteen or so medical graduates that year, he was probably alone as the only total black. In those days, medical studies were almost exclusively the preserve of the lighter-skinned Haitian elite. In truth, Duvalier was a beneficiary of the US occupation in that they encouraged a more expansive, less elitist, approach to such matters. Alongside his burgeoning self-confidence sat a growing awareness of Haiti's developing political landscape, and a determination to help exert change. With his friend and fellow intellectual, Arthur Bonhomme — later to be Haiti's Ambassador in Washington, and the man who would keep me abreast of Haiti's position in the Knox case — Duvalier co-authored *Trends of a Generation*, a short but significant appraisal of Haitian literature and its role in forming the character of the nation. This, together with the work he did for *Les Petit Impartial*, a publication specialising in trenchant political comment, indicated that his life was now to be that of physician-polemicist, tending sick people at the hospice by day, and attempting to heal the wider sickness of Haitian society by night. If Duvalier's shyness had kept him out of the fray in the past, he was now to emerge as very much involved in his nation's destiny.

In later life, Duvalier was to add the word 'Journalist' to his curriculum vitae, but he was not a journalist in any sense that a true media professional would recognise. His writings were not those of a properly trained news-paperman, but a budding politician with a particularly extravagant line in vituperation, who wished to get his views across in the public prints. Strident, sometimes hysterical, his work was markedly lacking in objectiv-ity, but it earned him something of a reputation among Haiti's thinkers, and that's what he required of it. In the first twenty-seven years of his life, Duvalier had witnessed much of what would, in truth, form the essence of Haiti's future. The blowing-up of Leconte, the poisoning of Auguste, the dismemberment of Sam and the long humiliation of US occupation rein-forced in his mind the need for stability — and the dismantling of the mulatto hegemony which had continued to create appalling social and economic divisions in Haitian society.

The gradations of the Haitian class structure were evident in the phys-ical structure of Port-au-Prince itself. Indeed, it would be hard to imagine any other place on earth where privilege and subjection were so clearly delineated. On the city waterfront, the sweltering slums: cesspits full of demoralised humanity wherein the horrors of disease and violence were the daily ration. Here, the jet-black urban peasantry lived in hovels of unparalleled squalor. In the city itself, the traders and vendors battling for business in the dusty haze of the streets, a riot of life where beggars and derelicts limped through a cacophony of hand-painted tap-tap buses and battered sedans. In the summer rains, this becomes a mudheap, vehicles sliding through brown slurry, swerving crazily to avoid open man-holes. Amid the chaos, elegant Haitian women of all ages carrying burdens on their heads. Sometimes, it might be a bundle of cane. More often, a con-tainer full of water. Once, Cole and I saw an impossibly slender maiden with four or five live hens strapped together on her head, all clucking and squawking wildly. This buzz of humanity existed on a shifting landscape of urban waste. Then, away from the malodorous downtown area, the scented slopes up to Petionville and Kenscoff, where cooler air and the fra-grance of tropical flora offered a life worth living. It was here, amid the poinciana, bougainvillea and hibiscus, that the wealthy lived, gazing down from their breeze-blown balconies and fretworked verandahs on to the melee below.

The chasm between rich and poor was social, ethnic, cultural and economic. Patrician mulattoes still owed cultural allegiance to France, their pampered womenfolk drawn to the salons of Paris. They thought European and denied any connection with the black hordes, even to the extent of declaring themselves and their families to have been eternally mulatto, with no genetic link with Africa at all. To emphasise their comparative sophistication, they spoke only French, regarding Creole as the language of their black underlings. Blacks like Duvalier, however, owed allegiance to Africa alone, and maintained their connections through voodoo, their colourful belief system, and the traditions of music and dance passed on through generations of slaves and their progeny. In 1934, one hundred and thirty years after the French scuttled from Haiti, under the lash of an illiterate slave force half a million strong, there was still everything to play for in this embattled land. Duvalier, the boy once mocked for wearing absurdly out-of-date clothing tailored by his grandfather, reached maturity as a man at a time when Haiti ought to have been reaching maturity as a nation. Alas, things didn't work out that way.

CHAPTER 7
THE ROAD TO POWER

As a respite from the rigours of the Knox case, the reporters returned to the waterfront nightclub, its multi-coloured fairylights festooned between posts round an empty boardwalk. Beyond the lights, nothing but the impenetrable blackness of a Caribbean night, and the gentle slap of water against the pilings. We sat at tables in a light breeze and the girls were once more paraded for our delectation. There were nine or ten of them, all attractive in their different ways, some short and slender, others buxom with heavy breasts slung casually in scant dresses. There were body types and hues aplenty: huge-hipped, caramel-coloured Dominicans with flashing Hispanic eyes; ebony Haitians with a gentler, more submissive air, their heads held high on slender necks. Some were stick-thin, others fleshy and commodious. Julia, the toffee-hued Dominican, ran to the reporter who had laid her last time, and threw her arms round him. Her tight-curled hair was plaited and pulled back, with small flowers woven into it. By any standard, she was delicious, but so small, almost childlike. They adjourned immediately to one of the small bedroom cubicles, where she rode him with enthusiasm, her breasts swinging wildly. Then she threw her head back, crying 'Si, si, si!' In English or Spanish, it seemed, orgasm was invariably in the affirmative. This time the reporter returned to the group holding her hand. Any girl who dispensed her favours with such abandon deserved, at least, a drink. She sat on his knee, strangely serene, stroking his hair and sipping fruit punch through a straw. Julia was nineteen, from Santo Domingo, and had crossed the border into Haiti in search of work. At the bordello, she paid half her ten-dollar fee to the owner, keeping the balance herself. By Haitian standards, this was very good money indeed.

The average per capita income in 1968 was about $250 a year. My income at the time, as a young reporter in Nassau, was about $10,000. At their nearest point, Haiti and the Bahamas were only sixty miles apart, but the disparity in wealth was enormous then, and is even greater today. Young reporters in the Bahamas today earn at least $25,000 a year or more tax-free. Haiti's average per capita income remains locked at about $350 a year. It is little wonder that its people are so desperate. Julia pined for home. She mentioned a child in Santo Domingo, but her English was poor and our Spanish virtually non-existent, so communication was rudimentary. I would have liked to have heard what odd conjunction of forces brought her west, from the Dominican Republic to Haiti, in search of work. Could Port-au-Prince really be better than Santo Domingo? Alas, it was impossible to find out: questions were met only with shy smiles and blank stares. What I knew was that fiery Dominicans always commanded a market among European men: their passion and warmth were legendary. So the raw forces of economics were at work again: supply and demand. Port-au-Prince's tourist trade was at a halt (thanks, according to Papa Doc, to the reprehensible Graham Greene, whose fiendish novel, *The Comedians*, had left his country in disarray and bereft of visitors) save for a trickle of adventurers like Knox, whose peculiar tastes were undetected, even by his wife and closest friends. In the press corps, the whores had found a concentration of very rich pickings, for all the journalists were 'on expenses', so they spent freely. One went through a Haitian and two Dominicans in less than an hour, and all for the discounted price of twenty dollars. "Three for the price of two," he said afterwards with some satisfaction, his eyes heavy from his exertions. Prostitution wasn't the only profession in which Haitians and Dominicans had engaged in joint ventures. Mixing of the two had always gone on to some extent, though their respective nations dwelt alongside each other uneasily, and often in an atmosphere of open hostility. At the root of the discord was the Haitian peasantry's own remarkable capacity for insinuating themselves into the lower reaches of other countries' economies.

In the Dominican Republic, in Cuba and, in more recent times, the Bahamas, Haitian political and economic refugees have implanted themselves in jobs which natives of those countries have been unwilling to do. In the modern Bahamas, an estimated 60,000 Haitians (the figure varies depending on the source) now do all the yard jobs Bahamians forsook long ago as beneath them. With their ever-present machetes, these industrious people take up their familiar crouching positions to hack away at soil and undergrowth for hours on end, in the broiling heat of the midsummer sun. The black Bahamian *nouveau riche*, who arose after the democratic ejection from power of the white rulers in the Sixties, showed no reluctance to embrace the elitist ways of their former masters. Though they had rejected, quite rightly, the racial elitism practised by the white merchants known as the Bay Street Boys, they soon adopted superior airs on social and intellectual grounds, and the Haitians became the butt of their new-found ascendancy. There is little evidence that Bahamians embrace Haitians as fellow blacks, or even empathise with the continuing despair of their homeland. There is no pretence of fraternal feelings. Black Bahamians, and especially black middle-class Bahamians, see Haitians as inferior in almost every sense, with no regard for their deep culture. They have adopted the proprietorial airs of the European bourgeoisie they once reviled. 'My Haitian' is a term which has now become common currency in the more sedate black suburbs of Nassau. However, though the Haitian presence represents low labour costs, and an endless supply of menial workers, there is little evidence that it is universally regarded as 'a good thing' for the future welfare of the Bahamas.

As I write, a restive air is apparent over a perceived 'Creolisation' of Bahamian society. Local teachers are being asked to learn Creole. Complaints are growing over the spread of Haitian shanty settlements. There is unease over the way they dispose of their dead, the way they relieve themselves into holes in the ground, the way they show total disregard for Bahamian laws. Suddenly, there is a growing feeling that things are getting out of hand, that the Haitians who once adopted deferential and servile airs were now becoming more sure-footed, and hence, more assertive, in their adopted land. The aforementioned Jeffery Cooper, who made it his personal mission to dismantle Haitian shacks in the pine barrens of Abaco, was forced to confront a stark manifestation of this growing assertiveness in the spring of 2006, when an elderly Haitian woman emerged from her shanty home, lifted her dress, pulled down her pants and said: "Kiss my backside, I ain't goin' nowhere!" Cooper and his helpers were shocked.

The Haitian interlopers were no longer servile. Though living for the most part on commandeered Crown Land, they felt secure from eviction, reassured it seemed by the Bahamian Government's apparent reluctance to take action against them. In a sense, this capacity of Haitians for insinuating themselves into alien societies has been at the root of the Dominicans' unease. At first, Haitians were needed to cut sugar cane, a particularly onerous task rated lowest in the jobs table, but their presence began to provoke an increasingly hostile response which had savage and bloody consequences. Since the Treaty of Ryswick at the end of the 17th Century, Hispaniola had, at least nominally, been two separate territories, the western third of the island eventually becoming French-speaking Haiti, the eastern two-thirds destined to become the Spanish-speaking Dominican Republic. However, the east was to mature quicker than the west, and the Dominicans' suspicions and reservations about their near neighbours were to harden into a real desire to put distance between the two. Through two centuries of turmoil, Haiti has now become known to its neighbours as the basket-case of the Caribbean, a land jinxed and cursed by untold forces. From the time of its liberation, it was recalled by Cubans and Jamaicans as the land which glowed orange against the night sky, its homesteads burning amid its many savage spasms. 'Crazy place,' was the most frequent epithet applied. 'Mad people, mad nation.' Smoke from Haiti hung over a huge area. That acrid stench alerted all to the fact that this miserable land was burning again.

If Haiti has become known as the unruly madhouse of the Caribbean, imagine what its nearest neighbours — those obliged to share the same island — have felt about it over the years. Every outburst of political violence has sent terrified Haitians eastwards into the mountains towards the Dominican border. Their desperation, their misery, has created enormous crises of conscience in Santo Domingo. It has also deepened the Dominicans' contempt for the country and its people. The friction between the two reached its zenith at the appropriately named Massacre River in 1937. What happened there is marked as a barely tolerable memory in a land of intolerable memories. America's withdrawal came, of course, in the midst of the Thirties Depression, five years after the Wall Street Crash. It's hard to imagine that a country so routinely depressed as Haiti would feel the impact of more of the same, but it did. Peasants had been trekking in droves over the mountains to the cane fields of the Dominican Republic in search of work and catching boats across the Windward Passage to

Cuba, where sugarcane planting was a staple of the island's economy. In good times, Haitian labour — cheap, reliable and productive — was welcome, enabling growers to profit from higher margins.

One unfortunate by-product of Haiti's chronic economic woes was its people's distressing lack of bargaining power. The dictators Rafael Trujillo and Fulgencio Batista were happy to exploit their vulnerability to the full when world sugar prices were high, but their attitudes changed dramatically when their countries suffered economic setbacks of their own. The Massacre River incident occurred in a year when Haiti reached its economic nadir. It was the product of Trujillo's brutish nature and, it seems, his deep-seated resentment of his Haitian origins. Haiti's abysmal failure to make its way in the world had diminished its citizens' status to a point where utter contempt was the prevailing attitude of its Caribbean neighbours. From my earliest encounters with them in the Sixties, when they were herded off captured sloops at Nassau waterfront, often prodded and whacked by police batons, I was appalled at the way Haitians were treated. There was undoubtedly a feeling among Bahamians then, and it's still largely true, that Haitians were of inferior stock, almost sub-human. Their inability to speak English was part of the problem, but their differences ran much deeper than that.

In the early years of the 20th Century, trade between Haiti and the southern Bahamas was common. Fruit, vegetables, household goods, even clothing and toys, were carried on small sailing boats between Inagua and Mayaguana, the southernmost isles of the archipelago, and northern Haitian ports like Cap Haitien, Port-de-Paix and Gonaives. Eventually, however, as communications improved with the Bahamian capital, Nassau, remoter islands felt less need to trade with foreign nations to the south. Hence, Haiti became more remote in every sense, and its adherence to voodoo gave it a mystical dimension among God-fearing Bahamians which drove an even wider wedge between them. This suspicion was even more marked in the Dominican Republic, which was becoming increasingly restive about the uncertain nature of its nearest neighbour. There was a strong feeling that continued migration from the west would introduce volatile, toxic and even satanic strains into Dominican blood that would ultimately destabilise the Spanish-speaking east. There was a genuine fear that whatever it was that kept Haiti in a state of chaos would be transferred to their own domain. Anti-Haitian feeling took on a frantic edge. One of the most notable characteristics of Haitian migration is that it is invariably one-way, with no reverse gear. Haitians, once settled outside of their homeland, have little desire to return, though they will speak long and loud about the delights of its mountains, its verdant valleys, its intoxicating rhythms and vivid, colourful art. In fact, their love for Haiti is genuine, but there is sad resignation among many, and probably most, Haitian refugees that the country will never be a happy place. Hence, Haitians have become natural expatriates, settling easily in other lands but always keeping their culture intact.

When the depression forced closure of the Dominican Republic's sugar mills, Haitians already living east of the border showed no inclination to move west again. Thus, Trujillo found himself with tens of thousands of foreign mouths to feed — all potentially a threat to his land's national bloodstock. As everywhere else in the Caribbean, where Europe's social, linguistic and cultural impact is all too evident, Dominicans' desire to preserve their whiteness remained a powerful dynamic. If it is still strong today, it was irresistible in 1937, when Trujillo engaged in his own brand of ethnic cleansing. In what became known as 'The Parsley Purge', his troops identified Haitian peasants by asking them to name the sprigs of parsley they carried with them through the cane fields and into the hills. If the Creole word *pelegil* emerged instead of its Spanish equivalent — *perejil* — the speaker was condemned. In the space of five weeks in the fall of that year, Trujillo's thugs chopped and bayoneted 20,000 Haitians in his version of what Adolf Hitler would later term 'The Final Solution' in relation to the Jews. In fact, the parallels were remarkable: like Hitler, Trujillo saw the interlopers as a threat to both his country's economic stability and its racial purity. They had to die.

As Hitler recoiled from the Jew others claimed to see in him, so Trujillo recoiled from the Haitian in his own body and soul. Their unfathomable inner conflicts found release in mass murder. Massacre River, which forms part of the border between the Dominican Republic and Haiti, ran red with Haitian blood, according to folklore, and the slaughter has gone down in Haiti's history as an outrage and an abomination never to be forgotten. The bloodletting began on the personal instructions of Trujillo, whose visit to the border town of Dajabon convinced him of the scale of the immigrant problem and the extreme measures necessary to solve it. The massacre reawakened all the vile excesses of Hispaniola's past, with indiscriminate elimination of defenceless people. Those who somehow escaped Dominican blades scrambled for the border. Others lost limbs and suffered unimaginable horrors before dragging themselves to Cap Haitien, where Trujillo's savagery was first revealed to the outside world. Eventually, Trujillo was to compensate Haiti for its loss with a cheque for half a million dollars, though there were doubts that any of the money reached the families of the victims. At twenty-five dollars a head, Haitians came cheap, as they always did. However, life in Port-au-Prince is probably even cheaper today (2005) as lawless gangs roam Port-au-Prince killing at will.

Duvalier, having completed his early in-house training at St Francis Hospice, moved on promotion to a government-run home for the elderly, some miles outside of the capital. Here he went about his work with quiet diligence. Though medicine gave him respectability and status in a land where markedly black men were rarely accorded either, it was politics that really caught his imagination. He joined an intellectual group called *Les Griots* – The Bards – and was inspired there to read avidly and pursue his literary interests. Trujillo's savage treatment of the Haitian peasants, and especially the racial undertones of his actions, was another seminal event in Haiti's history which left scars in Duvalier's mind. He and his fellow nationalists countered the widespread assumption of white superiority with a heightened reverence for blackness, and specifically African blackness. In their regular meetings, *Les Griots* harkened back, repeatedly, to the vast continent to the east where their forebears had been torn so brutally from their roots. They developed a deep reverence for the Sudanese and Ethiopian civilisations of old, playing on the black man's ascendancy in Africa at a time when European whites were still in caves. In these discussions, Duvalier was rarely among the most assertive contributors. He was painfully quiet and subdued, a man whose nature was so introverted, he was easy to overlook. However, it was among fellow intellectuals that his political philosophy matured.

In 1939, as the Second World War loomed in Europe, Duvalier was to take a step that would have a lasting, and largely beneficial, impact on his life. He got married. Typically, it was not Duvalier himself who instigated the match. Friends all too aware of his social deficiencies arranged for him to meet Simone Ovide, a woman who was far from socially confident herself, but who was to become the true dynamo in the Duvalier household. It is astonishing that so many black rulers in Africa and the Caribbean have followed predictable marriage patterns, choosing elegant and taller wives of lighter hue. Simone Ovide, illegitimate daughter of a prominent mulatto merchant, fitted the mould perfectly, though she was initially as retiring as Duvalier himself. At thirty-two, and now established as a government-employed physician, Duvalier remained a subdued, rather enigmatic, figure, but Simone was to provide, in the fullness of time, the true backbone of their partnership, with husband Francois drawing strength from a match that was to prove durable, if somewhat turbulent.

Like many of her type before and since, Simone Duvalier was eager to put her past behind her. As her husband progressed, socially and politically, she adopted airs suited to her new-found role. Typically, too, she quickly squashed all discussion of her origins as the unwanted daughter of a maid, and reinvented herself as a strong-minded matriarch who would become, in the 1950s, the shadowy but undoubtedly vital presence behind the most notorious tyrant of the western world. Reluctant to disclose her date of birth — a move presumably intended to block inquiries into her family background — Madame Duvalier was to become a fascinating subject for conjecture in Port-au-Prince's higher echelons. Thought to have been born in Leogane, in southern Haiti, around 1913, she was the product of a fleeting liaison between her young mother and the businessman-cum-scholar Jules Faine, who seduced her while she was working as a scullery assistant at his home. Simone was given away, an embarrassing and accidental by-product of a loveless tryst, and ended up being taken in by a waifs' home in Petionville, the mulatto suburb overlooking Port-au-Prince. Her light skin won her favours she might otherwise have been denied. Children at the orphanage were encouraged by the mulatto elite to learn occupational skills. And it was while working as a nursing aide that she met the diffident, tongue-tied young doctor, Francois Duvalier. Thus began an extraordinary partnership which would last for more than thirty years, ended only by the dictator's death in 1971, and in which she would figure as the almost spectral force behind the throne.

The aftermath of the Massacre River incident, and the years spanning the Second World War, were to prove a powerfully important period in Duvalier's life. His marriage to Simone, at St Pierre's Church, in Petionville was the beginning of his transformation from shy junior doctor to mystic scholar, polemical writer (though, it has to be said, not an especially good one) and political aspirant. The main dynamic in the remarkable rise of the young Duvalier was negritude, the active repudiation of the prejudices which — to his way of thinking — continued to condemn blacks to second-class status in a society which, even a hundred and thirty years after independence, was stratified along the colour lines which had bedevilled its past.

In many respects, Haiti's social structure of the 1940s was similar to that of Great Britain, where the masses were kept down by a privileged, but essentially mediocre, 'higher order' whose existence depended on control of national wealth and a network of clubs and fraternities whose objective was to maintain the status quo at all costs. Duvalier and his friends in *Les Griots* were obsessed with obtaining anthropological evidence to rebut all the old assumptions. They wanted blacks to emerge and triumph politically, certainly, but more important still was to provide incontrovertible proof of their intellectual worth. Enmeshed in this process was a growing recognition of voodoo and its mystical links with the negroes' African past. Running alongside Duvalier's intellectual and political development was his growing prowess as a voodoo adept, and his eventual emergence as a fully-fledged *houngan*, or priest, a development which would have a profound influence on his political life and prove a telling factor in the creation of the incomparably ghoulish figure called Papa Doc. All this was taking place against a backdrop of further political change in Haiti.

The Massacre River incident effectively disabled President Vincent, leaving him impotent and at the mercy of Trujillo, who took advantage of the situation to exert further control over his unpredictable neighbour. Dominicans were coming to recognise that the solution to the continuing 'Haitian Problem' lay in effectively annexing the country, reducing it to a virtual satellite state. Trujillo achieved this to a limited extent by engineering the ailing Vincent's replacement by the compliant Elie Lescot, an avaricious, loose-living mulatto who sailed to power in Port-au-Prince on a flood of Trujillo money. Lescot had been Haiti's Ambassador in Santo Domingo in the mid-1930s. He used this posting to inveigle his way into Trujillo's favour and emerged as something of a court favourite, sharing the Dominican strongman's taste for excess in all things. While Vincent was out of the country seeking treatment for encroaching blindness, Lescot was installed at the National Palace, a move that was ultimately to have disastrous consequences. One was a further period of tension between Haiti and the Dominican Republic (culminating in a plot by Trujillo henchmen and a Haitian death squad to kill him), the other was a widening of the racial chasm in Haiti, where the new President proceeded to assert mulatto supremacy in ways that would deepen the blacks' bitterness.

Part of Lescot's strategy was to connive at, if not actively encourage, the Catholic Church's campaign against voodoo, which blacks saw as a vital component of their heritage. For Lescot, this had a dual purpose: to reassert the mulattoes' European mindset and undermine a belief system that accentuated black identity. Through a series of promotions, he was also to catapult to prominence the man who would become Duvalier's immediate predecessor as President, a charismatic black called Paul Magloire. As police chief, and later head of the palace guard, Magloire had ringside seats at most of the major political events in the immediate post-war era. He studied the machinations of Haitian politics to good effect. When Lescot, now at odds with the Dominican Republic and the United States, was eventually forced out of office by growing unrest over his high-handedness, Magloire was in a striking position he was to exploit to the full. Meanwhile, Duvalier, still learning his trade as a government physician, went quietly about his work. So quietly, in fact, that his taciturnity became legendary among colleagues. He was sometimes referred to, behind his back, as 'The Dummy' or 'The Dumb One'. Beneath the silent facade, however, a fervent political spirit stirred. This spirit was reinforced by an astute mind and a strong streak of pragmatism. Haiti would hear from Duvalier soon enough. And his voice would produce enduring echoes.

By the time World War II was over, the Black Movement in Haiti had gained impetus. Trujillo continued to exert influence in Port-au-Prince through the US-trained Colonel Petrus Calixte, a black who commanded the largely black Garde, which had been formed to stabilise the national institutions and ensure the security of any popularly elected government. Calixte had initially enjoyed prominence under President Vincent, but when Vincent dismissed him for suspected collusion with Trujillo, he took a commission in the Dominican Army, only to rebound later with a significant role to play in the swiftly changing Haitian political scene of the mid-to-late 1940s.

It was Calixte and his Garde that hastened the departure of Lescot in 1946 after the President's elitist attitudes had rendered him unacceptable in the newly-emerging order. The three-man junta that took over following this mini-revolution included the aforementioned Major Paul Magloire. Initially, the intention was to introduce democratic civil rule, but the officers were unskilled in the nuances of such a transition. As they dithered, public unrest demanded action. The result was the election of a National Assembly in May, 1946, and a presidential poll which included Calixte as the MOP (*Mouvement Ouvriers Peysans*) candidate. Also running was the estimable Dumarsais Estime, Duvalier's former schoolmaster, who commanded wide support among working and middle-class blacks, especially in the traditionally radical and volatile northern areas. Considered moderate, and, therefore, relatively safe, Estime was installed at the Palace after two rounds of voting. Haiti appeared to be on course for better times. Like Duvalier, Estime was from humble stock. He was also passionate in his stand against mulatto elitism. His initial intentions seemed honourable enough, his stated objective being to uplift the poor. In many respects, he was, by Haitian standards, quite successful, expanding the school system, establishing agricultural co-operatives and extending black representation in the civil service. However, his radicalism did not sit well with the mulattoes, who sought every chance to undermine him. He fell foul of them on several fronts, but the two that were to prove crucial were business and religion. His income tax measures were not welcome, and his promotion of voodoo as an authentic religion outraged the Europeanised elite, who were intent on resisting the spread of African influence at all costs. Isolated from power, appalled at the financial burdens placed upon them, the elite began plotting, enlisting ambitious officers within the Garde to support their cause. When Estime, sensing the gathering storm, tried to force through constitutional changes that would have extended his presidential term, the Garde — now renamed the Haitian Army — moved in to secure his resignation.

As Estime left for exile in Jamaica, the same junta that replaced Lescot resumed office as an interim government. The deposing of Estime provided hard lessons for Duvalier, who had secured his first ministerial post under his former tutor. As Estime left Haiti, Duvalier lost his job in the Labour Department. However, the experience was to impress itself upon him in ways that would produce consequences a few years down the line. Duvalier realised that the Army, the one institution with the wherewithal to change regimes at will, could not be depended upon. It was a realisation that would ultimately produce the Tontons Macoute, one of the defining features of the Duvalier regime. The removal of Estime in 1950 was another of those seminal events that left deep impressions on Duvalier's mind. It forced him to recognise, once again, that mulatto influence was powerful – in fact, nigh unassailable – whoever occupied the National Palace. Always, it seemed, they would manipulate events from the rear. And always, it seemed, they would use their financial power to buy military intervention when things were not going their way. However, the Estime regime, short-lived as it was, helped to further the black nationalist cause, and intensified the resolve of Duvalier and his fellow intellectuals in their determination to break down the old order once and for all.

For Duvalier, the first political break had come via the MOP Workers Movement, which represented urban and rural blacks. This became a force in Haitian politics under the astute leadership of Daniel Fignole, one of two figures who would mentor the young physician, as he applied himself to humdrum administrative tasks in the movement, at the start of his inexorable rise. Fignole and the sullen voodoo priest, Lorimer Denis, were to provide the early momentum in Duvalier's climb. And behind them all lay the long shadow of Dessalines. If Haiti had always been torn between its European and African influences, then now was the time for realignment. The spirit of Guinea and the Congo were to shape the future of this troubled land. The result, as always, was enduring turmoil.

CHAPTER 8

THE VIEW FROM HOTEL OLOFFSON

From its balconies, the detached observer gazes across abundant tropical vegetation towards the city in the valley. Cradled by hills, Port-au-Prince looks placid, pleasant even, from here — an old Caribbean colonial capital steeped in sunlight under a thin haze of woodsmoke. Far off, cockerels crow loudly, a reminder that city and country live cheek-by-jowl in this scary but enchanting land. The Hotel Oloffson has seen it all, and possibly too much. Its location has given it a grandstand view of tumultuous events for more than a century. When the ill-fated President Sam found himself without a palace after the summary elimination of Cincinattus Leconte in 1912, it was the Oloffson that was to provide refuge. For Sam, it enshrined many memories, for the gingerbread edifice on its hillside perch was the old family home. Since then it had progressed through various incarnations (it was even a military hospital during the US occupation) to what it was in 1968 when Cole and I sipped Barbancourt under a ceiling fan on the verandah. Then, as now, the Oloffson offered its guests a kind of shabby gentility, a cool and wholly incongruous retreat from the urban madness. Graham Greene met his friends here frequently until he was declared persona non grata by Duvalier. Visiting writers — and especially journalists — liked its Bohemian insouciance, its take-it-or-leave-it air. Somehow, unaccountably, it had survived as a raffish reminder of better days, or what seemed like better days in retrospect. Truman Capote was here once to work on a musical play, foppishly amusing as he and the producer Peter Brook took sustenance at the Oloffson bar. Greene was in Haiti three times, firstly during the relatively relaxed Magloire years, when the Europeanised mulattoes were enjoying what appeared to be their political swansong. It was during his third visit, in the steamheat of August, 1963, that he was inspired to write *The Comedians*, and to recount the horrors of the Duvalier regime, which by then had revealed its true nature. Greene told his publisher that he would have liked to return a fourth time before completing his book, but by then he had already been blackballed by the Tontons. He had to content himself with a journey along the Dominican border, trying to absorb a little more of Haiti's special aura. No doubt, as he gazed westwards over the hills towards Port-au-Prince, he spared at least a moment or two for recollections of the Oloffson. Cole and I were in our early twenties then, mere tyros in the world of journalism, but the Oloffson and the Barbancourt jointly induced pleasurable illusions of sophistication.

From this high perch in an exotic land, life looked ridiculously promising. If we could achieve this — the Oloffson and Port-au-Prince — so early in our professional lives, then multitudes of riches lay ahead. I was a smoker at the time, and I can recall, even now, the satisfaction induced by deep draughts of Camel smoke, toasted tobacco glowing red against the deep Haitian night. We moved to high stools in the bar, and I recall being entranced by a Haitian beauty, one of Duvalier's aspirant noirs, who looked at me with serene detachment. Cole wanted her, and so did I, but even Barbancourt-induced bravado did not stretch so far as to make a move on her. Not here, where the Tontons fed severed testicles to the cats. "Too upscale," said Cole, "Black bourgeoisie. Probably Papa Doc's daughter." "Yes," I said, "Hanging by my extremities in Fort Dimanche does not appeal to me greatly." "No," he agreed. "Emphatically, no." Even so, I became convinced then that Haitian women, at their very best, were probably among the most beautiful on earth, with their sculpted cheeks and ebony sheen. Cole looked at her longingly and released a long murmuring sound. "Mmmm!" he said. "Absolutely," I replied. The Oloffson became 'The Trianon' in Greene's novel. Doctor Philipot was found dead in the pool, as I recall, the same pool, if memory serves, where the couple made love. Over the pool towered the Gothic splendour of the hotel itself, with its fretworked flourishes, toytown towers and breezeblown verandahs. Greene thought there was a touch of Edgar Allan Poe about it: he expected to find bats hanging from the chandeliers. It's tempting to think the Oloffson is somehow immune from Haiti's more reckless excesses, but this was not true in President Sam's time. It was from here — his makeshift palace — that Sam fled to the French Embassy, from which he was dragged to be impaled on the compound fence. US marines moved in, soon afterwards, in an attempt to calm the agitated populace and stayed for nineteen years.

When the girl rose and left, our attention was claimed by a very different character. He was a spectacularly well-dressed dandy who spoke English with a kind of bogus Oxbridge accent. There was a touch of the thespian about him. With his gold-topped cane and two-toned shoes, he might have been straight off the set of a 1940s Fred Astaire movie. Certainly, he was too fastidiously attired to be a journalist, but that's what he was. Aubelin Jolicoeur gained fame – infamy, maybe – thanks to Greene. It was here, in the Oloffson, where they almost certainly met, that Jolicoeur emerged a few years later as the ubiquitous Petit Pierre in *The Comedians*. Petit he certainly was, but physical slightness did not curb his success with women. Sexual prowess was one of the many legends attached to this prancing boulevardier, who oiled his way into people's confidence with a enticing mixture of charm and sheer persistence. Jolicoeur, superficially, was Port-au-Prince's equivalent of a big city gossip columnist. He charted the comings and goings of Haiti's transient celebrities, name-dropping shamelessly to gain access to circles in which he was probably not wholly welcome. In his white suits and silk ascots, he might even have been a Haitian Tom Wolfe. Certainly, he knew how Haiti worked and played the system to his considerable advantage.

Truman Capote introduced Jolicoeur to Greene in 1954. Though I have no evidence that the Oloffson was the location for this seminal event, it almost certainly was because, for the best part of half a century, the tiny newsman used the 19th Century hotel as his personal domain. It was here, where the local rum and lingering cigar smoke produced the unique aroma of Caribbean decadence, that Jolicoeur hob-nobbed with film stars, novelists, journalists and others from the glamorous worlds of New York and Hollywood. With a mixture of solicitude and quite shameless sycophancy, Jolicoeur inveigled his way into even the most defensive coteries. Using flattery, buffoonery and no small degree of personal vanity, he developed his appeal as a peculiar but hugely entertaining gadfly. Jolicoeur liked to characterise himself as a consummate public relations man. Mr Haiti was one of several soubriquets he adopted, hinting at his role of professional 'greeter', but more astute observers detected other, more sinister, sides to the dandy's life. When Jolicoeur materialised at Francois Duvalier International Airport to meet every major international flight, he was, on the face of it, part of Haiti's promotional package, an amusing mascot for a nation whose bleakness and despondency were sometimes all too apparent. In truth, however, he was monitoring incoming traffic for his 'father' – the word he always used – Francois Duvalier, who saw Jolicoeur as a useful tool in off-setting the more negative aspects of Haiti's image. If Haiti was home to this colourful jester, whose love for life was palpable, how could it possibly be the homicidal hell-hole depicted by Greene? Therein lay Jolicoeur's appeal for Papa Doc, but it went further than that: he was always suspected of being a palace informer. To deduce from this that Jolicoeur was a shallow, unprincipled popinjay would be quite wrong, though vanity was certainly a feature of his character. In fact, he was a hard-working and capable journalist who, when appropriate, turned his penmanship on those he considered vulgar or inept.

During Papa Doc's reign, Jolicoeur was a kind of cultural correspondent, impressing Haiti's intelligentsia with arcane literary references. Under Baby Doc, he adopted a more vituperative style, ridiculing the regime and what he considered to be Haiti's preposterous delusions about democracy. Under the flippant veneer, Jolicoeur was also a serious commentator. And his contacts were unmatched. When Cole and I caught sight of him, Jolicoeur was working his beat, flouncing on to the porch with a click of his heels and a tap of his cane. There was something quaintly anachronistic about him, hinting at Gershwin and Cole Porter. Close up, his deep black skin possessed an almost unreal sheen, as though he used potions to enhance what were, by any standard, quite remarkable facial features. There is no doubt that Jolicoeur had established an impressive rapport with Duvalier. On one level, this was surprising because it would be hard to imagine two characters more different. While Jolicoeur was the consummate showman, an extrovert extraordinaire, Duvalier was lost in deep vaults of silence, the ultimate introvert whose inner thoughts were rarely shared. However, something more profound provided the foundation for their affinity: their blackness. Both men were reared at a time when blackness was a social obstacle in Haiti, a virtual guarantee of failure in a society where mulattoes reigned and European mores predominated. Against mountainous odds, and in sharply contrasting ways, Jolicoeur and Duvalier had 'made it' to positions of prominence and power in Port-au-Prince. They were two noticeably small, and noticeably black, go-getters who upset the odds with style.

At the Oloffson, Jolicoeur targeted the women first. He flirted outrageously (his twelve children by twelve women testified to his persuasive powers) and seemed to acknowledge men more out of duty than commitment. Of course, he would have known why we were there: the Knox trial was the talk of the town, and the morning papers had listed all the names of the visiting correspondents. His interest in us, however, seemed cursory. Greene's depiction of Jolicoeur in *The Comedians* is not exactly flattering. He emerges as a plausible sneak whose overdone geniality concealed a deeper purpose, to collect intelligence for Papa Doc. However, Jolicoeur himself seemed unfazed by the international notoriety he achieved. Unlike Duvalier, he revelled in the celebrity Greene bestowed upon him. At the Oloffson, he was never allowed to buy a drink. Jolicoeur tracked Haiti's misfortunes for nearly half a century, but it was the rise of Duvalier he most favoured and admired. He genuinely believed that Papa Doc's way of doing business was the only realistic option for a country whose nature was so emphatically self-destructive. In his dotage, more than thirty years on, Jolicoeur and a Duvalierist friend spent their final days reflecting on more ordered times, when Papa Doc brought discipline to a fundamentally unruly land.

Jolicoeur was born in 1924, during the US occupation, in a Jacmel cemetery. His mother had gone into labour and delivered him among the tombstones. By the time *Les Griots* and the MOP began advancing the black cause in the immediate post-war era, he was a young man on the make, taking care to learn immaculate French so that he might ingratiate himself with his social betters. From his inauspicious start, Jolicoeur progressed quickly, winning over influential mulattoes and their international friends with a charm which, though somewhat syrupy for most tastes, they found hard to resist. One of Jolicoeur's undoubted virtues was a capacity to see good in all things. He constantly and diligently advanced Haiti's cause, insisting that it was not as brutal and hopeless as its popular image suggested. Privately, though, he acknowledged the truth, developing a contempt for his own people encapsulated in a single sentence. "In every Haitian there is a thug," he said. The dandy he became was, it appears, a conscious reaction against what might have been had he not escaped his background. As a working journalist, he was never wealthy in his own right, but he set out to become the embodiment of an old adage that newspapermen are paupers who live like princes. In a sense, that's what Jolicoeur achieved, hobnobbing with the Oloffson's glitterati, trading off what became a formidable array of contacts.

When *The Comedians* was published in 1966, and Petit Pierre became an internationally renowned character in modern fiction, Duvalier grew apoplectic with rage at Greene's impudence. But Jolicoeur revelled in his new-found notoriety. Greene lovers travelled far to meet him. Jolicoeur held court in the Oloffson, the diminutive dandy in his element, and did more than justify the entertainment potential attributed to him by the writer. As Greene said, the irrepressible Aubelin had the quick movements of a monkey 'swinging on ropes of laughter'. True enough, for Jolicoeur was always laughing in a land where there was little to laugh about. On the night Cole and I saw Jolicoeur, the Oloffson lights went out. This was an accepted part of Port-au-Prince life: the utilities were unreliable, and public lighting came and went as if on an official's whim. Candles were lit on the bar and a faint glow was cast on the looming shrubs and bushes outside. I recall the cicadas scraping in the trees like a million electric razors, and huge moths hovering towards the pinpricks of light, some as big as birds. Jolicoeur did his rounds, a quip here, an aside there, and all in his strange little high-pitched voice as he collected gossip for his paper, *Le Nouvelliste*. Jolicoeur was an agronomist in his early life, but the inquisitive instincts that were to take him into journalism were well-established by the time the Black Nationalist Movement began seriously challenging the mulatto hegemony in the early post-war age.

The rise of Paul Magloire would create fertile terrain for Jolicoeur's socialising, and it was during this comparatively gilded time that he began mixing with the stars. Duvalier, meanwhile, began the slow transformation from backroom drone to political high-flier. His progress was to be built on the strong foundations of his strictly unglamorous past. Under Estime, Duvalier had acquired his first ministerial experience and had become something of an expert on land reform and other agrarian issues. This helped to underpin a reputation already well-established in Haiti's rural areas by his tireless efforts in combating yaws, a disease which played havoc with the peasantry. It was during his wanderings among the farmsteads that a powerful image evolved of Duvalier riding his donkey up treacherous mountain paths, carrying his potions and medicaments on his mercy missions deep into the countryside. During these peregrinations, the quiet, contemplative and compassionate Duvalier was in the ascendant. He became known for his unassuming diligence. The poor, who lived at the mercy of a savage tropical climate, the insect-borne diseases it spawned, the economic depradations of their homeland, and the capricious nature of its politicians, were pathetically vulnerable in almost every sense.

The Anti-Yaws Campaign was a US-funded initiative to eliminate a debilitating affliction which had left thousands of rural Haitians disabled. A contagious bacterial disease, it primarily struck children under fifteen and was incubated and nurtured by moist tropical conditions. Almost invariably, yaws flourishes among the poor, encouraged by inadequate sanitation and social congestion. In its early stages, it creates ugly skin lesions but, untreated, it can cause severe physical deformities, twisting bones and joints. Though virtually unknown in First World societies, yaws thrives in Third World conditions in Africa, Asia and South America, and is easily passed from human to human in overcrowded conditions. Haiti, with its rampant poverty, chronic overcrowding, poor sanitary arrangements and widespread ignorance in medical matters, was a fertile breeding ground for the disease. Before the mass treatment initiatives of the 1950s, up to 100 million people worldwide were estimated to suffer from yaws. By the 1980s, these had been reduced to a few hundreds per year, though a resurgence was recorded later in the Far East and South Sea Islands.

Duvalier's role in combating yaws was, in truth, relatively modest. He was sincere enough in his endeavours, and was certainly not lacking when it came to covering the ground needed to make a worthwhile contribution, but his critics were later to claim that he made the most of his involvement for political gain. The man of compassion was a useful image to nurture during his presidential crusades, and he was soon to adopt a paternalistic posture towards his patients. "The peasants love their doctor," he said, "and I am their Papa Doc." Reserved, considerate, solicitous, Duvalier was as far removed from a ruthless tyrant as one can imagine, but power prompts men to perform unusual contortions. In his case, the contortions were such that the physician with an almost missionary zeal became a monster. Even those who knew him best were at a loss to explain how this appalling transformation came about. As part of the Estime Government, Duvalier learned much about the machinations of departmental affairs. As Director-General of the National Public Health Service between 1946 and 1948, he continued the battle against yaws and achieved significant political mileage in the process. In 1948, he was appointed Minister of Public Health and Labour, a job he was to keep until Estime's overthrow. For a time thereafter, Duvalier returned to the US Sanitary Mission, extending his medical knowledge in the field of hygiene and disease-control. It was now that he formulated his strategy for political advancement. Enraged by the Magloire junta's expulsion of his hero, deeply annoyed at the resurgence of the mulatto elite, appalled at the stalling of the negroes' cause, Duvalier had plenty to occupy his mind during the first three years of the new decade. It was now, during this crucial period between 1950-53, that Duvalierism began to take on a shape of its own, for the once diffident doctor was increasingly becoming recognised by his political foes as the central figure in the opposition fold. From once being the shy man with nothing to say, Duvalier became the embodiment of black nationalism in Haiti. It was a role he was to savour for many years to come.

CHAPTER 9

MAGLOIRE

THE rise of Paul Magloire, a charismatic black soldier of soaring ambition, helped to harden the resolve of Francois Duvalier as he moved to set the black nationalist cause back on track. In practically every respect, Magloire represented what Duvalier most despised among the general run of Haitian presidential aspirants. That he was the main force behind the removal of the revered Estime was but one aspect of the problem. More significant still was that he had mulatto interests at heart, and was an enthusiastic black advocate of their cause. Physically, Magloire was at the far end of the spectrum from Duvalier. He was tall, handsome, extrovert, expansive...in fact, an attractive lover of life, whose dynamic demeanour was as far removed from that of the furtively quiet Duvalier as can be imagined. These were not kindred spirits. Magloire was a swaggering, uniformed leader of men who believed passionately in the military's capacity for manipulating the political landscape to its own advantage. Duvalier was a deeply suspicious critic of the Army who resented its power and treachery. From the earliest days of the Magloire presidency — and it was to last six years — it was clear that a collision course had been set between these two influential but contrasting figures, and that the impact, when it came, would have sickening consequences. For the time being, however, Duvalier lay low, carefully cultivating his connections and working towards what he saw as the crucial next phase in Haiti's political development. It was a period when his image as a compassionate man of the people gained credence. For Haiti itself, and especially gadabouts like Jolicoeur, the Magloire era was to be reflected upon in future years as something of a gilded age. If Estime's reign would be remembered for its social advancement, especially in the field of education, Magloire's would become stamped upon the minds of the international glitterati, as the period when Haiti blossomed into one of the world's most romantic, and intriguing, destinations.

At its best, there was no doubt that Haiti possessed charms that most of its Caribbean neighbours found hard to match. Topographically, it was an enchanting riot of rolling forested hills and fragrant valleys. Climatically, its enveloping warmth was dampened down by torrential and refreshing summer rains. Culturally, it was a bewitching blend of European and African influences, the self-consciously elegant former often at odds with the colourful, vibrant, uninhibited latter. Artistically, it was an extravaganza of vivid images, mostly daubed in prime colours and inspired by voodoo. Musically, it was both quaint and dynamic, the drumbeat a defining motif of its native rhythms. This enticing mixture of attractions, all overseen by the benign Magloire, became irresistible for the rich international set of the early 1950s. Literary icons, movie moguls, Hollywood starlets and vast armies of pretenders and hangers-on, all began converging on fashionable Port-au-Prince, a fundamentally glamorous city whose potential had always seemed blighted by the vagaries of its politics. Its natural beauty and cultural riches were enhanced in the eyes of its fun-loving visitors by a frisson of danger, an element of the unknown, and for six magical years, it became 'the place to be' on the global celebrity circuit. It was at this time that the English homosexual playwright, Noel Coward held court, no doubt trawling for boys on his excursions to Haiti from his Jamaica home. The composer, Irving Berlin was also attracted by the new regime, along with the aforementioned Truman Capote, who, with Coward, introduced new dimensions of camp behaviour to the Port-au-Prince scene. Suddenly, the Oloffson became the place it was always intended to be, a gingerbread palace for the creative classes.

Across the water, only sixty-odd miles away, lay another island enjoying a gilded age, the Cuba of Batista, where international mobsters held court among the less cerebral, less cultured, elements of the celebrity circuit. Between them, the islands gave the Caribbean a patina of glamour it was subsequently to lose, as first Duvalier, then Castro, fell like heavy curtains across this colourful stage and its immense cast of characters. Inevitably, this surge in Haiti's popularity was helped along by restoration of the mulatto elite's fortunes. Under Magloire, the light-skinned upper middle-class felt comfortable again on the balconies of their hillside villas, gazing down on the heaving slums of the downtown area, reassured that their interests were being taken care of. It was during Magloire's reign that Haiti celebrated the 150th anniversary of its independence. And it was then that the apparent immutability of its race and class stratification became most evident, much to the annoyance of Duvalier and his political sympathisers.

While Washington feted Magloire, and the American press made laudatory but ludicrous comparisons between the Haitian President and Dwight Eisenhower, Duvalier was working tirelessly in the shadows, far from the glitzy gatherings the President hosted and relished. This was a time when the repellant US Senator, Joe McCarthy, was conducting his witch-hunts against alleged communists among America's actors and writers. There was a fever of anti-communist feeling throughout the land, and Magloire traded on the trend by adopting anti-Red postures of his own. It was one of the few areas in which he and Duvalier shared views, and both were to trade on it unabashedly, in seeking to procure American aid. Magloire, in fact, was to preside over the last relatively civilised period in Haitian history. It is no exaggeration to say that everything has been on a downhill slide since his day, and older Haitians still reflect on the early 1950s as a serene interlude between the humiliation of the US occupation and the insanity of the Duvaliers.

Magloire was a man of marked military bearing, and no wonder. His father was a general and the discipline of military life had been instilled into him from an early age. He had grown up to believe that the army was the one constant element in a land of chaos, and that its force was vital to the ordered progress of the nation. When the US departed in 1934, Magloire emerged as one of its most illustrious products, a rising young officer in an army formed to assert itself against the caprice and intrigue of the politicians, whose motives and methods could never be trusted. At the time he helped overthrow the calamitous regime of Elie Lescot in 1946, he also became aware of the destructive potential of Marxism in the new Cold War setting. Haiti's student uprising of the time reflected the new infatuation young intellectuals felt for Left-Wing ideology, and Magloire vowed to combat it at every turn. As a product of the black bourgeoisie, Magloire was quick to appreciate the spoils of elitism and showed no reluctance to embrace the monied mulatto milieu, who continued to control Haiti's economy. Though markedly black himself, he was not averse to accepting the patronage of the mulatto business interests and was quickly identified as their champion. When Estime showed a disturbing tendency to promote more than a token number of blacks in his own administration, it was Magloire's junta that once more brought about change at the mulattoes' behest.

For the best part of a decade, Magloire was seen as the elite's negro strong-man, a military leader capable of unseating unacceptable presidents almost at will. However, the cyclical nature of Haitian politics would soon catch up with him. If Duvalier's political hero was Dessalines, and Estime identified closely with Toussaint, there is no doubt that Magloire's inspiration was King Christophe, who built the famous citadel in northern Haiti, and shared the national territory with the mulatto Alexandre Petion after the downfall of Dessalines. From 1807 until 1811, Christophe was President of northern Haiti, while Petion ruled the south, but a short civil war left him as King Henri I at the beginning of a nine-year reign which, though tyrannical, achieved some notable economic successes. Christophe, born in Grenada, was a military leader whose expertise had been burnished by the revolutionary turmoil of the times. During the American Revolutionary War, he fought at Savannah, Georgia. Then, in 1790, he involved himself in the various rebellious convulsions which were ultimately to give Saint Domingue its independence. Under Toussaint, he served as a Brigadier-General and, in the fiery aftermath of Dessalines' short and brutal reign, he inevitably found himself at the head of one of the two competing factions.

Like Magloire, Christophe was not averse to self-aggrandisement. He possessed an expansive attitude to life which found expression through grandiose building schemes, the Sans Souci Palace and Citadelle Laferriere being the most notable examples. What's left of these two impressive edifices have become major tourist attractions in more recent times, though as I write (2005), tourism in Haiti is strictly for the recklessly intrepid, as the country moves into new realms of chaos and disorder. Ultimately, Christophe was unhinged by a stroke in 1820 and took his own life as insurrection erupted around him. It was not a happy end for a man with monarchical instincts, and lofty ambitions for his adopted homeland, but it was very much in keeping with the ebb and flow of Haitian political affairs. Once the strong hand of the tyrant was loosened by disability, the people ran riot in the streets. It was a theme that was to find many a reprise as Haiti made its uncertain way in the world.

The parallels between Magloire and Christophe were noted by the internationally renowned dancer, Katherine Dunham, whose book *Island Possessed* (Doubleday 1969), cites the similarities with special reference to their African maleness, their liking for material wealth, and the boundless well-being they were able to acquire at the expense of the Haitian peasantry. Indeed, this oft-repeated trend among Haitian presidents, a raft of good intentions followed by an uncontrolled taste for exploitation, was to set the pattern for two centuries of political non-development. Magloire was egregiously acquisitive, even by Haitian presidential standards, and fell into all the traps that were later to become so evident in post-colonial Africa. He liked uniforms, medals, oil-painted portraits, grandiose sur-roundings, all the glittering trappings of office, and saw the impoverished Haitian people as buttresses for his high opinion of himself. Perhaps it's a throwback to tribalism, but emerging black nations have, almost invariably, fallen into this pattern of lionising maximum leaders in stretched limos decked out in ostentatious regalia. Magloire was the archetypal post-colonial leader at a time when they were in short supply, for Haiti achieved its 'freedom' – the freedom of the abattoir, its people offered up for slaughter – long before other European possessions around the world.

Ms Dunham, who saw Haiti as her second home, was in a better position than most to judge the three outstanding Haitian leaders of that immediate post-war era. As a global celebrity in her own right, she gravitated naturally into presidential circles, and evidently revered Estime, who she regarded as a genuine reforming force for good. In Magloire, she recognised an opportunistic early manifestation of Third World grandiosity and extravagance, a man whose type would later emerge rather more grotesquely in the form of Idi Amin, the appalling Bokassa and, of course, Robert Mugabe. With his broad chest and military bearing, Magloire liked to stand in front of a life-size portrait of Christophe, adopting a similarly regal posture. He also developed a passion for building things, another post-colonial excuse for misdirecting First World aid. His Cite Magloire was a forerunner of Duvalier's own aborted urban monument, Duvalierville. Having been close to Estime, Ms Dunham felt guilty at her developing friendship with the man who unseated him. But, as she wrote in her book,

Magloire was hard to resist, particularly as he displayed such a partiality for all things European, especially the English. Magloire and his strong-willed wife, known somewhat sarcastically as Madame la Presidente, fell into patrician ways, viewing the peasantry as children to be manipulated with arbitrary cash handouts and other gestures of presidential benevolence.

For Ms Dunham, their behaviour was strongly reminiscent of the Perons in Argentina, where Evita saw herself as the mother of the people, achieving iconic status among the poor. By her own admission, Ms Dunham and her large travelling entourage of musicians and dancers were well-treated by the Magloires. This, no doubt, would have been partly due to the President's natural magnanimity. But it would also have been influenced, in no small part, by his liking for celebrity, and especially 'cultural' celebrity. The presence of Ms Dunham, and her close affinity with Haiti, would have added cachet to the Magloire regime, and the President was the type to utilise her friendship to the full. At the same time, however, Ms Dunham was doing whatever she could to ease the travails of her old friend, Estime. The Magloires never seemed to resent this fact.

Whatever his excesses, Magloire is viewed, with hindsight, as a force for good in Haiti, especially relative to many other presidents. It's true his early ideals were tainted somewhat by his liking for power and his determination to hold on to it at all costs, but he provided some tangible benefits during his six years in charge. Notable among these were road improvements, which could never be taken lightly in a country where overland communications had never been good. He oversaw the surfacing of major routes out of Port-au-Prince, replacing pot-holed tracks with at least something akin to modern highways. Asphalted roads to Petionville and the near-completed route to Cap Haitien were tangible memorials to a president whose mis-appropriation of government funds, and renowned drunkeness, were later to besmirch his name. However, the roads proved that at least some of his intentions were honourable, even though corruption was ultimately to overtake him, as it had so many of his predecessors.

While Magloire luxuriated in his presidential role, taking the plaudits of the mighty, and especially of the US government, his wife engaged in Evita-style charitable works. Again, this trait among presidential wives to succour the poor is very much a Latin American archetype. Its purpose is at least two-fold: to salve whatever consciences might survive inside the

National Palace, and buy the support of the people. Though effective, at least in the short-term, it has never been enough to halt the natural ebb and flow of political fortunes. However many gourdes Magloire and his wife tossed from the presidential limousine into the imploring hands of the poor, their tenure would ultimately be curtailed by the caprice of an unpredictable nation. On reflection, the Magloire years followed a foreseeable path. No matter how benevolent, how well-meaning, a Haitian leader is at the start, there are certain political imperatives that have to be acknowledged. One is the notorious impatience of the Haitian people, the readiness of dissidents to challenge the status quo. This, in turn, provokes the need for repression in one form or another, and a growing inclination to lay hands on the spoils of power while the going is good. With its record of short-term presidencies, it is no wonder that Haiti's leaders acquire a mood of frantic desperation. The National Treasury becomes their insurance policy and they loot it in anticipation of hasty departure. Magloire was not immune to the usual pressures. As time passed, idealism gave way to avarice, and disillusionment grew among those who had hoped against hope for a new age under the charismatic soldier. However, it took the forces of nature to create the decisive cracks in the Magloire regime.

Hurricane Hazel in 1954 wreaked havoc in Haiti, causing untold misery at one level, but also laying the ground for political upheaval. Francois Duvalier, having kept his head down for so long, was able to discern the trends and capitalise on them to the full. Estime had opened the way for Magloire on several fronts, firstly by elevating too many blacks for the mulattoes' taste, but also by confirming voodoo as a legitimate alternative to the established Catholic Church. Moreover, he legitimised the trade union movement and introduced income tax policies which unsettled the monied classes. Though Magloire did not repeat Estime's mistakes, he committed egregious errors of his own, alienating his traditional power base, and leaving the country at the mercy of the sinister country doctor and his brutal henchmen. Haiti, whose history had been deeply shadowed by a succession of poor leaders, was about to descend into a new dark age of unimaginable oppression. The deep night Graham Greene mentioned in the introduction to *The Comedians* was about to fall across Haiti's slumbering hills. Tens of thousands of its people did not live to see a new dawn.

CHAPTER 10

THE ELECTION

MP, the taxi-driver, manoeuvred his lumbering gas-guzzler up the drive and rolled to a halt outside the lobby of the Castelhaiti Hotel. It was just after 8am, but the day was already hot, and he had to unwire the bonnet to quench the engine's thirst with water from a molasses can he kept on the front passenger seat. The cicadas were already buzzing as Cole and I emerged from the gloom of the lobby into the piercingly bright sunlight. MP cranked open the back door of his car — he was the only one who knew the procedure, for a large dent in the panel had messed up the lock mechanism — and we settled into the commodious bench seats. One thing about those American cars of the 1950s was that they offered plenty of room. Everything about them was extravagantly proportioned, not least the voracious engines. MP lifted the door as he shut it, and it occurred to me that, in the event of a crash, we would probably never get out as the gas-tank exploded around us. Then he climbed in, juggled the column-mounted gearstick and jerked his battered limo into life by fiddling with wires under the dashboard. In moments, we were gliding down the drive for the long descent into Port-au-Prince, the car rocking gently on its haunches. Cole and I were out early with nought to sustain us but half an orange and a cup of black sludge-like coffee. We needed to be early because we had an appointment with a man who for me remains one of the oddest, most incongruous, yet fascinating characters in Duvalier's Haiti.

The night before, we had somehow managed to make contact, via Haiti's uncertain telephone system, with Gerard de Catalogne, who was Editor of *Le Nouveau Monde* — one of Port-au-Prince's daily newspapers — and Press Aide to the President. Together, we had hatched a plan, exclusive to ourselves, to seek an interview with President Duvalier. As we had learned from older, wiser and infinitely more experienced heads in the Oloffson bar more than once, seeking an audience with Duvalier was as hopeless and forlorn a mission as one could imagine. He despised journalists and — especially since the unforgiveable indiscretions of Graham Greene — refused to have anything to do with them. The word 'journalist', for him, could be used only in a pejorative sense, meaning something akin to treacherous vermin. Correspondents from New York were united in saying 'no chance' as Cole and I mulled over the possibilities, yet we decided to have a go anyway. All I would say now, forty years on, is that young journalists ought never to under-estimate the power of naivete. The old saying about the bumble-bee, that it is an aerodynamic impossibility but no-one has told it yet, always springs to mind as I recall our approach to the haughty de Catalogne. "We'd like to see the President," we said. "See the President? What for?" he asked, as though the request had broken new bounds of absurdity and impertinence. "We would like to interview him," we said. Incredibly, de Catalogne did not dismiss us out of hand. "He does not speak to the press," he said, "but, in accordance with procedure, I will forward your request to the National Palace. Call at my office in the morning, first thing." Thus, Cole and I were sprawled in the back of MP's cab as it spluttered and coughed its way through Petionville, choking up blue smoke under arches of bougainvillea. "What will he say?" I asked, 'What are the chances?' "Nil," said Cole, "but it was worth the try."

When de Catalogne appeared before us, he was a dead ringer for Alfred Hitchcock, the famous film producer with a taste for horror. Pudgy-faced, translucently white, he was like a giant suet pudding wrapped in an oversized tropical white suit. Like most immensely fat men in tropical climes, he mopped himself incessantly, scooping globs of moisture from his jiggling jowls. Patches of sweat seeped through his jacket, with extensive concentrations near his armpits. How, I wondered, did someone so blindingly white find favour in a regime so resolutely black? The answer was to prove complex but intriguing. At first, de Catalogne showed surprise at being confronted by journalists so young. It must have seemed obvious, from the start, that he was dealing not with seasoned correspondents from big-time agencies, but gauche tyro reporters from small papers. He was right, of course, but unworldliness sometimes pays. In his thick, gallic accent, de Catalogne said: "I have good news for you. The President has agreed to see you." Cole and I looked at each other with incredulity. "When?" we asked as de Catalogne shuffled papers on his desk. "This afternoon," he said, "be sure to wear a jacket." Hence, we secured an audience with Duvalier, an experience which — in the context of the times —was as surreal as meeting the Wizard of Oz. No-one, even his own people, seemed sure that Duvalier actually existed outside the myth. Even when he appeared before them in person, there was an ethereal aspect to his presence. Now the two of us, junior journalists from Nassau, were to have him materialise before us. It was only later, much later, that I came to appreciate the significance of de Catalogne in the life of Papa Doc. He needed to be special, I knew that, because Duvalier's anti-whiteness was renowned, yet here was a top adviser who was as bleached as alabaster, whiter than a swan's rump. I wondered how anyone could live in a land of per-petual sunshine and remain so ashen. It was one of the many mysteries enveloping Monsieur de Catalogne. Our experience at the palace has already been related — the hollow, menacing stares of Tontons guards, the shabby sparseness of its interior, the hugeness of Papa Doc's desk and the almost pathetically inadequate physical presence of the President himself.

Much later I was to write: "He looked peculiarly vulnerable behind his huge mahogany desk. With his pebbled specs, grizzled head, and unusually large hands, he was most people's idea of a frail and ailing granddad." His physical self was, however, always at odds with the gruesome reality. Just a few months before, he had personally supervised the execution of nineteen army officers, all suspected of trying to unseat him. And a huge revolver lay in his pending tray, lest an adversary somehow found his way into his inner sanctum. "Watching him during my forty-minute audience, I tried to square this tottering hunchback with the vile deeds attributed to him. He signed a copy of his little red book of Duvalierist ideology and handed it to me on my way out. His huge signature was bisected by what graphologists call a suicide line. But self-destruction was not in his nature. He died three years later in his bed, the kind of quiet and dignified end denied his victims."

De Catalogne, it transpired, was much more than a press aide, a media go-between. Interestingly, this noticeably pallid Caucasian was, in truth, Duvalier's political mentor, the man who was behind his dynastic philosophy and his controversial decision to name himself President-for-Life. Though alien in most respects to his adopted land, de Catalogne was astute enough to know how the Haitian psyche worked and to exploit it to his own considerable advantage. He also insinuated himself into Duvalier's life in a way that was to prove crucial to the character of the family's protracted rule. In one sense, de Catalogne was to the Duvaliers what Niccolo Machiavelli was to the Medicis, a kind of political guru with extraordinary insights into the nature of power. However, there was a Svengali-style element to de Catalogne's make-up which enabled him not merely to advise Papa Doc but to mould him into what he needed to become, if he were to survive the uniquely precarious nature of Haitian political life. De Catalogne sought to impose upon Haiti a dynastic style of governance reminiscent of the French monarchs. Heavily influenced by the French thinker Charles Maurras, he believed stability in Haiti was only possible if the uncertainties of its past were jettisoned in favour of hereditary rule. In the 1920s, de Catalogne became acquainted with Maurras, at a time when the thinker was working out ways of re-establishing the French monarchy, reasoning that the vagaries of post-revolutionary government could only be ironed out in the context of a properly structured hierarchy.

As an author and scholar, de Catalogne had the gifts required to articulate ideas which Duvalier found very much to his liking, and he used Maurras's work as a foundation for his theories on hereditary transmission. In his preface to Duvalier's book, *Oeuvres Essentielles*, de Catalogne leans heavily on Maurras's texts and propounds the virtues of passing power from one generation to the next. Maurras's thinking on hereditary transmission is delightfully simple and, in relation to Haitian political affairs, undeniably seductive. It rests on the thesis that sons of presidents are much more acquainted with the machinations of governance than the sons of carpenters or lumberjacks. By being immersed in politics on a day-to-day basis, the children of rulers are instinctively equipped for assuming power in a way that outsiders never could be. Far better, therefore, that the potentially chaotic implications of democracy be subverted by a dynastic structure, in which presidents assume power with all their expertise and knowledge in place. Under de Catalogne's persuasive influence, Duvalier formulated ideas for a dynasty which would dominate Haiti for generations to come, using force and, if need be, brutality to bring his unruly fiefdom to heel. Thus, by the time Papa Doc died in his bed in 1971, his corpulent son Jean-Claude was already in place as his successor, adding another fifteen years to a family reign that brought the country close to ruin.

By the time Cole and I met de Catalogne in 1968, his influence on Papa Doc was already well advanced. Duvalier was by then President-for- Life — a fact spelled out in lights on a traffic island near the National Palace — and plans were in hand to elevate his Bunteresque playboy son to the presidency when he reached the end of his own earthly tenure. The Machiavellian parallels are, in fact, appropriate because the old Italian schemer also favoured hereditary succession, reasoning that such transfer of power eliminated many of the hurtful and destructive elements of the conventional democratic process. Watching modern democracy at work around the world, it is easy to see the wisdom in his words. General elections are so often steeped in corruption and violence, so often the touch paper for civil disorder, that one frequently wonders whether a simpler and more orderly process might not be preferable. Haiti, alas, is as good an example as any. Its tentative attempts at democracy have been calamitous. Polling days have traditionally reduced the country to savage explosions of violence, with ballot queues raked by machine-gun fire, polling stations blitzed by bombs, and prospective voters intimidated into taking refuge inside their homes rather than run the risk of voting. The prince who assumes power by heredity, reasons Machiavelli, slides into position without the routine resistance of election time. Having been granted authority on the basis of his birth, he arrives at the throne with his inherited blend of authority and expertise in place. If the prince is able to rule effectively without provoking the ire of the masses, there is no reason why his dynasty should not endure for centuries. European monarchies survived on this basic principle: only gross abuse of power brought them down. Astonishingly, some are in place even today, though bereft of their traditional authority. Nonetheless, they provide dependable keystones in governmental structures which might otherwise crumble in the democratic scramble.

Duvalier, having grown to understand his people during his rural ramblings, achieved power with a pragmatic view of his country's short-comings. As children, he thought, the Haitian people needed paternal guidance and, if need be, the kind of chastisement that keeps delinquent juveniles in line. With governments changing every few months, it also needed stability of a kind which could only be provided by dynastic rule. Elections, he thought, were no more than organised excuses for chaos and disruption. To his supporters, Duvalier's approach was no more nor less than a logical response to Haiti's unusual predicament. Hence, following months of mayhem in the wake of the Magloire regime's collapse, Duvalier saw himself as well-equipped to assume the presidency. He was intent on a no-nonsense approach to righting Haiti's traditional wrongs, uplifting the black masses and curbing the excesses of the mulatto elite. At last, he thought, he had an opportunity to realign Haitian politics in a way that would grant power to those who deserved it. The days of elitist exploitation, of rank racial injustice, were now coming to an end, he told his supporters.

The first four years of Magloire's tenure were among the most productive, and successful, in Haiti's century and a half of independence. Under the President's guidance, the national campaign against yaws — the deadly, crippling disease that was ravaging the country's rural poor — reached its peak. Duvalier, as an employee of the Inter-American Co-operative Health Service, was a key figure in the fight against the disease. But it was in the wider world that Magloire made most impact, elevating Haiti's presidency to unimagined heights in the international community, mainly by adding colour, vibrancy and celebrity appeal to a country which had always been seen as troubled and embattled. Although elitist by nature, Magloire established a superficial levelling of the races. Even more importantly, he introduced order and discipline as a platform on which to build national prosperity. Haiti's relationship with its old adversary, the Dominican Republic, was more than adequate (Trujillo resisted any inclination to interfere in his neighbour's affairs) and the United States was more than satisfied with Magloire's apparently successful formula for ruling a volatile land. Having unseated Estime, Magloire began to emulate him, continuing some of the reform programmes initiated by his predecessor, especially in promoting industry, encouraging tourism and improving the country's health and school systems.

Foreign investment was attracted by Magloire's success and Haiti was better able to hold its own in the world coffee market. As inward investment mounted, so did international goodwill. As the celebrities began flying in, and Magloire became ever more flamboyant in dress and gestures, it seemed that Haiti was, at last, establishing itself as a credible player among western nations. In fact, Magloire's munificence knew few bounds. Big names from the outside world were flown in to be decorated by the state, fairy lights were festooned in the square outside the National

Palace, the President himself was featured on the cover of *Time* magazine, and high society balls became commonplace. All the while, Magloire indulged his taste for extravagance and ostentation. As host at lavish receptions and investitures, he was resplendent in military attire laden with medals and ribbons. His goodwill reached a peak in 1953 when he laid on a magnificent state funeral for former President Estime, who had died in exile in New York. His old adversary was laid to rest with full military honours and Magloire was accorded due praise for his magnanimity. Astutely, Magloire managed to leaven his reputation as a military strong-man with a measure of compassion, a combination which might well have produced a pattern for the future. But by 1954, the rumblings of unrest were already evident, and Francois Duvalier was at least partly responsible for the gathering gloom. The radical element in Haitian politics began to see Magloire's presidency as fundamentally decadent, a throwback to old-style paternalism. The grand balls and receptions were all very well, but they sat awkwardly alongside the harsh reality in the hills: the continuing poverty of the Haitian people.

Magloire was making headway, providing new roads, dedicating a soccer stadium, furthering the traditions of Estime, but there was still too much of the 'toy soldier' about him for more serious tastes. It was as though Magloire saw the presidency as a theatrical opportunity, a means of fulfilling fantasies of international glory in an atmosphere of glitz. There is no doubt his reign brought light to a land of darkness, but this was never enough for the revolutionary forces among Haiti's black intellectuals. At a rally outside the National Palace early in 1954, Magloire warned workers of his resolve to quell the agitators. Daniel Fignole was arrested for distributing subversive literature and inciting revolt. Later that year, Magloire was warned of Duvalier, and the middle-aged doctor's use of his medical activities as a front for political manoeuvreing. Although Magloire was later to maintain that he never intended to arrest Duvalier, the scheming physician took no chances and went into prolonged hiding, at one point finding refuge in the home of a Catholic priest, Jean-Baptiste Georges. In moving from one haven to another, Duvalier sometimes had to resort to pure pantomime, dressing up as a woman on one occasion and falling over his skirts as he tried to avoid the gaze of the President's soldiers. All the while, Duvalier's anti-Magloire stance was hardening. Ostensibly, Magloire remained the internationally acclaimed President of Haiti as 1955 dawned, but fissures were already evident. While he was being feted in New York and Washington by President Dwight D Eisenhower early in the year, underground forces were chiselling away at the foundations of his regime. By the time Vice-President Richard Nixon arrived to stay at Magloire's marble villa in the hills, the opposition was already building a significant momentum.

By the spring of 1956, student unrest — alleged to have been Duvalier-inspired — shook Port-au-Prince and the troops were out on the streets to restore order. Reports of government corruption leaked back to Washington. After six years, the Magloire administration began to tremble on its plinth, like a grand monument with structural defects. As so often in Haitian political history, another presidential term was about to end in disorder amid fury over different interpretations of the national constitution. By the time the 20th Century had reached its midway stage, radical constitutional changes since independence had already reached twenty, and there were more to come. The unrest surrounding Magloire's departure was over whether President Estime's version of the constitution ought to prevail — with May 15, 1956, being the official end of his presidential term — over the incumbent President's own amended constitution, which added another year to his tenure. As students took to the streets, prompting savage police response, Duvalier worked diligently behind the scenes to ride the flowing tide of history. As rioting and pillaging escalated, Congress declared a state of emergency. Anti-Magloire brochures littered the streets as soldiers tried to maintain control and dampen down growing tension. It was not an easy task.

Haiti's youth was on the rampage. By now it was clear that the dazzling veneer of the Magloire era was being tarnished by the smoke from street fires. And Duvalier, incongruously attired in his sombre suit and black hat, was readying himself to emerge from the shadows. In citing his qualifications for succession, Duvalier pointed to more than a decade of solid political preparation. He also cited his medical work for the poor, emphasising his role in the fight against yaws. A Magloire acolyte, Clement Jumelle, was emerging as a rival for the presidential crown, but this did nothing to unsettle Duvalier's studied calm. One of the characteristics which did more than anything to deepen Duvalier's mystique was the apparent gulf between the would-be President's almost apologetic physical presence — even at this late stage he remained a diffident figure — and his implacable ambition. Duvalier was disarmingly harmless in appearance. That was his strength, for no-one believed that he could have anything to do with the eruptions of disorder that now became a daily feature of the Port-au-Prince scene.

As sporadic explosions rocked the old Iron Market, Magloire himself discounted conspiracy theories implicating Duvalier, declaring him too great a patriot to be caught up in such treachery. He also discounted suggestions that Duvalier had used his medical work with the Americans to curry Washington's favour and lay poison in preparation for a takeover. The expansive, genial Magloire was too trusting. Duvalier, like a termite, was gnawing at the struts and supports of the President's power structure. If Magloire was by now feeling uneasy, he was no more so than the Cuban dictator Fulgencio Batista, who was beginning to feel the first flutterings of a revolt that would result, three years later, in a revolutionary takeover by Dr Fidel Castro. As Haiti girded itself for elections, and the nation-wide troubles that invariably accompanied such events, Batista was obliged to take severe action against upstarts in Havana, where police shot and killed six Cubans taking refuge in the Haitian Embassy. This prompted, in turn, protests in Port-au-Prince, where students saw this infringement of national sovereignty as another excuse for disruption.

Two Caribbean nations known for bloody political conflagrations in the past were now on the brink of more ferment. As bombs burst in the streets of Port-au-Prince, sending crowds screaming in panic, no-one was looking in the direction of the kindly, bespectacled doctor of medicine. Yet historians are now virtually certain that Papa Doc was behind this campaign of violence, and that he was using unrest in Cuba to advance his own anti-communist cause in the eyes of the ever-watchful Americans. If there is one aspect of Duvalier's political career that best explains his longevity as leader, it is his passionate dislike of Leftists. His thinking dovetailed neatly into Washington's anti-communist obsession during the mid-to-late fifties, and established Haiti's role in the Cold War, as the East-West frost intensified. Duvalier, with one eye always trained on his country's need for American aid, traded on his loathing of communists to the limit. When Castro descended from the hills in battle fatigues in 1959, imposing communist rule on Haiti's near neighbour, Duvalier's stance became even more reassuring for Washington Right-Wingers, convincing them that at least one corner of the Caribbean was free of the taint of Marxist ideology.

The need to ensure Castro did not extend his sphere of influence in the region became a dominant theme of US foreign policy at this time, and Duvalier was to emerge as one of their most reliable allies in the cause. As pressure on Magloire mounted towards the end of 1956, it was clear that his attempt to manipulate events in his favour had failed. There was no way he would survive until the May of the following year, which was the date he had chosen to stand down. However, possibly out of pique, but more likely because he wished to stave off impending chaos, he decided to ignore procedure and introduce another period of military rule. It did not bring the desired effect. Haitians brought the country to a standstill by refusing to work. Businesses closed and resisted all Magloire's entreaties to open again. Sensing that his authority had evaporated, told by young officers that the army was no longer behind him, Magloire took the hint and flew into exile, first in Jamaica and later in New York, where he maintained a passionate interest in his country's affairs to his dying day. Haitians, always eager to embrace change, were jubilant at what they thought was to be another stab at democracy. After two centuries of mismanagement, they never stopped dreaming of better times ahead.

As an army plane lifted off from Port-au-Prince, with the Magloire family aboard, Haitians danced and sang at the prospect of a golden future. From the balconies of the Oloffson, Haiti's gilded visitors looked down upon a changing tableau. For them, and the mulatto elite, this was a kind of political sunset. For the poor, however, the departure of Magloire was being viewed as yet another promising dawn. What they failed to realise was that Haiti's future was already behind it, and that this false dawn would outstrip all others in its failure to deliver high expectations.

The reign of the Duvaliers was to bring new realms of misery to this beautiful but hopelessly stricken land. Haiti had tried and failed to introduce a semblance of democracy in the past. As far back as Petion, the first President, voting rights had been acknowledged as a base on which to build the nation. In practical terms, though, adult suffrage was an elusive ideal. The general election of September 22, 1957, was the country's first real exercise in democracy and, predictably, it was to lead to chaos, confusion and protracted recrimination. Following Magloire's departure, Haiti descended into nine months of civil disorder, with provisional governments coming and going in a blur. At one point, it seemed that civil war was a real prospect as families were torn asunder and old enmities flared. The people on the receiving end of the violence hoped against hope that election day would restore a modicum of discipline to this benighted land. And many saw their future in the shape of the unimposing Francois Duvalier, a quiet man of compassion, it seemed, whose role in defeating yaws was repeatedly cited as his most significant claim to the presidency. It was probably Duvalier's unusual calm that appealed to them most. In a country where volatility and irrationality were built into the national psyche, it was a tempting prospect for many that Haiti might yet enjoy a few years of relative equanimity. From bombastic military leader to a sombre rural physician seemed a long hop for any country to make — especially one in which sheer force had invariably shaped its political destiny — but Duvalier appeared to present the most appealing credentials as the big day approached.

The four-way fight for the National Palace reflected all the old divisions of Haitian society. Apart from Duvalier, there were three other major candidates for the presidency, including the black populist Daniel Fignole and the aforementioned Magloire acolyte, Clement Jumelle. For Duvalier, however, the real threat came from the urbane mulatto Louis Dejoie, a cultured patrician who epitomised all that Duvalier most reviled about Haitian society. There is little doubt that, with Dejoie in the Palace, Haiti would have had more of the same: subjugation of the black masses, elevation of the beige elite, and no prospect of social advancement for the impoverished rural peasantry. The confrontational nature of the election — with Duvalier versus Dejoie emerging as the main feature — was most marked with the forcible removal of the rabble-rouser Fignole, who was kidnapped by soldiers during the campaign and jettisoned into exile in the United States, under suspicion that he was plotting to corrupt the poll. This was followed by the withdrawal of Jumelle, a sophisticated economist who, as Magloire's finance minister, presided over a period of reckless profligacy which helped bring down the six-year regime. Fignole, ambitious, charismatic and incredibly accomplished in playing the crowds, had achieved the presidency for just three weeks during the kaleidoscopic sequence of events following Magloire's downfall. It was poor reward for one so dedicated to

Haiti's future, but inevitable when one considers in retrospect the behind-the-scenes manoeuvreing of Duvalier.

The full extent of the doctor's chicanery was gradually becoming clear to at least one of the contenders. Jumelle, with some justification, felt the election process was being manipulated by Duvalier interests — notably the army — and that Dejoie faced certain defeat. His decision to quit the race before the nation went to the polls left Haiti with its usual 'salt and pepper' choice. Duvalier was the pepper, the emphatically black preference of the negro multitude. Dejoie was the darling of the Petionville upper classes, but he was at an overwhelming mathematical disadvantage.

The election itself was the usual Haitian combination of high comedy and low cunning. Voters had the nail of their right little finger clipped as they deposited their ballots as a means of preventing multiple voting. Then the finger was dipped in scarlet ink. Soon, ballot stations took on the appearance of abattoirs, with chopped nails and splatters of red everywhere. In Port-au-Prince itself, tension overflowed into scuffles and fist-fights. There were riotous scenes as supporters careered round the city with their placards and favours. Truck horns blasted to drown out the usual din of garrulous women and crowing cockerels. Duvalier played hard on Haiti's unconscionable contrasts in wealth, espousing the cause of the poor, promising to right wrongs and reverse an unjust order. Invoking the spirit of his political hero, Jean-Jacques Dessalines, he promised a no-nonsense solution to Haiti's woes. Interestingly, Duvalier also used the campaign to promote voodoo as a crucial component of Haitian life. It was the first time he had proclaimed his interest in this mystical belief system so openly. He was laying the groundwork for a regime in which voodoo would play more than an ancillary role. Superstition was to help Duvalier and his son occupy the palace for three decades.

The final count — which gave Duvalier a more than two-to-one majority over Dejoie — was significant for many reasons. Firstly, it represented, for the first time in Haitian political history, a triumph of rural Haiti over the capital. Dejoie won Port-au-Prince, but Duvalier swept the countryside. Secondly, it highlighted Duvalier's unusual capacity for generating enthusiasm for his cause in a low-key way. Thirdly, it reflected the army's power as a 'persuader' of the people. There is no doubt that the cajoling of the troops, especially in rural areas, was a decisive factor. The vote was greeted by the usual flurry of charges and counter-charges. Corruption was alleged by the losing side, as indeed it was by Duvalier himself, who claimed that Dejoie's followers were buying votes at two gourdes a time in the urban slum areas. When the dust had settled, however, it was Duvalier who was destined for the National Palace, buoyed up by peasant fervour and a disputed vote. Haiti would live to regret its decision. To paraphrase Graham Greene, this troubled nation was about to lose itself in a long night deeper and darker than any it had ever known.

Papa Doc, Dr. Francois Duvalier, at a ceremonial occasion in the 1960s after he had declared himself President-for-Life

(Tribune photograph)

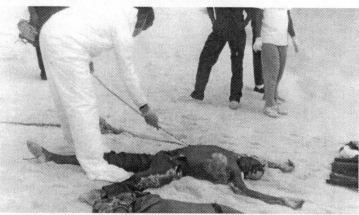

Bodies of drowned Haitians awaiting burial at Bitter Guana Caji the Exumas, where
their bid for freedom ended in tragedy

(Tribune photograph)

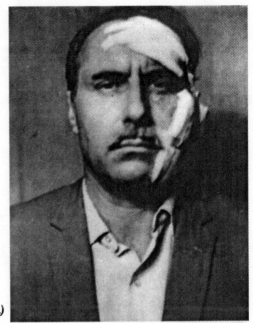

This police photograph shows Knox, his face bandaged, shortly after his arrest in Port-au-Prince.

(Tribune photograph)

David Knox listens intently during his trial in Port-au-Prince. Interpreter John Pickering is at far right of picture.

(Tribune photograph)

David Knox contemplating his defence
(Tribune photograph)

David Knox and wife, Phillippa arrive in
Nassau from Miami after his ordeal in
Haiti.

(Tribune photograph)

CHAPTER 11
THE CHIEF

Power changes men, invariably for the worse. It leads them to believe the myth, to heed the chanting of the mob. Conceit blooms into self-destructive hubris, which ultimately heralds the slide into oblivion. Oddly, Dr Francois Duvalier did not fall into the Third World presidential stereotype. He did not become a bemedalled behemoth orchestrating crowds, nor did he don a gilded crown and call himself king. His own insecurity in the face of persistent plotting never allowed hubris to intrude into affairs at the National Palace. And whatever conceit he might have harboured was hidden under the blank countenance of inscrutability. However, he certainly changed, and those who knew him best were astonished at how those changes seemed to transform the physical man. Throughout his medical and political career, Duvalier adopted a low-key, almost apologetic, attitude towards his fellow men. He traded heavily on compassion, professional solicitude, an almost slavish devotion to the Hippocratic Oath.

In the campaign against yaws, he was the diligent hands-on carer with a commitment to easing the burdens of the rural poor. In the 1950s, when Duvalier was actively treating the affliction, yaws had reached its height, crippling millions in under-developed tropical countries. In Haiti, rural peasants were at its mercy, for the bacterial disease flourished in unhygienic conditions, and young children were its most vulnerable victims. Transmitted by direct contact with infected skin, the disease causes unsightly rashes and lesions, ultimately leading to facial disfiguration, destroying the nose and palate and attacking the throat. Duvalier was a small part of a worldwide programme which eventually led to treatment of more than 160 million people in 46 countries. With penicillin the primary weapon against this appalling source of misery, thousands of physicians working under World Health Organisation guidance eventually got it under control. Unlike its related disease, syphilis, yaws rarely kills its victims, but Haiti's countryside was littered with affected peasants, many hideously deformed by its more extreme effects. Duvalier was to them a doctor of mercy, sympathetic to their pain, conscientious in his treatment of their tormented skin.

When he entered the National Palace for the first time as President, Duvalier was still seen as the quiet, caring man of Haitian politics, in spite of hints during the election campaign that there was more to him than his renowned taciturnity and professional diligence suggested. In their book, *Papa Doc: Haiti and Its Dictator* (published in 1969), Bernard Deiderich and Al Burt referred to Duvalier's altered demeanour and wondered at the zealot who emerged from the tiny frame. In the run-up to election day, he had roused public emotions by accusing his rivals of vote-buying in the city slum of La Saline. As he raised his arms and yelled abuse at his adversaries, his jacket flew open to reveal the handgun in his belt. As a doctor, Duvalier was a saver of lives. As a politician, however, he would not be averse to taking them in abundance. Suddenly, the true nature of this sinister, enigmatic little man became evident. Those who saw him as a kind of Albert Schweitzer, dedicated to uplifting the afflicted, also had to acknowledge the brutal spirit of Dessalines, which the new President imbibed voraciously and without apology. Duvalier's rise to power brought with it unparalleled opportunities. Emphatically black, with the cachet of a medical doctorate, he was in a unique position to tap into the aspirations of the masses. His knowledge of voodoo gave him an additional edge: he was spiritually aligned to those who found solace in their unusual beliefs.

As he took up residence at the National Palace during that momentous year, downtrodden Haitians had every right, and justification, for thinking this was the beginning of an age of liberation. Magloire had, by Haitian standards, been markedly benign, but his interests were always with the monied classes. His wife, a chic, petite and beautiful woman with the kind of savoir faire that won friends in high places abroad, was very much in the tradition of Latin American first ladies. Like her husband, she was a free-spending socialite who liked the trappings of office, but fundamentally both were indifferent to the cries of the people. The Duvaliers, on the other hand, were far less ostentatious in style, far less attractive in appearance and manner, and much more earnest in their approach to the business at hand. At first, all this was interpreted as natural for altruistic people with the nation's interests at heart. However, events were to prove those early impressions to be entirely illusory.

If Deiderich and Burt were alert to those radical changes in manner during the 1957 election campaign, it was left to Katherine Dunham, the dancer, to capture the absolute transformation of the man in all its complexity. In her fascinating book, *Island Possessed,* she wrote of the 'chemical change' that seemed to have taken place between her first and last meetings with Papa Doc, in 1956 and 1962. Here she ponders whether Duvalier actually worked on creating a sombre and sinister persona, apeing Baron Samedi, the symbol of the graveyard, in an attempt to strike fear into the people. She recalled attending a ceremony in the Palace auditorium at which the Haitian poet, Carl Brouard, was to be honoured and being bemused by the disturbing changes in the President's entire demeanour. He was so changed chemically, physically and in personality that he appeared to be a different man altogether, she thought. Although they had met several times before, at which her international status had been duly acknowledged, he seemed not to see her at all during this encounter. It was as if Duvalier had been overtaken by the challenges of power, leaving him somehow transmuted and diminished. Was he ill? She did not know. However, what she recognised, and certainly with hindsight, is that Duvalier was by this stage already engaged in the extreme measures he was to adopt for the preservation of power. He was already creating the force that would counter treacherous elements in the army, mobilising thuggish elements of his support system into the brutal band later to be called the Tontons Macoute. Having studied Machiavelli, and having listened intently to the insistent philosophising of Gerard de Catalogne, Duvalier was getting to grips with the reality of power, its possibilities and requirements for its retention. If genuine concern for the welfare of his fellow men had once been a true component of his thinking, it was quickly subverted by cruel pragmatism. In Haiti, soft men did not last. Hard, uncompromising rulers triumphed in the cauldron of Latin American politics and Duvalier quickly became attuned to the extreme demands of the job. In changing so radically, he probably became what he needed to be.

The President's transmogrification was a talking point among the people. It was fuelled by a traditional belief in different body states. Zombieism had long been part of the Haitian belief system, a kind of sub-life induced by burial, a separation of body and mind. Whatever one's colour or status in Haiti, zombieism is seen as at least a possibility, if not an incontrovertible fact, an off-shoot of mystical traditions dating back to pre-slavery days in Africa. There are several definitions of the zombie, the half-life theory mentioned earlier being one, the result of burial followed by swift resur-rection. However, there are other versions, including the revival of the dead by black magic. Sorcery is never far from Haitian minds, and leads them to closely observe the dead until decomposition sets in lest the cadaver regain life in a corrupted form. A third version is the herb-induced coma which, following interment, renders the victim a compliant follower, an unquestioning automaton. In such an environment, Duvalier's chemical change was attributed to many things, all inspiring a measure of fear in his people. The 'other worldness' of Duvalier, the blank stare behind the heavy spectacles, became a defining characteristic of the man and his regime. While outsiders found him mystifying and intriguing, those obliged to live under his rule were rendered tremulous and wary at the very sight of him.

For the fourteen years he was in power, the people of Haiti were never certain he had a soul, that he was a mortal man. No wonder they became transfixed by the image, the understated presence. The idea of the unquiet soul, the dead come to life, was deeply implanted in Haitian thinking. It was prevalent in Guinea, in the Congo, in Senegal and Dahomey, and had crossed the Atlantic in slave ships. Slaves who jumped overboard to escape the horrors in the holds were not choosing death but another kind of life. The ocean offered an unfathomable embrace for them. Little wonder that Duvalier was seen as someone who had crossed a spiritual, pathological or psychological threshold into realms only the spirits understood. Here was a man whose mortality could not be depended upon. The belief that only a silver bullet could kill him was only a short step away. Though Katherine Dunham showed admirable understanding of Magloire and Duvalier, having known both well, she was wrong in at least one very important respect. She refused to believe that the rather prosaic, humdrum Duvaliers were as rapacious in their material demands as the Magloires and doubted in her book that the couple were spiriting the nation's money into Swiss bank accounts. That the Duvaliers were less colourfully demanding, less obviously avaricious, than the Magloires is true enough, but they proved just as mercenary.

Time would show that Papa and Mama Doc were as greedy as any of their predecessors, looting the treasury to secure their future. After the President's death, his son and widow would live on the proceeds of their kleptomania for the best part of two decades. In every sense, Duvalier was more, or less, than he seemed, a bewildering anomaly. With hindsight, it is possible to see the Duvalier regime as remarkable in many respects, not least in the sheer exuberance of its brutality, but its longevity was also incredible in the context of Haitian politics. How was it achieved? In building his power base, Duvalier shrewdly created a mixture of the upper reaches of the proletariat and the lower reaches of the bourgeoisie, a blend of loyalties which neutralised, to some extent, the traditional power of the mulattoes. It was the first real effort to blur the ethnic and social divisions which had so bedevilled Haiti's past. The Tontons Macoute was founded on the ruthlessness of black hardmen like Franck Romain, the red-eyed prosecutor of David Knox. This terrifying force gave status to elements in Haitian society who had been denied their share in the governmental process for the best part of two centuries. Like Toussaint and Dessalines before him, Duvalier was rearranging the social and racial order, and lubricating the process with the blood of his enemies.

There was, however, another factor which helped Duvalier stay in power, and that was the rise of Dr Fidel Castro in neighbouring Cuba. When Castro descended from the hills in battle fatigues in early 1959, leading his guerrillas to victory over the Batista regime, he became the focus of Washington's notorious anti-communist paranoia. For nearly half a century that paranoia has persisted through a succession of US presidencies, and Duvalier was able to capitalise on it for the entire 14 years of his own incumbency. During those early years, via the 1961 Bay of Pigs 'invasion' and up to, and including the missile crisis in 1962, America was obsessed with Castro. When John F Kennedy was assassinated on November 22, 1963, suspicions were focused, at least partly, on the troublesome Caribbean isle to the south. There were real fears that Cuba's sphere of influence would eventually extend throughout the Americas, posing a potent threat to the USA's hegemony in the region and infecting the West Indian islands with Marxist ideology. Duvalier, sensitive to Washington's concern, proclaimed himself a stout bulwark against any such eventuality. He was ruthless in hunting down Leftists and declared himself the enemy of those who would challenge and undermine the capitalist system. If Duvalier shared Castro's ideals in elevating the masses, he challenged his methods of achieving those ideals. State control was not part of the Duvalierist agenda, and nor were the kind of bureaucratic structures Castro created, in keeping his country on track.

If there were similarities between Duvalier's Haiti and Castro's Cuba, then they were in the area of human rights. Under both regimes, dissent was ruthlessly crushed, freedom of the press abolished, and presidential authority promoted to the detriment of those obliged to live in its shadow. However, Castro introduced positive social developments which countered, to some extent, the horrors of oppression. The spread of free medical services and free education were, over the space of 30 years, to give Cuba a significant edge in these areas. Even Castro's most implacable foes had to admit that impressive strides were made in health care and schools. Under Duvalier, however, Haiti made no such strides, even though the reforming spirit of Estime was supposedly an inspirational force at the Palace. Only in the fields of torture and brute force, in which the Tontons Macoute were acknowledged masters, did Haiti eclipse its communist neighbour.

Within a few years of the two regimes existing side by side, it was Haiti that claimed pre-eminence in the area of sheer brutality, and that's because the nation's blood-drenched soil had nurtured men who were accomplished practitioners in the black arts of physical and mental cruelty. Given the unpredictable nature of Haitian governance, the country's record of violence and political intrigue, it was no surprise that Duvalier should find himself under pressure from the start. There was always an over-riding suspicion that Duvalier had grabbed power by illicit means. And there was no doubt at all that his rule was unwelcome among those who lived in closest proximity to the National Palace. The Duvalierist vote had been centred, almost exclusively, on the countryside, where the peasantry saw the new President as a paternalistic saviour. In Port-au-Prince itself, however, his support was far from solid. The mulatto elite was implacably against him, and the urban blacks were more inclined to favour Daniel Fignole. Hence, Duvalier's paranoia set in early, as did the plotting against his regime. There was never a true 'honeymoon' period for the little tyrant: he was a target from the start, but he soon came to understand that whatever his government lacked by way of organisational ability, his opponents lacked it, too.

Bureaucratic ineptitude was always a feature of the Duvalier regime, but it began to take on a patina of efficiency alongside those who would wish to depose him. Even before he moved into the palace, the signs of insurgency were all too evident. Sporadic explosions, random gunfire, gratuitous violence and a general air of unease left the Haitian capital tense, and expectant, in the immediate post-election period. Had Duvalier received the unswerving support of the merchant class, things might have been different, but he knew that the old Magloirists were deeply resentful of his ascent to power and, even more significantly, of the way he had achieved it. With the urban masses also less than ecstatic at his success, there was little to make Duvalier sleep easy at night. Thus, he began to underpin his shaky power base with ruthless loyalists who would be his eyes and ears throughout the city. Recognising that the army, too, would have to be closely watched, he began to fashion this cold-eyed rabble into a force to reckon with. The Tontons Macoute became globally renowned as pitiless enforcers. Duvalier might well have set out with wholesome ideals. The welfare of the masses had certainly been his predominant concern throughout his medical career. There was always a desire to uplift levels of prosperity and promote a more equitable distribution of wealth. However, with conspirators all around, he became preoccupied with retention of power against formidable odds, consigning social reforms to the backburner.

Historians are left to wonder whether he might have become a force for good, had there not been so much desire, among his opponents, to dislodge him. Whatever his altruistic tendencies at the start, they were quickly subverted by an almost manic lust for revenge against those who wanted his head. Within a week of the election, Dejoie's supporters were on the streets, protesting at an alleged rigged vote and forcing businesses to close amid chaotic scenes. Once again, Port-au-Prince was in a state of ferment, and once again presidential power was required to enforce order. In this respect, at least, Duvalier was equal to the task. Those among his supporters who had kept their brutal instincts in check during the campaign no longer needed to show restraint. Wielding guns, facing down the crowds, Duvalierists ordered shops to reopen and restored order with a mixture of brute force and callous intimidation. The matrix had been laid for a regime of terror. The crushing of the strike was only the beginning of Duvalier's ongoing war with his adversaries. Even when he held his first post-election press conference, it was against a background of unrest as anti-Duvalierist insurgents harassed army sentries and sought to undermine any symbol of government authority. "The people love their doc," he told reporters who sought explanations for his victory. Describing himself as "the indivisible bicolour of the Haitian people", he promised unity and peace. Over the next fourteen years, he would achieve neither, except the sombre peace of the graveyard, which many of his adversaries were to experience in short order.

CHAPTER 12
THE ENFORCERS

As David Knox was sentenced to death, Haiti's carefully constructed facade of judicial respectability disintegrated before our eyes. Its attempt at justice, unsophisticated as it was to First World eyes, was no more than a rather squalid sham, reinforcing all Graham Greene's assertions, and reminding its detractors, that the dark republic was still aeons adrift from the expectations of the wider world. Franck Romain revelled in the spectacle as Knox was dragged away. As a symbol, it was hard to imagine anything more potent than the sight of a white man in distress, surrounded by soldiers of Haiti's rag-tag army, as he was strong-armed from the courtroom to God knows what hell-hole. By Haitian standards, of course, this was justice at its height. There had been at least a semblance of due process, though Romain's oft-expressed prejudice would have offended most western courtrooms, and this alone was at odds with the arbitrary methods of enforcement usually favoured by Duvalier and his henchman.

An Italian friend once told me of an alarming incident at Port-au-Prince waterfront when she was aboard a cruise ship which had called in for the day. Peasants were leaping into the sea to retrieve coins thrown to them by passengers from the upper decks. The sight of screeching street people throwing themselves into the water, then struggling for their lives as they tried to scramble ashore, was both touching and disturbing. "Their desperation was almost unbelievable," she said. If it was disturbing for the ship's passengers, it was even more so for the Tontons Macoute, who promptly arrived in cars and began shooting the peasants as they dog-paddled in the water. Soon the sea was scarlet as the beggars screamed and sank amid panic and fear. In the distorted minds of Duvalier's enforcers, the beggars' antics were an affront to the regime, an insult to Haiti, a harrowing reminder of the truth, which was that Papa Doc's oft-proclaimed benevolence had yet to percolate into the lower reaches of society.

The gulf between Haitian and conventional western thought was evident, too, in the treatment of political foes. At one point, passengers arriving at Francois Duvalier International Airport were greeted by a bloated corpse sitting in an armchair: Papa Doc's way of reminding outsiders, and especially the Americans, that he was on top of the job, resisting the communist onslaught. The sight of the pop-eyed cadaver, and its attendant stench, gave the visitors much to talk about as they caught a cab into town. What kind of place had they come to? They might well have asked: by then, Haiti had descended into new realms of implausibility. As Knox was hauled away to his fate, it occurred to me that he might well have ended up as a grisly trophy on the airport road, still in his beige suit and chukka boots. Worse things had happened. Duvalier, echoing the extremities of Dessalines, was not beyond parading severed heads through the streets of Port-au-Prince when it suited him. If there was one man who best epitomised the severity of the Duvalier regime in its early days, it was Clement Barbot, an acolyte-cum-fixer who was to become Papa Doc's first true enforcer. Barbot was of a type known to all tyrannical Third World regimes: an almost robotic, unquestioning hardman who heard his master's voice and never challenged its demands.

The Nazis had the Gestapo and the cold-eyed Himmler. Papa Doc had the Tontons Macoute and Clement Barbot. Ideologically, 1930s Germany and 1960s Haiti were not far apart. A fervent anti-communist doctrine was not their only similarity. The Nazis' racial policies were the product of innate feelings of supremacy. Contempt for Jews, gipsies, mongrels and blacks was built on Aryan pride. Papa Doc's racial prejudices were the product of two centuries of rage. Whites and mulattoes were as reprehensible to him as Non-Aryans were to Hitler. Both regimes also nurtured powerful feelings of hatred against those who would dislodge them. The result in both cases was a fear-inducing knock on the door in the middle of the night. If the Gestapo was feared by Jews, that fear was no more intense than that felt by Duvalier's foes when the Tontons arrived in the dark hours. Stories abound of the grotesque extremities of their brutality, but the militia was to survive throughout the reign of Papa Doc and into the only marginally more tolerant era of his son, Jean-Claude. The mirrored shades, the blank inscrutability of their countenance, the brazen disregard for human life...all became symbolic of the Tontons years. And Barbot was the chief enforcer, the man whose word decided whether others lived or died.

In Nazi Germany, opponents of the regime dreaded the roar of the black Mercedes leviathans which brought the Gestapo to their doors. In Haiti, it was the death rattle of Barbot's DKW Jeep that heralded terror in the night. With his black spectacles and sombre suits, Barbot was a ghoul who relished his work and gloried in his resultant notoriety. The people, already diminished by poverty, were at his mercy. What the Haiti Democracy Project was later to call 'a wave of death' in the early Duvalier years — a tsunami of pitiless oppression and slaughter — was largely inspired and initiated by the execrable Barbot, whose barbaric activities were experienced at every level of Haitian society. Taking his lead from Papa Doc himself, Barbot imprinted the dead hand of Duvalierism on every institution considered inimical to the regime's survival. Almost from the start, the President imposed a system of what the HDP called 'state terrorism' and rode recklessly over the nation's laws. Barbot proved a most enthusiastic henchman, encouraging the Tontons Macoute in acts of criminality, extorting money and eliminating opposition with unimaginable savagery. Death, in fact, became more than a daily reality for Haiti's long-suffering people, it quickly came to define Duvalier and his mindlessly destructive philosophy.

There was no rationale behind this hasty descent into bloodletting and arbitrary victimisation, just a growing obsession with death itself as a final solution to problems of opposition. Papa Doc and Barbot, both perpetually attired in black, were twin symbols of a macabre era in Haiti's history. HDP said in reviewing the book, *The New Face of Macoutism, Headless Cadavers* by Jean-Claude Bajeaux, that Haiti under Duvalier quickly began to self-destruct, and cited an attack on a policeman by children as a symptom of the nation's unnerving descent into butchery. They cut off the officer's head, an act that was to gain favour among the President's own men, as opposition to the regime grew in the early 1960s. After the unsuccessful invasion attempt in May, 1968 — the military expedition resulting in David Knox's capture and trial — the heads of rebels were paraded on pikes through the streets of Port-au-Prince. Papa Doc himself kept the head of a detractor on the side of his bathtub. Decapitation for him had a reassuring finality about it with the added advantage of heaping humiliation upon his victims. And heads, for the voodoo adept, could always be relied upon to yield their secrets. "When the victims are chosen at random, this roulette game does not only destroy one life, it destroys the reason to live altogether, and animalises the relationship between people," said HDP. "A regime of this type, predator and murderer, becomes the centre of corruption, a kind of apocalyptic animal, the master of terror who imposes silence and obedience."

Democracy has always been a flexible concept and can mean whatever governments want it to mean. Fidel Castro claims to be democratic, and the Cuban electoral structure is such that it's hard to counter his assertions, even though he has effectively been a dictator for half a century. If the people elect an assembly which then goes on to elect Dr Castro as its leader, it's difficult to argue that the voice of the populace is not being heard. In Duvalier's case, restricted elections, warped by corruption could be made to produce whatever results the National Palace demanded of them. It was an approach which was to lead, ultimately, to Papa Doc's presidency-for-life. In its many incarnations, the Haitian constitution has been made to reflect the whims of successive dictators, usually with the purpose of extending their tenure. Hardly ever have those changes been a force for good for the people. When I met Papa Doc, however, the one point he wished to impress on journalists was that his country was a democracy, wherein the people's voice was heard and their best interests served. It was, of course, a travesty of the truth, but brave was the man who contested his claims, for such treachery led to a cell in Fort Dimanche and possible extinction against the prison wall. But it illustrated once more the extent to which democracy can be fashioned to mask totalitarianism, and present a moderately acceptable veneer of respectability to the world. In the eyes of his opponents, however, Duvalier was no more a friend of democracy than the self-serving presidents who had preceded him.

Perversion of the electoral process had been part of Papa Doc's strategy from the start. In dislodging Magloire, his followers were not averse to spreading terror with explosions and gunfire. And, almost immediately after Duvalier was sworn in on September 22, 1957, Barbot's crudely armed thugs — using archaic weaponry from the palace basement — began their vile campaign of terror and extortion, brutalising all whose existence offended them. The media was, inevitably, an early target. The labour unions, the student body and eventually the Roman Catholic Church swiftly followed. Any institution which represented resistance fell under Papa Doc's baleful gaze until most descended into a deep and protracted silence. As turbulent priests were expelled, and recalcitrant students were spirited away in the night, Haitians began to absorb the reality of rule under the supposedly benign doctor. Exile, jail or death appeared to be the options for those whose views did not accord with his. Many of those who could afford the privilege jetted to foreign lands, viewing events in Haiti from afar with growing alarm. Intellectuals and professionals who could not escape often found themselves incarcerated without trial. The least fortunate were those tortured to death in Fort Dimanche, which became Duvalier's slaughterhouse for the elimination of his detractors.

Throughout this gruesome and dispiriting process, Duvalier underwent his transmutation from compassionate physician to ruthless psychopath. Moreover, he became an enthusiastic participant in the process of death, a man seemingly happy to watch foes being tortured and to oversee executions. Barbot, complete with machine-gun, which he brandished menacingly at the slightest provocation, led the Tontons thugs on their nocturnal crusades, which systematically extinguished opposition and helped fuel the dictator's lust for power. Within six or seven years, Haiti was sufficiently cowed to absorb, if not accept, his inevitable claim to permanent incumbency of the palace. By then, internal dissent was all but quelled. If the tyrant was to be unseated, it would require extraordinary determination by an outside force. But history did not favour such expeditions, which almost invariably ended in failure and bloody retribution. So it was to prove as exiled rebels tried repeatedly to end Papa Doc's reign. From the summer of 1958 onwards, Barbot assumed leadership of the National Security Volunteers and became the self-styled 'Chief of the Secret Police.' This sounded high-minded but was, in truth, the beginning of a prolonged and barely believable nightmare.

The Tontons Macoute were not an organised force, nor did they have any constitutional rights. However, such technicalities had little relevance in the age of Duvalier, when force was the decider. The Macoutes were a brutal rabble coaxed from the slums and encouraged to persecute their compatriots with the promise of presidential patronage. Unsalaried, uncontracted, they found their remuneration in criminality, spreading misery while preying on the poor. A fringe benefit was the freedom to torture at will, something they did with increasing relish as the years wore on. From the outset, Duvalier knew that conciliation was unworkable in the hot-house of Haitian politics. Utter ruthlessness was the only practical means of retaining power, and his ghoulish henchman and the Tontons militia were more than equal to the task. The army had proved unreliable in the past and needed to be neutralised. This became the Tontons' prime purpose. Duvalier saw Haiti's armed forces as a termites' nest, a potentially lethal conglomeration of malevolent irritants who, given the chance, would gnaw away at the regime's support structure. His bogeymen identified politically ambitious officers and kept them under surveillance. Suspicion and mistrust were everywhere in and around the National Palace and Casernes Dessalines, the ochre-walled barracks in the centre of Port-au-Prince.

This tension eventually spawned a succession of purges, with army personnel vanishing in the night. It also led to virtual elimination of anything resembling due process, for the regime began to create 'laws' on the hoof, using them for the arbitrary disposal of troublesome people. Eventually, Haitians came to recognise that their rights under Papa Doc were of no account. They fell under the gaze of the Tontons' mirrored shades, which offered nothing by way of empathy or consideration, just the ever-present possibility of big trouble, usually for no good reason they could understand. The first attempt to dislodge Duvalier came in the year following his election. Haitian exiles backed by Cuban guerrillas landed in southern Haiti in an attempt to spark insurrection. Haitian soldiers, aided by US marines, repelled the force, such as it was, and Papa Doc survived. But he was unnerved by the experience and sought revenge. As usual, it was the military who fell under suspicion. He reacted by reducing the army's numbers, replacing senior officers with younger men and closing the Haitian military academy, traditionally the training centre for junta leaders. For too long, reasoned Duvalier, the army had seen itself as the nation's political arbiters, kingmakers and power brokers. It could not be allowed to continue.

Along with his assault on the army came a ban on political parties. A curfew was imposed to cut the risk of insurrection. The lights of Port-au-

Prince, uncertain at the best of times, now dimmed early as the city took on a haunted calm. As the military was forced to accept its reduced role in Haitian political life, Duvalier created a new palace guard, cold-eyed trusties with obsolete small arms whose fate was closely linked with his. Having been hauled from the cesspits of Bel Air and La Saline, where poverty and disease vied for ascendancy amid broken shacks and filthy lean-tos, they knew where relative prosperity lay. So long as Papa Doc reigned, they were guaranteed comforts they had never known before. His removal, however, would bring bloody retribution.

The Tontons stayed focused, and their methods became renowned. In the annals of extortion and terror, their exploits have rarely been equalled. Barbot was their mentor, their leader and their inspiration. In May, 1959, Duvalier had a heart attack, a blow to his health which was to intensify his feelings of vulnerability and deepen his paranoia. This setback appeared to reinforce the deepest misgivings of the voodoo adepts, who considered the presidential chair 'range', a Haitian witchcraft term suggesting spiritual meddling. Leaders who had occupied it had been deposed with such haste, and often with so much violence, that its very existence seemed to induce unfathomable foreboding. Engulfed by conspirators, weakened by illness, Duvalier was emerging as just another short-term presidential transient, a mere rural physician out of his depth in the bloody vortex of Haitian politics.

The spectres of Dessalines, Leconte, Sam and others who had suffered the people's wrath must have haunted the palace staircase many a time during these troubled early months. But his enemies had not accounted for Barbot and the level of trepidation he managed to engender, during the crucial early stages of the administration. Opponents hauled in by the Tontons faced Barbot's uniquely persuasive powers of interrogation. Those who stayed silent died. Few were allowed a middle course. It was to prove an astonishingly effective tactic. The militia chief's reputation spread fast, creating alarm in the slums and suburbs of Port-au-Prince. The growing number of amputees in the city's streets testified to the efficiency of the bogeymen as they haunted the festering byways. The peasants scattered like dogs as the Macoutes descended on neighbourhoods in their black sedans. Over this grim tableau hung an awful silence. Only voodoo drums in the distant hills, the shrill call of roosters, the snapping of dogs and the crackling of summer storms intruded upon this strange quietness.

CHAPTER 13

TORMENT

While trying gamely to cling to power, and eliminating his foes in the process, Duvalier was eager to preserve an illusion of stability as Haiti stumbled into a new phase of institutionalised horror. In so doing, he began adopting methods which more civilised areas of the western world found hard to understand. At one point, as mentioned earlier, he left the bloated cadaver of a political opponent sitting in an armchair, outside the arrivals hall at Francois Duvalier International Airport in Port-au-Prince. The few tourists who trickled into Haiti at this time found this offensive. Severed heads were another Duvalier speciality which upset the stomachs of those from more decorous regions of the world. Worst of all, though, was an incident relayed to me, via a friend, from an Italian tourist who was aboard a cruise ship at Port-au-Prince waterfront, during the early years of Papa Doc's reign. This was at a time when Barbot was still at his height. Peasants were leaping off the wharves into the sea to catch coins tossed to them from the ship's upper decks. Shrieking with excitement, fighting for position on the dockside, the stick-thin men and women of the streets were throwing themselves into the oily water to retrieve the tourists' largesse. "The sea was alive with them," the tourist said, "they were in a state of hysteria, fighting in the water for whatever they could grab. The passengers thought it was all part of the tourism game."

It was the kind of scene you might witness at scores of ports around the world, especially in the Third World. However, the Tontons evidently thought this was demeaning to Haiti and the President, Papa Doc. It was an insult to his regime, an indication that not all was well, that the government couldn't feed its people. "Suddenly, a big black car appeared on the dockside, screeching to a halt. Tontons Macoute leapt out with guns and began firing at the peasants in the water. Soon the sea was scarlet with blood and the peasants shrieked and turned over like logs, dying where they lay. Some dived underwater to escape the bullets. Others tried hard to scramble clear. Many, wounded and unable to swim, simply disappeared. Within minutes, noisy hysteria had been replaced by total silence as corpses twitched around the ship." The tourists stood on the decks, horrified and in some cases traumatised. It made us realise that we were in an alien land where western standards did not apply, were not even remotely understood. When their job was done, the Tontons Macoute climbed back into their car and sped off. Killing people was nothing to them. It was their work and conscience was never allowed to intrude – if, indeed, it ever existed.

From the beginning of Duvalier's reign, the President's thugs had been engaged in what they considered a 'clean up' of the capital. This came in several forms. At a purely political level, it was intended to exterminate the verminous opposition, whose disruptive exploits made Papa Doc feel uneasy. Within only six months, the militia's terror tactics were already paying dividends, driving anti-Duvalierists underground and silencing the critics. George Petit, Editor of *L'Independance*, was taken into custody after his office was ransacked by Duvalier's police. The *Miroir* newspaper was also attacked, having been accused by the enforcers of printing anti-government lies. Monsieur Laferriere, Mayor of Port-au-Prince, made clear Duvalier's intentions, when he warned opponents that the Presidential forces had been mobilised to quash dissent without mercy. He pledged a bloodbath in such explicit terms that the US Embassy felt compelled to complain, saying it did not want a situation to arise in which their citizens would feel threatened. International indignation was such that Lafferiere was dismissed, but this did nothing to slow down the inexorable move towards totalitarian rule.

The dark hours were now being used as cover for Barbot's neighbourhood purges. His swaggering cohorts turned machine-guns on the homes of known anti-Duvalierists. A rigidly enforced curfew enabled Tontons hardmen to search and destroy at will, operating in small autonomous groups to control entire districts of the city. In the early days, the militia wore hoods, but shades were later to become their hallmark. Inscrutability undoubtedly helped their cause. People shrank from their gaze and fled when they heard clips of ammunition being loaded into their high-powered weaponry. The term Tontons Macoute (which roughly translates as Bogeymen) became their unofficial soubriquet, purloined from Haitian childhood horror tales and given an extra edge by Barbot's nocturnal excesses. There were elements in the early Duvalierist pogroms which had echoes many years later in the Taliban in Afghanistan or the Mugabe regime in Zimbabwe. These were a rigidly enforced puritanism and a rabid appetite for irrational persecution. Traditional street games and certain Creole songs were banned. Prostitutes and pan-handlers were outlawed. Night raids were inflicted on entire communities. Many people came to believe their very existence was offensive to the regime.

Mopping up opposition, silencing press critics, cleaning up the streets and ingratiating itself with Washington DC, became the principal thrusts of Duvalier's administration during the early months and years. When the US dispatched a small unit of marine advisers to help improve the Haitian army, he made much of it, emphasising repeatedly his country's strong affinity with the Americans, its willingness to help Washington strategically wherever possible, and his own personal revulsion towards those who would harm this great nation's interests. In truth, there was always a deep ambivalence in Duvalier's relations with the United States. He had opposed the US occupation of Haiti and felt profoundly the humiliations heaped upon his black brothers in the American south. At the same time, he acknowledged that his medical training was due largely to American generosity, and that his country could only survive economically with US support.

Financial aid was never far from Papa Doc's mind, and the need for it drove many of his key decisions. As a result, he embarked on public relations campaigns, whenever he could, to laud America's progress in the field of civil rights while burdening his own people with restrictions, which outsiders found hard to understand. It would have been interesting to know what Dr Martin Luther King Jr would have made of Duvalier's torture-and-kill tactics, or his penchant for snatching dissenters away in the night. Even more intriguingly, what would he have made of Fort Dimanche and its institutionalised terror? While Papa Doc was at least, theoretically, in favour of civil rights in America, he gave them scant regard in his homeland. Even as Barbot imposed his evil will on Haiti, bombing *Le Patriote* newspaper as part of his crusade to silence dissident voices, his master at the palace was extolling Washington's role in the cause of freedom. The irony was ignored. Papa Doc felt Haiti had unique problems for which unique remedies were required. Idealism could wait awhile, until the dirty business of securing power was complete.

The supposedly jinxed presidential chair inside the National Palace was never comfortably held by Duvalier, who, by the time I met him in 1968, had already repelled eight attempts on his regime. Few of these, it has to be said, were professional operations involving first-class military men, but they had the effect of deepening his feelings of vulnerability. If the infamous Bay of Pigs invasion on Cuba in 1961 was shambolic, it was nothing alongside the vaudevillean exploits of Duvalier's exiled foes. Time and again, largely inept and poorly financed attempts were made to dislodge Papa Doc, but each had the effect of reinforcing his regime. In the end, the dictator was so emboldened by his enemies' lame attempts on his life that he adopted military airs, even donning a soldier's helmet following the notorious Dade deputy sheriffs' onslaught in 1958, when a small band of adventurers tried to topple Papa Doc by posing as tourists aboard a 50-foot launch called the Mollie C.

The climax of this attempted coup occurred on the barracks square, across which David Knox was to march ten years later, to the makeshift courtroom at Casernes Dessalines, just a few hundred yards from the National Palace. It was here, an oblong parade ground where rag-tag soldiers swept crowing cockerels aside with gun butts, that a shoot-out reminiscent of the OK Corral occurred in the steamheat summer of 1958. Extraordinarily, this ill-conceived and ultimately doomed venture almost brought the required result. The eight-man mission nearly pulled off what would have been the most bizarre overthrow of a tyrant in the entire history of the Americas. At the time, Haiti was — in tourism terms, at least — still basking in the afterglow of the Magloire regime, with its expansive 'live and let live' philosophy and its determination to let the good times roll. Tourists were still flying into Port-au-Prince, from New York and Miami, to sample the exquisite charms of a country which, despite its never-ending challenges, always offered depths of culture most Caribbean destinations lacked. The lingering lure of the Truman Capote era was still enough to bring a sizeable influx of romantic and intrepid types to the old French colony's shores, and dollar-wielding blancs always found a welcome among the black hustlers on the beaches and the pimps in the bars.

From the outset, the Mollie C and its unusual crew were intent on insinuating themselves into this scene of jollity and *joie de vivre* as they negotiated the Florida Straits and moored in Gonaives Bay. Florida sheriff Arthur Payne did not look out of place as he stumbled ashore in bathing trunks with a smile on his face. According to the inevitable folklore which followed, he even took several straw hats from vendors and piled them on his head to have his photograph taken. However, Payne was not in reality in holiday mood. His visit had a more serious intent: to overthrow the government and provoke an insurrection. Aboard the Mollie C were enough arms to create havoc around the palace and a mixture of men whose reasons for being there must have been as varied and unusual as they were. Payne, an imposing man in his mid-thirties, was accompanied by fellow Dade County sheriff, Danny Jones. Three other Americans, including the boat captain Joe Walker, were also involved along with three disaffected former Haitian army officers, Henri Perpignan, Alix Pasquet and Philippe Dominique. This was an odd assortment of rebels, but not as odd as the tactics they deployed for execution of their scheme.

The original idea had been to organise a lift into town from the seaside resort of Deluge, but an army patrol was alerted to their presence and came under fire when they went to investigate. The three patrolmen were mortally injured in the skirmish while Payne received a bullet hole in the leg. It was not an auspicious start for the invaders, but they made the best of a bad job and grabbed the officers' jeep and sped off towards Port-au-Prince. En route they abandoned the jeep and hired a tap-tap, one of the colourful buses that ply trade in Haiti, and continued their journey into the city full of high hopes of a military victory. From the start, there was a mad-cap dimension to this plot, but Payne and his fellow conspirators did not see things that way. Papa Doc's regime, they reasoned, was a precarious edifice bolstered by terror. Once shaken from within, it would crumble under the weight of its own unpopularity. If the theory was sound, the practice turned out to be something else, and the consequences were horrific.

In some respects, the Dade deputy sheriffs' coup attempt was similar to Dr Castro's attack on the Presidential Palace in Havana the following year. While the Cubans used a delivery van to storm Batista's defences — the vehicle still stands in the grounds of Havana's revolutionary war museum, its sides punctured by bullet holes — the Haitian party made do with the tap-tap, a truck converted for passenger use with odd religious slogans painted on the front. Charging through the streets of Port-au-Prince, with gung-ho desperadoes clinging on for life, it must have caused a few heads to turn, even in a city where madness was routine and bad driving the norm. As they approached the gates of Casernes Dessalines, Pasquet bellowed instructions in Creole to the waiting sentry, telling him they were bringing in prisoners, and received in return a half-hearted salute and a signal to pass. So far the bid to bring down Papa Doc had been easier than even the eternally optimistic Payne had imagined. As the tap-tap crunched to a halt on the barracks parade ground, he and his colleagues leapt out and swiftly took control of the office quarters, where a guard sacrificed his life by drawing a gun on them. In less time than it takes to boil an egg, the insurgents had imprisoned all the soldiers they could find and prepared to incite a Haitian uprising.

Pasquet, as a former barracks commander, knew this territory well, but made one appalling blunder. He thought he and his men would have instant access to the barracks arms store, but Duvalier had taken the wise precaution – no doubt inspired by his eternal suspicion of army loyalties – to move all the guns and ammunition into the palace basement, where they would have been overseen by Tontons loyalists. Hence, the invaders, far from having the unlimited firepower they expected, were in truth cornered in a compound at the mercy of Duvalierist forces. Even by Haitian standards, the gory scenes that followed were considered harrowing. The eight-man 'army' banked heavily on creating the impression that they had more men than they had in truth. The ruse worked inasmuch as even Duvalier himself was preparing to flee the palace, believing that a sizeable revolutionary force was literally within yards of his study with the wherewithal to blow him and his family apart. However, when word leaked out that only eight invaders were involved, the President abandoned his plans to seek the protection of a foreign embassy and mobilised his forces against what was, in effect, a suicide squad.

Pasquet had called the palace by telephone to issue a warning that an uprising was about to begin, and that exiled troops would storm the presidential stronghold to extinguish the regime and all who sustained it. At that point, their objective was just about attainable, but hesitation undermined the enterprise, and Duvalier was able to summon sufficient reinforcements to repel whatever the rebel band could muster. Makeshift riflemen were dragged off the streets, Tontons thugs were forced into the firing line, and even vendors and bootblacks were enlisted for the cause.

Guns were thrust into the hands of reluctant heroes and pressure was gradually applied to the tiny and ill-advised guerrilla force behind the barricades. The public, meanwhile, were bemused onlookers as history unfolded before them. As armed Duvalierists took up positions in the square outside the barracks gate, the city's street people gathered like cattle, naively inquisitive and uncomprehending. Once gunfire began spurting from the palace, they scattered, with cripples dragging their crutches behind them and beggar boys shrieking.

Barbot, the Tontons torturer, was in the thick of the fight, leading a grenade charge which led to Pasquet's death, part of his head being blown away as shrapnel exploded around him. Payne was dispatched while wrapped in bedding, pleading for his life, while Dominique was cut to pieces by machine-gun fire. Hickey, one of the Americans, was picked off by a sniper, and Perpignan was stripped and brutalised by the mob, a fate suffered by Dessalines and Sam before him. Another American, Levant Kersten, suffered a similar fate, being sliced up as he fled the barracks alone, his remains dragged like a battered trophy through the streets.

With hindsight, it's easy to depict the Dade Deputy Sheriffs' invasion, as it has come to be known, as just another ill-conceived tragi-comedy in Haiti's long history of bloodletting. But it did, in fact, include air support which never materialised, as the Feds confiscated the plane and its contents before it took off from Florida. Hare-brained as it appeared, the venture came perilously close to success, but sheer bad luck hampered its progress almost from the start. The capture of the aircraft, with sixteen 'troops' aboard, was undoubtedly a major blow, but Duvalier's astute move in shifting weaponry from the barracks was the really decisive factor. Once the invasion force's real numbers were known, the initially tentative Duvalierist counter-attack gathered force and ultimately prevailed. Like most assaults on Papa Doc, this was hardly a glorious military exercise, but the commitment and courage behind it were real enough. The fact that all eight invaders ended up dead is stark testimony to that. The triumphant President, meanwhile, was treated to the sight of Perpignan's savaged corpse, which was carried to his study, and the acclaim of his followers. With a soldier's helmet perched ridiculously on his head, Papa Doc celebrated quietly at another successful defence of his realm. The legend was taking on new dimensions of indestructibility.

CHAPTER 14
CHAMBER OF HORRORS

As I gazed out across the barracks yard at Casernes Dessalines, trying to look contained as I sucked on a tipless Camel, the Tonton flicked his camera shutter inches from my face. 'The personification of British imperialism' I might have been, in the mildly derisive words of an esteemed colleague, but there was in truth little self-assurance in my demeanour, because Haiti had the capacity to unsettle even the hardiest of men. Casernes Dessalines, the ochre-walled hub of Haiti's military might, was a far cry from Sandhurst or West Point, but nonetheless represented for Haitians both the best and worst of its institutions, for the army had become known for installing and deposing regimes at will, acting as the primary power-broker in the land. It gave, then deprived, Haiti of Magloire and helped to some extent in creating the ogre that Duvalier was to become. The day I watched Knox marching hollow-eyed across that square, his suit a size or two too big, I thought also of the Dade Country deputies and their foolhardy attempt on Papa Doc's regime. As the Tonton sized me up, focused his lens, snapped pictures from right and left, and sometimes from behind, I pondered the prospect of being incarcerated like Knox, by a government seemingly oblivious of the demands and expectations of western society.

This was not, after all, a western society, but a transplanted satellite of Africa, where the spirits exerted more power than the constitution, and where human welfare was a consideration hardly worthy of the name. The Tonton said nothing, just fired away. For him, I was an exhibit, a weird product of a distant civilisation which he presumably had no desire to know or understand. "Tell him to fuck off, John," said Cole, confident that the bogeyman did not understand. "Tell him to boil his fucking Tonton head in a cauldron." "I tell you what," I said, "I'll get the Creole translation for you. Then you can tell him." There was laughter all round. The cockerels scattered. A soldier in baggy fatigues and oversized boots shifted uneasily, probably sensing that mockery was afoot.

Pickering the translator scuttled past, holding his backside as usual, as though his bowels could not be relied upon. Poor old Pickering, a perpetually frightened man, his rolling eyes jutting from skull-like features. The fear in his face seemed to sum up all that Haiti was about. His interpretation of everything said in court would help decide Knox's fate, and probably mine. It was a far from reassuring thought. I would never forget the way he laboured over my name. Jean Markee. Tontons are thugs, by Jean Markee. And the words of the seasoned New York correspondent. "Take my tip, old boy, be on the plane out tonight," he advised. Cole said: "Do you wish you'd flown out? I mean, this Tonton bastard is overdoing it a bit, isn't he?" The camera clicked again. Mmmmm. Yes, he was insistent. "What if you end up in the nick? Not a nice thought."

Casernes Dessalines doubled as a jail. Like the National Palace basement, it also had a prominent role in Duvalier's torture system. Men were routinely kicked in the testicles as they lay in their cells here. In fact, bloated testicles became a mark of the regime. Shortened limbs, blinded eyes, crippling back injuries and savaged genitalia were all part of the prisoner's portion. Mercy, blessed release, even a modicum of compassion were always in short supply, but torture was doled out daily, not for any special reason, merely in response to the President's blanket directive to make life unbearable for the *kamouken*, the pestilential enemy.

In fact, Knox was rarely subjected to Duvalier-style violation during his time in custody. Though he was apparently roughed-up more than once, he was never physically maimed. There was the inevitable intimidatory interrogation, and implied threats, but never a disabling kick in the groin or jab in the eye. When he emerged finally to face the tribunal, he looked haunted and thin, but there was nothing to betray violence. Whatever his suffering, it was psychological rather than physical. He still managed to march, like the former military man he was, with a certain bearing, his moustache twitching, his nose flaring, under the close watch of Haiti's rag-tag army. For the most part, he was kept in the barracks hospital, where he had a proper bed and room to work on plans for his Madeira home. Unlike most of Duvalier's prisoners, he was allowed a degree of hope. Even so, the unpredictability of the regime, its notorious savagery, must have weighed heavily on his mind during that long, hot summer of incarceration. Apart from visits by Charles Sanderson, the British envoy from Jamaica, and Greg Bentley, the special branch officer from the Bahamas, Knox's imprisonment was largely solitary. He had long hours in which to ponder his plight, and foremost among his thoughts must have been Fort Dimanche, the former ammunition depot built on marshland just outside Port-au-Prince which Duvalier used for housing and disposing of enemies.

Throughout the Duvaliers' long reign, Fort Dimanche took on almost mythical dimensions. It loomed large in the Haitian psyche, as did the supposed indestructibility of Papa Doc and the appalling mystical powers at his disposal. It was a place where unimaginable suffering took place and from which many, and probably most, prisoners never emerged alive. From the outside it was nondescript, a scattering of low-slung buildings behind wire-traps. It had none of the gauntness, the sense of foreboding, of the world's most infamous prisons — Dartmoor, Changi, Alcatraz and San Quentin among them — just the sullen indifference of a place where joy was routinely denied. It was here that the Duvalier regime's contempt for its enemies found its most articulate expression.

With several men to a cell, and all invariably infested with black lice, there was no space for anything resembling privacy or dignity. Inmates used brimming slop-pails to urinate and defecate, with one per cell assigned to empty them each day. When the pail was full, the prisoners relieved themselves where they lay, so that cell floors were frequently covered with an indescribably malodorous slurry. The guards, meanwhile, maintained an attitude of callous indifference. Those fortunate to emerge alive added considerably to Dimanche folklore. They told of skeletal prisoners rolled up in filthy mats waiting to die, of execution days when prisoners were marched out to face the firing squad, of scant food and dirty drinking water. Even Tontons who had fallen foul of the regime, were tossed into the Fort, among prisoners they had probably previously tormented, in pursuit of their foul calling. Inmates who died were rolled up in their mats and laid outside the door for the guards to collect. Death was so much part of life in Fort Dimanche that cadavers were as common as vermin.

Life was without value, an irrelevance. Deprived of even the most basic of human decencies, the inmates were reduced to a state of resigned inertia, staring blindly at stained walls while their fellow captives vomited and relieved themselves around them. There must have been worse places on earth, but where else in the middle years of the 20th Century were men so intent on debasing their compatriots?

It was as if Haiti were plumbing new depths after an already severely degraded past. If Duvalier echoed Hitler by installing an anti-communist tyranny and maintaining it with the help of a fearsome secret police force, he did so, too, by leaving prisoners to rot behind walls in unspeakable conditions. Less than 30 years before, Europe's liberators exposed the horrors of Belsen and Buchenwald, but the world's revulsion had done nothing to influence the excesses of Haiti's country doctor, who, by 1958, was implementing many of the terror tactics favoured by Germany's mad *fuhrer*. In Fort Dimanche, according to those who somehow escaped, many of the horrors of Nazism had found new expression through the Tontons Macoute and sadistic elements of the Haitian army. The difference was that there was no ideological message, other than a crude anti-communist stance fuelled primarily by a constant desire for American aid, and an almost manic determination to silence opposition voices.

Admission to Fort Dimanche was often quickly followed by an unconscionably vile induction process. This led to prolonged periods of standing, sleep deprivation and near starvation. Some prisoners stood so long, sometimes for days on end, that their feet ballooned alarmingly. Those who tried to sit or crouch to ease their exhaustion were beaten with sticks. Sometimes lacerations developed into abesses. Mosquitoes and lice were a perpetual irritation. Even the most robust of spirits were eventually broken by Duvalier's ghouls. Food was doled out grudgingly, and rarely in adequate portions. Even for those who pined for sustenance, the fare was hardly appetising. Usually, lumpy boiled rice was served with mashed vegetables and grain of indeterminate origin. If inmates were lucky, this would be washed down by weak, tasteless coffee. The poor diet inevitably led to disease. Diarrhea was common, and particularly distressing for those obliged to share the victims' cells. With slop-pails already full, uncontrolled evacuation of the bowels was not welcomed by those who had to sleep and eat in the same congested cell.

One of the most graphic accounts of Dimanche life appeared in Patrick Lemoine's book, *Fort Dimanche - Dungeon of Death*, first published in 1997. His own six-year imprisonment actually occurred in the 1970s, when Duvalier's son, Jean-Claude was in power, but the essentials of daily prison life had changed little from Papa Doc's day. If anything, they might have been marginally better, certainly not worse. Yet, his often harrowing account depicts life without hope, among people who often had little idea why they were behind bars at all. The arrest and detention process was so callous, so arbitrary and so unjust that many inmates were left simply bemused. Tontons discretion was wide-ranging: they could throw people into prison on a whim, and always with Papa Doc's tacit or even explicit approval.

In his book, Lemoine recounts the case of Justin Bertrand, who was always proud to tell fellow prisoners that his own incarceration was the result of his assassination of a Duvalier acolyte, Pierre Novembre. This gave him a certain cachet among the inmates, for most were detained simply for their suspected political leanings and nothing more. In Bertrand's case, there was a positive act to boast of, with the added delight that Novembre was Papa Doc's personal food taster, the man whose devotion to his master landed him the job of forestalling any poisoning attempt on the President's life. The surprise to Lemoine was that Bertrand had been spared execution, but his presence lifted a spirit or two. Most were less fortunate. Lemoine made it his mission after release to chart the full extent of the Dimanche horror under Baby Doc. In so doing, he admitted that the Papa Doc years were probably far worse, with untold numbers perishing inside the prison walls, including a large portion of Haiti's intellectual elite. Many died for no better reason than vague suspicions of Left-Wing leanings. Some were simply too poor to pay for intercession on their behalf. Those without power, without hope, prayed for death. More often than not, their prayers were answered.

By the time I met Papa Doc, in the late summer of 1968, his brutality had been well-chronicled, not just by Graham Greene, but the exiled Haitian movements dedicated to his overthrow. Benign as this strange little man appeared that day, his huge hands wafting before him like palm fronds in a sea breeze, his worst excesses were still to come. Within a few months of our meeting, and of the death sentence being passed on David Knox, Papa Doc was to embark on an orgy of barbarism against his own people, outstripping even the dark era of 1963-64, when Tontons massacres became so commonplace that the entire populace cowered.

For those who suffered most, 1969 was a new low point for Haiti, with Fort Dimanche swallowing up countless supposed dissidents like a voracious predator. In the bloodletting of that year, Duvalier did not allow gender, or youth, to intrude upon his conscience. Those perceived as enemies of the regime perished, usually without any hint of due process. The group Fordi9, dedicated to charting the full roll call of Duvalier's victims, each month honours victims of this age of despondency. One such was Gladys Jean-Francois, who was allowed to live only one month beyond her twenty-first birthday, before being dispatched by Papa Doc's pitiless henchmen. She was arrested as an activist and executed on July 29, leaving behind two young sons, who were subsequently raised by her mother. Her brothers, Raymond and Aimard died the same year at the hands of Duvalier's torturers. This family was but one of many that felt the brunt of the regime.

As summary executions gathered pace at Fort Dimanche, more and more supposed dissidents were dragged from the streets, or from their beds in the dead of night. Their misdeeds could be utterly trivial, like whispering anything vaguely anti-Duvalierist or giving succour to anyone deemed unsympathetic to the regime. Many years later, when Papa Doc had gone, the Inter-American Commission on Human Rights recorded some of the vilest of practices within the prison walls, and also in the nearby woods. Fifty metres from the rear wall of Dimanche is where executions occurred. When bullets grew scarce, and prisoners were no longer considered worthy of the expenditure, they were led away singly to be clubbed to death in an area later to be called Bayarons, Duvalier's secret graveyard. In this wooded area between the prison and the sea, faint cries of the dying could be heard as the soft clubbing sound was carried on the gentle sea breezes. Inmates in their cells claimed they could hear these dying wails.

Naturally, the government was later to deny these events, but the Commission was satisfied with the veracity of its evidence and recorded it in detail. In outlining Fort Dimanche's role under Duvalier, the Commission wrote of the 'depersonalising' of prisoners, a systematic reduction of inmates to an animal state. This began with a humiliating physical examination accompanied by verbal abuse from the jailer. The psychological conditioning continued with deprivation of all rights.

Speaking up, or answering back, was expressly forbidden, earning extreme punishment. Small ill-lit, virtually airless cells, which were three metres square in size, were used for accommodating between twenty-two and thirty-three prisoners, who would have to sleep in shifts because of the limited floor area. For the first three months, they lay on bare cement floors, then were granted a woven mat. In the long hot summer, the conditions were intolerable, with inmates bathed in sweat and tormented by mosquitoes, bed bugs, head lice and other forms of infestation.

As Lemoine and others have related, Dimanche was a place where urine came to serve multiple purposes. As water was in chronically short supply, urine was used for washing hands, bathing wounds, and sometimes even for quenching thirst. Lemoine records an instance where a dying man took his last drink by cupping his hands under a fellow inmate who relieved himself so that his friend could at least die with a moist mouth. No baths were allowed at Dimanche, only dead-of-night excursions to a standpipe which offered pathetic dribbles of water. However, with only five minutes allowed for each cell-full of inmates to make use of it, there was little time to stand under the water. Some gulped what they could, others opted to cleanse some part of their bodies. Those who lingered too long were beaten savagely.

The Commission also recorded the niggardly portions of food, most of it lacking nutrition. Corn mash was the staple fare, sometimes offered with macaroni, but there was no meat, fish, fruit or vegetables. And the filthy cell floor was the 'plate' from which they were forced to eat, guards taking delight in offering crockery, then taking it away again. Sometimes a single plate was shared between many, spreading whatever infections were lurking around. The roll call of prisoners who died from typhoid, loose stools and tuberculosis was depressingly long, longer even than the one recording executions. Vitamin deficiency, malaria and intestinal worms were also rampant.

The dead were usually carried by fellow prisoners to shallow graves, where wild dogs would often prowl in the night to dig up the corpses to feast as the inmates never did, devouring whatever flesh they could find and gnawing on the brittle bones. Most Dimanche inmates survived no longer than a year, and many died under torture from Enos St Pierre, a Duvalier ghoul who relished the suffering of his fellows so much that it became his life's work. He was part of the presidential guard, and his speciality was dunking prisoners' heads in buckets of excrement and watching them plead for water before they died. "We do not stop people from dying," he liked to tell them, mockingly. Fort Dimanche was eventually demolished in 1994, when the Duvaliers were long gone but as new convulsions gripped the land. It remains powerfully symbolic of Haiti's darkest days.

CHAPTER 15

CURFEW

Papa Doc was traumatised by the deputies' invasion. It re-emphasised the brittle nature of his regime and deepened the persecution complex which was to become the dominant feature of his life. A curfew descended on the land, quietening the streets and darkening an already dark city. Lights had always flickered erratically in Port-au-Prince, but were now more often off than on. When the sun went down, dipping into the Caribbean and casting huge deep shadows across the mountains, Haiti was left at the mercy of the Tontons. Barbot, chief ghoul, arch-torturer and principal architect of the military success against the Florida Eight, now had the President's full blessing to do whatever he needed to do in securing the state against its opponents. It was a task he undertook with the assiduity of the true enthusiast. As the bodies of Haiti's American attackers went back to Florida, and the dead former Haitian army officers were consigned to unmarked graves, Papa Doc began articulating for the masses the true significance of the invasion, its abuse of Haitian sovereignty, and its reckless disregard for the potential prosperity of those whose voices had been heard during the national ballot.

With his new-found swagger, and bellicose utterances, Duvalier was taking on a form never previously recognised or acknowledged by his people. From being a slightly reticent, and seemingly harmless, intellectual, he had morphed into a fiery gunslinger, determined to put down anyone who stood in the way of his objectives. The nature of those objectives became hazier as time elapsed, for the elevation of the masses, the equitable distribution of wealth, and the suppression of the mulatto elite were aims which soon fell

171

victim to compromise. The elevation of the masses never happened, and the equitable distribution of wealth was somehow lost amid the Duvalier family's growing lust for riches of their own. Dowdy and unexciting as they were alongside the Magloires, Papa Doc and his wife did not take long to warm to the caress of money. As looters of the national treasury, they were to have few, if any, equals. Looking back on his words now, it is impossible not to be struck by their staggering hypocrisy.

"The election was the victory of our miserable peasant masses for whom a just and equitable part of the national revenue is, henceforth, assured. This election signalled the victory of the working classes too long tricked who had decided to consolidate the conquests of 1946. This election signalled the victory of the middle classes delivered from a permanent fear of tomorrows." He depicted his presidential triumph as an assertion of provincial aspirations over metropolitan avarice, of black grassroots revolution over the entrenched financial interests of the grasping mulattoes.

Duvalier's command of language was never entirely sound, and it frequently tended towards contradiction, especially when he was emotionally aroused. But one message which came through clearly was that his election was a victory for the people, a blow in favour of the exploited, persecuted and oppressed. It was a claim that, in the fullness of time, would strike those obliged to live under him as bitterly and savagely ironic. The elimination of the political opposition got underway immediately. Barbot led an assassination squad against the brothers of former candidate, Clement Jumelle. The pair, Charles and Ducasse, were dragged from their beds and shot. Then their bodies were pulled into the street and photographed as part of Papa Doc's propaganda assault on what he saw as the forces of evil. The victims were portrayed in an official communique as bomb plotters and schemers involved in the July 29 incident. Jean-Jacques Monfiston, accused of harbouring the Jumelle brothers, was tortured to death in Fort Dimanche, as Barbot's thugs tried to extract from him the whereabouts of Clement Jumelle. His failure to speak up led to elimination of his family. It did not take long for the true nature of the Duvalier regime to reveal itself as darkness enfolded Port-au-Prince.

The brutal killing of Ducasse Jumelle, a respected middle-aged man of noble bearing, was a traumatic blow to Haiti's political fraternity, for it displayed an aspect of Duvalierism which was to become increasingly evident as time went on. It was an absolute absence of gratitude for past favours. During those difficult times when Duvalier had sought refuge from Magloire, it was Ducasse who hosted and succoured the Duvalier family. At great personal risk, Jumelle had supported and encouraged Duvalier in what had then seemed a worthwhile mission. But when Papa Doc's nature turned, it turned completely, disregarding friends of the past in a callous campaign for what he perversely saw as revenge. Having been so embarrassingly exposed by so small an invasion force, Duvalier's military arrangements were evidently in dire need of reform. Hence, a small contingent of US marines was summoned to Haiti for the dual purpose of training home-grown troops and providing a potent symbol of Washington's support.

For Duvalier, image-building was becoming an important part of his survival strategy. The presence of US military personnel in Port-au-Prince was, in his eyes at least, a token of his own legitimacy, a presidential imprimatur. If military enhancements were a priority during these uncertain days, financial worries ran them a close second. The Haitian economy was in shreds, largely because of the uncertainty created by the precarious political situation, and Duvalier felt compelled to underpin the country's dwindling finances. Anxious to prevent any suggestion that Haiti was in a downward economic spiral, the President ordered businesses to stay open, whatever their financial travails. Bankruptcies were explicitly forbidden, lest they created an impression of failure. With exiles eager to destabilise the regime from without, Duvalier was determined to preserve illusions of integrity within. Aware that his survival could not be guaranteed, he countered any move that might exacerbate unemployment and stir public agitation. Duvalier, having studied Haiti's past in fine detail, knew the nature of its people better than most. This was a hair-trigger situation where a single wrong move might ignite rebellion. As a show of strength, he acquired war equipment from Italy, including a squad of Second World War tanks to augment the six he already had. He also bought ammunition to fit newly-acquired rifles and machine-guns. Warming to his new image as a war commander, he also organised a military parade to mark the anniversary of Haiti's ejection of the French, then set about freshening up the senior ranks by compulsorily retiring older officers. US-trained younger men were brought in to supplant the general staff, which had been made up largely of experienced veterans with twenty-five and thirty-year records behind them.

In everything he did during the crucial early years of his regime, Duvalier was geared towards frightening would-be usurpers and ingratiating himself with the Americans. A combination of paranoia and penury made him feel embattled in almost every sense. There were times when it seemed he could not possibly survive. To make him sleep easier, Duvalier finally decided on the establishment of an elite presidential guard of unshakeably loyal soldiers to provide twenty-four security around the palace. These crack troops, with their sharp uniforms, pristine weaponry and more than ample food, became Papa Doc's insurance policy in a hostile world. They established quarters in the palace grounds, provided eyes and ears among less reliable elements of the armed forces, and dedicated themselves to the preservation of the regime.

Meanwhile, Barbot liaised with neighbouring Dominicans to ensure the border was secure. If sea approaches from the west were, by their very nature, vulnerable, and the air above almost impossible to patrol, Duvalier wanted at least to feel that the sole land approach into Haitian territory from the east was sealed. In December, 1958, he and Trujillo signed a pact aimed at mutual co-operation and support, with the declared aim of helping each other to suppress exiled upstarts and, more specifically, communist infiltrators. That same month, the Americans declared that their marine training mission in Haiti would become a fixture, with officers serving two-year terms at a time to provide an open-ended presence. The arrangement was reassuring for all parties involved, for it provided Port-au-Prince with a superpower's blessing and protection, and Washington with Duvalier's declared pledge of resistance to all Leftist agitators.

Just as the US and Haiti were settling into this cosy pact, events across the straits in Cuba took a dramatic turn. A gangling, garrulous, bearded figure in battle fatigues descended from the Sierra Maestra with his guerilla army to oust Batista from power in Havana. Castro's arrival was disquieting for everyone in the Caribbean, but especially Duvalier and his American friends. The Left-Wing rebel from the mountains was to unsettle the region for decades to come, though no-one knew it at the time. Duvalier, shaken and bemused, was unsure how to respond to this latest challenge. Warily, uncertain whether Castro would prove to be friend or foe, he opted to proceed with caution and bide his time. Duvalier's concerns centred partly on his friendship with Batista, a man whose rampant extravagance and flagrant Mob connections made him a natural target for rebels with the evangelical, and puritanical, zeal of Castro. He felt the new Cuban Government might turn its sights on him. More disturbingly, Cuba's close proximity to Haiti made it a potential base for exile raids. Having secured his eastern flank in his pact with Trujillo, he was now feeling exposed to the west. His initial response, therefore, was to soften his own line against Haitian agitators and make conciliatory overtures to Havana.

This involved sending a consignment of medicine to Cuba and releasing a number of political prisoners, including several of Leftist persuasion. Sensing that Castro was a no-nonsense revolutionary intent on developing a sphere of influence in the Caribbean region, Duvalier was disturbed lest his accommodation with Trujillo be interpreted as a Right-Wing alliance against the new Cuban leader, especially as Trujillo had been providing arms to Batista during the struggle against insurrection. This was not a happy time for Duvalier, and it would not get better. As things turned out, events forced Duvalier's hand. His former foe Louis Dejoie, darling of the Haitian elite, sought Castro's help in changing the political landscape in Haiti and was not rebuffed. Castro, high on success, saw himself now as leader of a regional movement against tyranny. His charismatic henchman, Ernesto Che Guevara, became actively involved with guerilla groups inside Cuba training to overthrow dictators elsewhere. Haitian exiles, inspired by Dejoie, received military training inside Cuba with the objective of replicating Castro's triumph in their homeland. Duvalier, in desperation, sent secret death squads into Cuba to eliminate the core of the exiled opposition, but without success. Recognising that the new Cuban regime had long-term aims inimical to his own survival, he was ultimately to resume his posture as a rabid anti-communist and throw in his lot with Washington. Looking back, it was the right decision. Whatever travails Haiti was to suffer in later years — and especially during the three decades of the Duvaliers — communism wasn't one of them.

CHAPTER 16

SICK AND TIRED

For those at the sharp end of Duvalier's terror tactics, life was becoming nigh intolerable. Barbot cared nothing for appearances and performed his duties with nauseating glee. Random assassinations became the norm, often in public. Chicago-style car chases frequently ended with the Tontons Macoute blazing away with machine-guns in crowded Port-au-Prince streets. Not all their work was undertaken in the dead of night behind closed doors. Frequently, bullet-peppered corpses were left on the streets, where stray cats sniffed round them. If the regime was beginning to look impregnable by the summer of 1959, the reality in the palace was somewhat different. Duvalier was already feeling the weight of his responsibilities and fearing the consequences of Castro's successful revolution in Cuba. Left-Wing ferment now became the rage of the age, with Right-Wing regimes of all kinds in the Americas susceptible to the chill winds of change. For Duvalier, more paranoiac than most, early fears were taking on dimensions of hysteria. He and Trujillo began to suspect that an emboldened Castro would exploit mounting revolutionary fervour, to stage an invasion of Hispaniola in pursuance of his Marxist dreams. There were fears in Washington that the 'Castro effect' would have awful repercussions throughout the Caribbean and into Central and South America.

Physically, Papa Doc was not a strong figure. There had always been a noticeable frailty about him, even in his youth. Unlike Magloire or Castro, both robust men with a powerful presence, Duvalier was stooped and studious, and the pressures of office soon began to take their toll. In May, 1959, illness almost achieved what his exiled opponents passionately desired but felt unable to achieve. First, he fell victim to an influenza epidemic which weakened his ailing frame, then he suffered a heart attack which almost ended his life. The mood at the palace was sombre. Loyalists who depended on presidential patronage to survive began to feel uneasy. Tontons Macoute enforcers who had become the ogres of modern Haiti started to feel that payback time was on its way sooner than they hoped. In his bed, Papa Doc looked worryingly weak. His physician friend Jacques Fourquand, himself a political activist with impressive medical credentials, administered insulin, fearing the President was in a diabetic coma. It seemed Haiti was about to be plunged into a period of yet more anguish and uncertainty, with Cuban communists awaiting their chance to exploit the country's woes.

To combat the disconcerting physical reality, Duvalier on his recovery began to take refuge in the mythical, spiritual and divine. It was around this time that he buttressed the faith of his followers by proclaiming himself to be beyond human form. "They cannot get me, I am immaterial" now became a mantra that Papa Doc used whenever events went against him. As if to convince themselves that what he said was true, Duvalierists began trading on the superstitions of the people by plastering "Duvalier is God" slogans all over Port-au-Prince. This sustained graffiti campaign was tied in with the President's evolving image, with the sinister voodoo deity, Baron Samedi, now constantly invoked as a kind of alter ego. As the threatening reality became less and less palatable, Papa Doc resorted increasingly to the spiritual and surreal, donning funereal attire — the signature dark suit and black bowler — to promote the Samedi image.

Few people are as susceptible to other-worldliness than Haitians, who have consistently sought salvation from their grim circumstances among their various gods. Duvalier, a voodoo adept, whose peregrinations as a physician had given him invaluable insights into the peasant psyche, now used his knowledge with an adroitness even his most fervent rivals had to admire. Papa Doc's smoke-and-mirrors approach paid off, for soon less sophisticated Haitians began to imagine that the myth and the man were one and the same. It's tempting for Europeans to see this shameless manipulation of the masses as evidence of a primitive, undeveloped society, but Papa Doc's tactics were not far removed from those of modern western politicians. Certainly from US President Richard Nixon onwards, western governments have increasingly relied on image rather than substance in promoting their imagined attributes. In Nixon's case, the image-makers had a huge job on their hands. They somehow had to transform a blue-chinned villain, with shifty eyes and unsavoury antecedents, into an electable Republican with the people's interests at heart. Somehow they did it, only to see brutal reality eventually win the day with the Watergate revelations five years later. Leaders like Ronald Reagan, a B-movie actor once described by Henry Kissinger as 'an empty jug', functioned successfully for two full terms by projecting an image of down-home affability, which voters were more than happy to interpret as a camouflage for an astute political mind. The possibility that he might have been a total ass seems never to have occurred to them. Similarly, the Democrat Bill Clinton utilised his Rhodes Scholar brain while offering his fans a carefully coiffed and eternally switched-on version of a coyly handsome Arkansas farmboy. Even with hindsight, it's difficult to discern exactly where the reality lay with these two well-regarded presidents, yet it's certain that image was actually far more potent than substance in both cases.

In Britain, this process of projecting fantasy-over-fact was taken to new extremes by the New Labour Government of Tony Blair. He engaged spin doctors for the explicit purpose of bamboozling the public. By creating the strange hybrid called New Labour, he managed to seduce Leftish conservatives while retaining Old Labour's traditional cloth-cap support. Spin doctors are now an accepted and indispensable component of a British leader's weaponry and their sole purpose is to create images for their leaders which don't necessarily accord with the truth. In each of these cases, political leaders traded off the susceptibilities of their people, a process Papa Doc had adopted some years before them. Perhaps they took their lead from the embattled Haitian President in his sugarwhite lair, for in each case, they achieved the political longevity Duvalier himself was striving for. Both Reagan and Clinton served two full presidential terms while Blair was British Prime Minister for a whole decade. Even the repugnant Nixon was elected for a second term, only to allow his innate criminality to get the better of him, forcing his departure after five years at the White House.

Papa Doc beat them all by remaining at the top for fourteen years. In his case, the spin doctors took several forms, none of them especially endearing to western minds. Apart from the voodoo *houngans* who proclaimed his immortality, and the graffiti artists who projected the myth in graphic form, Duvalier had the Tontons to reinforce his illusions. The latter's 'spin' came in the form of machine-fun fire, usually up back alleys during the dark hours.

Until recent times, western beneficiaries of the Enlightenment have adopted lofty airs in promoting the benefits of rationality and reason in government. They have imagined that democracies based on open debate are inherently superior to the more erratic governmental systems of 'lesser' societies. In truth, though, Duvalier's methods for retaining power were quite sophisticated. Like a good retailer, he knew his market and pitched for it with the assiduity of a super-salesman. Influenced by both Machiavelli and de Catalogne, he carefully erected a mystical base for his tyranny, then reinforced it by proclaiming the virtues of dynastic succession. Papa Doc was nothing if not shrewd: few imitators have applied his theories with such success. An academic, David Hawkes, who published a book about ideology and government in the mid-1990s, likened Duvalier's Haiti to medieval Europe, claiming that its people did not think in a post-Enlightenment manner. Irrationality rather than enlightened reason dominated their thinking, he claimed, because of their lack of education and reliance on the lowest levels of subsistence farming. Their constant battle against harsh conditions, with male life expectancy as low as 42, all worked against the possibility that they would ever be able to think like comfortably-off Europeans or North Americans. In the same way that poor men often can't afford to be honest, uneducated men in a fight for survival can't spare time for rational discourse. Their various preoccupations preclude it. What emerged from Haiti's deficiencies was the kind of society which was fast fading in Europe by the start of the 19th Century, one based on feudalism and a small, all-powerful elite.

Meanwhile, Haiti's beleaguered people took refuge in superstition and what passed for religion. Relying on divine power to retain control of government might have sounded absurd in the cynical Sixties or the sceptical Seventies, but by the early years of the 21st Century such ideas had become just as commonplace as they had been a thousand years earlier at the time of the Crusades. Not only did George W Bush invoke God as his guide, so did his arch-enemy Osama bin Laden and — astonishingly — even his British friend Tony Blair, who eventually confessed his heavy reliance on spirituality in 2006. In a sense, Duvalier was ahead of his time. Like his people, he believed most things were pre-ordained by supernatural forces. Debate leading to consensus was, therefore, an irrelevance. The descent into tyranny was but a short step away. To maintain mystique, whatever its form, often requires some bending of the truth. If Papa Doc were to remain unassailable in the eyes of his people, it was important to camouflage his vulnerability, physical or otherwise.

While the President lay stricken in his bed, Clement Barbot assumed power as Acting President, showing a taste for the job which Duvalier was to find discomfiting. Barbot was later to discover that over-conscientious understudies were not to the President's taste. All around, the cauldron of Caribbean politics bubbled threateningly, and Port-au-Prince itself was in a state of high tension. An attempt was made on the Cuban Ambassador's life (subsequently blamed on Barbot, acting in cahoots with Trujillo) and Trujillo himself was under threat from Dominican rebels operating out of Cuba, whose air and sea 'invasion' of their homeland reached an all-too-familiar conclusion, with all the exiles either killed in action or executed by the military. These were momentous times for the Caribbean region. With Cuba now established as a potent threat to all Right-Wing dictatorships in the Americas, and Castro, a socialist icon of the times, sitting astride the broad back of a successful revolution, it was no wonder that Trujillo and Duvalier were feeling shaky.

June 14 — the date of the ill-fated Dominican adventure — was engraved on Leftist hearts, in the same talismanic way that Easter 1916 became an inviolable symbol of Republican resistance in Ireland. The Castro effect was gathering force, with communists everywhere suddenly feeling a euphoric surge, as though the ideology was winning hearts and souls throughout the region. In the Dominican Republic, Leftist rebels saw no reason why Trujillo should not go the same way as that other Right-Wing strongman, Batista. In Haiti, the instinct was more muted but no less heart-felt. This was a bad time for tyrants. When a Cuban invasion force stepped ashore near a small village in southern Haiti on August 30, 1959, it seemed that a communist-style 'liberation' exercise was fully underway. In their battle fatigues, some lavishly bearded, the 'invaders' appeared to be Castro clones intent on extending the boundaries of the revolution.

Barbot countered swiftly, airlifting Haitian troops — fresh from US Marine training — into the area to resist the onslaught. It proved to be an uneven contest, with the Cubans handicapped by lack of forest cover and, of course, local knowledge. One unit was blasted apart while taking a meal by a stream. Another was slaughtered alongside the peasant family who had offered them refuge. Barbot then systematically eliminated all those judged to be collaborators, leaving a thick trail of blood through mud-hut villages where peasants were thought to have sheltered the invaders. By early September, what remained of the Cuban guerilla force had been eliminated. Pinpointed by air reconnaissance, flushed out by troops on the ground, the invaders died either in firefights or subsequently in stage-managed executions. It was all over in five days. Less than half a dozen survived and they were paraded for public display in Port-au-Prince, wretched examples of another failed force, and further confirmation of Papa Doc's invincibility.

As the 1960s dawned, Duvalier began to feel his feet again after the ravages of his illness, and the second failed attempt to topple his regime. Though he didn't know it at the time, he was entering a decade of celebrity which would, ultimately, bestow a kind of fame upon him, too. It seems ridiculous, in a sense, to imagine that Papa Doc became a 1960s icon alongside Bob Dylan, the Kennedys, Martin Luther King and the Rolling Stones, but he did, albeit for the least wholesome of reasons. Perversely, Papa Doc's celebrity rested upon the depths of terror he induced and his peculiar preoccupation with death. There were enough aficionados of organised murder around for him to be accorded an unfathomable reverence, mostly by those who were not obliged to suffer life under him. With bombs going off all over Port-au-Prince, rumours of military preparations being made offshore, and international disapproval mounting against him, Duvalier began the decade in the familiar role of embattled ogre. With his country crumbling around him, and the glow of the Magloire years fading, he had to find a way to attract foreign aid in the face of intensifying opprobrium. This was not easy.

The United States, prime target of Duvalier's appeals for help, found itself in a quandary. Having occupied Haiti for the best part of two decades, it felt that it had invested heavily — both financially and emotionally — in the country's welfare, yet had little to show in return. Apart from the Magloire years, when it seemed Haiti might yet shake off the hideous legacy of Dessalines, there had been little to show but the usual shambolic presidential mismanagement and gratuitous abuse of its citizens. Washington had good reason to feel fatigued by Haiti's inability to raise itself, and resist its cries for help when all past endeavours had been met with such reckless ingratitude. But Castro's presence made it imperative for Americans to maintain a paternal concern for Duvalier's tiny fiefdom. The tyrant had only one ace in his hand, but he was to play it adroitly for many years to come. If slaughtering his people was to be the main preoccupation of his presidency, maintaining his position as 'a bulwark against communism' was to run it a close second.

CHAPTER 17

EXODUS

By mid-1960, the march of the Left in the Caribbean region was being sharply felt in Haiti, with students taking up the cry of Castro and applying it to their own stricken and forsaken land. For the western world, and especially emerging nations, this was to be a decade of dramatic change, when colonialism would begin its final spasms before expiring, and racial segregation would be outlawed in pursuit of progress. With the young, bearded lawyer Castro now bestriding the most dynamic island in the Caribbean, and the Civil Rights Movement gathering pace in the United States, it was a time when oppressed people everywhere were being encouraged to shake off their tormentors. And these included the Right-Wing tyrants of the Americas. For Duvalier, the implications were serious. Though, in his own warped way, he saw himself as a radical reformer, he was viewed by international political observers as more aligned with the Trujillos and Batistas of the world than the young progressives. When Haiti's student union began adopting extreme Leftist postures, Duvalier found himself pitched irrevocably alongside the reactionaries, a man to be removed by the onward sweep of the socialist revolutionary movement. In the eyes of radicals, he was part of a dying order founded on cruel oppression and, therefore, expendable. Though emotionally and instinctively sympathetic to the likes of Dr Martin Luther King Jnr, who was to die leading the progressive march of America's blacks, Duvalier felt bound by his own paranoia to adopt methods more akin to those of the old slavemasters when it came to dealing with his own people. The more troublesome they became, the more ruthless was his response.

With the Left in the ascendant, and US aid an essential component in Haiti's strategy for survival, Papa Doc found himself locked between diametrically opposed forces. Whatever his reforming inclinations at the outset, they were compromised by his reliance on US financial support and his almost manic desire to retain power at all costs. In the end, he had to settle for expediency: crushing the Left became part of his formula for staying the course. As the nature of the regime became increasingly apparent to those obliged to live under it, the Haitian exodus began in earnest. In the north, especially, political ferment combined with hopeless poverty drove even the least enterprising peasants to make life-or-death decisions about their future.

Sixty miles from Haiti's northern shores lay the southernmost islands of the Bahamas chain. For the next four decades and more, the limestone rocks, swiftly abandoned by Columbus in 1492, would become the yellow brick road to freedom for many thousands of Duvalier's people. At first, the flight northwards was an arbitrary and haphazard process. Peasants hacked down trees to build crude sloops which, grossly overladen, frequently overturned in the turbulent straits between Haiti and the promised land. Countless refugees perished in those waters, many in the most heartrending circumstances, with children torn from their mothers by strong currents. Some were victims of the elements, others of their exploiters, who came to see human trafficking as a lucrative alternative to whatever else they did to eke out a living in a severely deficient society. From Port-de-Paix, in north-west Haiti, they set out in droves, tiny boats packed solid with frightened souls. Many were tucked below deck, others clung to the sides. Wafted north by offshore winds, they were at the mercy of skippers who, with not so much as a compass to guide them, relied on God's mercy and the stars for guidance.

The Bahamas then was still a British colony, and it found itself spending an increasingly large slice of its annual budget repatriating people, whose hit-and-miss attempts at liberation were to become the islands' most pressing social predicament in future years. By mid-1963, the Bahamas had become the target of a concentrated influx of illegal immigrants. Between January and May of that year, the Bahamas Government deported nearly 1,500 people, many of them women and children. Those who were rounded up by police and shipped home would live to try again. A few escaped into the bush, to be absorbed into Haitian communities which were to grow alarmingly over the next forty years. But many more died in the perilous waters between Inagua, the southernmost Bahama isle, and Tortuga, an outcrop of Duvalier's republic off Haiti's northern shores.

In Miami, Senator Spessard Holland made it clear that the Haitians reaching the Bahamas should not seek asylum in the United States. He and his compatriots were vigorously opposed to any such influx, an attitude very much at variance with that towards Cubans escaping Castro's clutches. Yet the desire to flee onward to Florida was quite strong among some Haitians because they believed, quite seriously, that Papa Doc's thugs, the Tontons Macoute, were already firmly established in Nassau and ready to persecute them. Bald statistics tell their own story as pressures mounted in Haiti. *The Tribune*, Nassau's daily newspaper, reported that 700-plus Haitians were deported from the Bahamas in 1959. Over the next three years, the annual figure was 550, 600 and 935. Then, in 1963, it jumped suddenly to 2,879, followed in the next twelve months by 2,028 more. For a time, Duvalier's government monitored departing boats, but the exodus from Haiti became so pronounced by the mid-1960s that his government had virtually given up trying to stem the flow. For the refugees, it was a mixture of poverty and political oppression which drove them north.

In Haiti itself, rumours abounded that an enormous bridge was being built from Paradise Island, less than half a mile from Nassau, the Bahamas capital, to Grand Bahama island some 120 miles away. With little geographical knowledge and total ignorance of Bahamian laws, Haitians were drawn by the prospect of hundreds of labouring jobs being created by this engineering phenomenon, with no thought given to possible immigration regulations. In fact, a much more modest structure was being erected to link Nassau with Paradise Island itself, and a boatload of arriving Haitians cheered wildly when they passed under it, believing this to be their salvation. As the sloops sailed north, the Haitian diaspora developed into one of the most harrowing tales of migration anywhere. Desperation drove the Haitians to recklessness and the sacrifices they made were enormous.

The full story of the ensuing horror can never be told. Haitian lawyer Eliezer Regnier admitted to me many times that it is simply not known how many refugees died in their bid for freedom. However, a large number of the boats checked out of northern Haiti never made landfall and their passengers, mostly non-swimmers, were never heard from again. Young Yves Excius was among a group earmarked for deportation aboard the Mayaguana vessel Frecil. But while guiding a dinghy ashore, he was lost as the boat capsized in heavy seas. His body was later found floating off-shore, with his shoes tied to his arm. Whatever Yves sought in escaping from Haiti, he was never to find it. He was dead before his twenty-second birthday, one of the many whose flight from Papa Doc was to prove their undoing. The story of Michel Sylvain, 29, was almost as cruel. He made it to Nassau, only to be shot during a robbery. The bullet severed his spinal cord, and left him paralysed from the waist down. Eventually, he was taken back to Haiti in a wheelchair under Red Cross escort, where there were family members to look after him. His injury was so bad that there was no prospect of recovery. He was another whose flight to freedom was to prove disastrous. For Duvalier, loss of population was no hardship. It was a relief for his crippled, dysfunctional country not to have to bear the burden of those who wanted to be elsewhere. The economy was in such a parlous state that it offered no respite from the misery the people were suffering, so the fleeing boats were seen as little more than a tiny safety valve in a country which could blow its seams at any time.

Washington, meanwhile, was in a dilemma. While Duvalier continued to develop his reputation as the ghoul of the age, Castro achieved iconic status among Leftists. Worse still, Cuba's revolution was hailed and ultimately bolstered by Soviet Russia at a time when the United States was still almost neurotically preoccupied with the global threat of communism. The Caribbean, an area all too close to American soil, was full of colonial or former colonial territories still trying to find their way in the world. At the height of the Cold War, the blandishments of Moscow and its Havana satellite were much to be feared. Not surprisingly, Duvalier began playing on US nerves unashamedly. His country, he said, had a choice to make between the two dominant powers and their opposing ideologies. In a country as ravaged and desperate as Haiti, he said, there was little to choose between capitalism and communism. Poor was poor, whatever its ideological base, and his mission was to make Haiti better.

The US, fearful that Haiti might veer Left, giving communism a twin power-base in a strategically important region, was pretty much obliged to fall in with Duvalier's aid demands. Almost immediately, Cuba's sugar quota to the US was cut and Haiti's given a twenty-five per cent boost. In addition, economic aid was increased throughout Latin America, with the obvious exception of Cuba, which Washington now regarded officially as an outcast state. President Dwight D Eisenhower saw this tactic as a worthwhile precaution against proliferation of the Reds. Duvalier, skulking in his study at the National Palace, became a willing — though still resentful — recipient of US largesse.

Meanwhile, Duvalier's suspicion of everyone, even those closest to him, intensified with every week that passed. The ambitious Barbot, by now deposed as chief of the Tontons Macoute, was arrested in the high summer of 1960 and thrown into Fort Dimanche. This was the most classic example to date of Duvalier's capricious nature. During Duvalier's ascent to power, Barbot and his family has been close friends of the Duvaliers, even sharing the same roof at one point. There was an almost uncanny rapport between them, which earned the dapper but ruthless militia boss considerable kudos during the early days of the regime. But Duvalier was nothing if not perceptive. He detected signs of possibly subversive ambition in his outwardly loyal henchman, and had his opinions confirmed by a casino deal in which Barbot attempted self-enrichment at his master's expense. Encouraged by rivals who sought the presidential favour Barbot had enjoyed for some years, Duvalier neutralised the former Tonton by sending him to the Dungeon of Death.

In the streets of Port-au-Prince, student unrest continued to blight the regime. Duvalierist and anti-Duvalierist factions were now openly at odds, a conflict that inevitably spilled into the Catholic Church, which was expressing alarm at presidential excess. When the Archbishop, Monsignor Francois Poirier, was accused of making financial donations to communist agitators, his expulsion opened a fissure between Duvalier and the church hierarchy which was never satisfactorily bridged. Bundled on a plane to Miami, Poirier came to symbolise the religious argument against murderous tyrants. Among his supporters, he took on a saintly visage. But to Duvalier, he was typical of a disruptive minority who were trying to drive a wedge between Port-au-Prince and The Vatican. It was probably this one act, as much as any, that reinforced Graham Greene's implacable opposition to everything Duvalier stood for. As a Catholic convert, the writer found it hard to countenance any move against the Church, and specifically a well-regarded priest moved to act by humanitarian ideals. Rumours spread in Port-au-Prince of Duvalier's excommunication, but he defended his stand by lauding the concordat between his government and the church. In the days which followed, however, Papa Doc's proclaimed good intentions towards Catholics were sorely tested.

As students stepped up their demonstrations into a full-scale strike, Poirier's successor, Bishop Remy Augustin — the first Haitian to achieve such high office in the church — and four other Catholic priests were thrown out of the country. In the President's mind, at least, communism and Catholicism were now becoming inextricably entwined. In response to the threatening forces all around, he imposed a curfew, closed down the university, and imposed censorship on all voices contrary to his own, including a Catholic newspaper. The Vatican hit back by giving substance to the rumours. Duvalier and his government were excommunicated. With Haitian youth, anti-Duvalierist factions and God Himself against him, Duvalier hunkered down and began to use indiscriminate violence to silence the hordes. The true nature of his regime was now to find full expression, largely through the Tontons Macoute and its new boss, Jean Tassy, whose dedication to brutality and no-holds-barred extermination was even more pronounced than Barbot's. As 1961 dawned, Duvalier was intent on restoring order by whatever means he deemed necessary. If the past four years had plunged Haiti into a 20th Century dark age, it was nothing alongside what was to follow.

CHAPTER 18

DEATH OF A STRONGMAN

The Tontons' grip on Haiti tightened in the middle months of 1961. The best and most loyal of them were granted special status. From a ragged rabble of undisciplined enforcers, they became a properly structured unit, with the higher ranks now attired appropriately in sharp dark suits and wrap-around shades. While the foot soldiers in the provinces retained their denims and coloured neckties and bandanas, the metropolitan officer class took on the appearance of well-heeled mobsters, hardware bristling from their hips as they perfected a menacing swagger to back up their baleful gaze. Duvalier's dependence on the Macoute deepened in May of that year when his neighbouring tyrant, Rafael Trujillo, was shot dead in the back of a car. The dictator's death was immediately interpreted as another successful blow for the Left, because it further fragmented what had been a strong 'necklace' of Right-Wing tyrannies across the northern Caribbean. Until early 1959, Cuba, Haiti and the Dominican Republic were all ruled by maximum leaders of Anti-Left persuasion – Batista, Duvalier and Trujillo. The Cuban Revolution had left Haiti exposed on its western flank. Now, with Trujillo's removal, Haiti seemed vulnerable to the east as well. For Papa Doc, the omens were clear: having once been poised between two roughly like-minded regimes, he was now apparently surrounded by hostile Leftists.

The Tontons Macoute's power increased dramatically from this time forth. Duvalier bought their loyalty by declaring them to be the true defenders of Duvalierism. They were granted perks and privileges and virtually unlimited power, seductive incentives for men of their kind. Trujillo's demise was deeply troubling for many reasons. Firstly, his longevity as the Dominican dictator was unmatched in the region up to that time. For more than thirty years, he had lorded it over his country with a mixture of arrogance and paternalistic solicitude. Whatever his faults, and there were many, he was seen by some Dominicans as a stabilising influence in a region where stability could no longer be taken for granted. Typically, Trujillo was bound for an illicit tryst with a new mistress when the end came on May 30, 1961. As his chauffeur drove him in an unmarked and unprotected sedan along a lonely road near Santo Domingo, plotters raked the car with rifle fire. Trujillo died in the fusillade, bringing to an end one of the most enduring regimes in Latin America.

Duvalier, on learning that Trujillo's assassins were close associates of the dictator, was both fascinated and appalled. Until this moment, his paranoia had been marked: now it became the defining feature of his regime. It's tempting, given its bad press over so many years, to see Haiti only in the bleakest terms because of the insanity of its politics, but there has always been much more to it than that. Artistically and culturally, it had always outflanked most of its Caribbean neighbours, but as Duvalierism took hold, and the vicious lunacy of the government became apparent, the country began to lose its best and brightest, who took their talents abroad and left their homeland to wallow in a mire of deepening despondency. The northward trek to the Bahamas was undertaken almost entirely by peasants, mostly from the northern areas around Port-de-Paix, Gonaives and Cap Haitien. These were the Haitian underclass who would ultimately establish themselves in the lower reaches of Bahamas society, taking on the low-paid jobs Bahamians didn't want.

More tragically for Haiti, however, was the leakage of the business, artistic and professional classes, who finally came to recognise that Duvalier was destined to lead Haiti to a new low in its affairs. They headed, not for the Bahamas, but the United States, Canada and Europe, where their skills would be recognised and rewarded. Duvalier's racist attitudes were certainly a factor in this exodus of talent, but it was the viciousness and irrationality of the regime that really did the damage. In the process, Haiti was deprived of any hope it might have had of a worthwhile future. The flower of its creative and academic ability was driven abroad by Papa Doc.

In response to Trujillo's death, Duvalier felt compelled to bolster the image of Duvalierism in ways which led his detractors to suspect the onset of insanity. Increased reliance on mystical and spiritual forces was a factor, but more disturbing still was a drive to immortalise himself in more concrete form. The city of Duvalierville, some twenty-five miles outside of Port-au-Prince, was intended to be a Haiti showpiece. With its rum distilleries, industrial plants, cane refineries and other enterprises, it would become a potent symbol of Haiti's progress, in a world whose attitudes towards it had traditionally been dismissive and sceptical. It was, in truth, Haiti's answer to the 'new town' and 'garden city' craze prevalent in Europe at the time, though whether he actually drew inspiration from them is unknown. The village of Cabaret was chosen as site for the venture, with the ambitious deputy from the area, Luckner Cambronne, in charge of the development project.

In Papa Doc's eyes, Duvalierville would be the ultimate vindication of his view that Haitian blacks could match anyone at anything. Though self-aggrandisement was undoubtedly among the motives, he was also fired by a xenophobic desire to show that — given the right leadership — Haiti was capable of excelling in areas traditionally regarded as the white man's domain. Duvalierville, he said, would become a 'flower city' designed to attract and transfix tourists, a gemstone of urban development in a rural setting. The problem for the doubters — and specifically the doubters in the business and professional classes — was the funding. In a country as impoverished as Haiti, where the average per capita income was so pitifully low, grand gestures like Duvalierville were inappropriate, especially when Haitians themselves were expected to finance it under the Tontons' duress.

According to the Dierderich and Burt biography of Duvalier (*Papa Doc: Haiti and Its Dictator, 1969*) the President's financial expectations extended not only to businessmen and others who could afford it, but also families struggling to pay their children's way through school. Parents making huge sacrifices to meet school fees were now being urged to 'volunteer' dimes towards the Duvalierville project. Alongside such examples of presidential excess, the Tontons began moving blatantly and unashamedly into extortion, often citing the Duvalierville enterprise as justification for their demands. Those who demurred were frequently dealt with savagely. Haiti's thinkers were now beginning to acknowledge that the country was in the grip of a madman. As government restrictions tightened, those who no longer felt able to live under the regime sought escape. Members of respected and well-established Haitian families pursued their futures else-where. Those who were unable to fly out found refuge in foreign embassies in Port-au-Prince, as Duvalier had planned to do, when the Florida deputies descended on Casernes Dessalines, during their failed attempt at insurrection. It was as if the forces of darkness were taking over.

Trujillo's assassination resonated with Duvalier for many reasons, but their obvious tactical similarities were probably the greatest cause for alarm. The 1937 slaughter of 20,000 black Haitians — recounted in an earlier chapter — established Trujillo's pedigree as a brute: there was never any doubt from that point on that Trujillo was a vile and vicious dictator with no regard for human life. He also used his almost total political control of his country to amass great wealth and — like many dictators of his type — tried to establish in the public consciousness a close affinity between himself and God. His nation's capital, Santo Domingo, was renamed Cuidad Trujillo (Trujillo City), and neon signs proclaimed 'God and Trujillo' at prominent points in the urban landscape. While frequently hosting lavish state banquets, he was also carefully siphoning part of the national revenue into his own foreign bank accounts. Like Batista and Duvalier, he adopted self-serving pro-US policies while crushing his people underfoot.

Washington's support for such heartless Caribbean regimes prompted critics to suggest that the US was ready to set aside human rights considerations for political expediency. It was Trujillo who prompted US Secretary-General Cordell Hull's famous aside: 'He may be a son-of-a-bitch, but he is our son-of-a-bitch.' Whatever his excesses, Trujillo remained popular among some Dominicans, while others developed an almost obsessive hatred of the man and everything he stood for. During the late 1940s and into the 1950s, opposition against him gradually gathered impetus and — as with Duvalier — he began to lose the approval of the Roman Catholic Church. Whatever the Vatican said, however, Trujillo saw only one way to rule a land as potentially volatile as his, and that was by brutal force if necessary. Unfortunately for him, oppression led only to a hardening of the resistance against his regime.

The Catorce de Junio Movement, named after the June 14 invasion attempt, became the focal point for the Trujillo opposition, and exile groups worked assiduously to add muscle to local dissidents. Their work ultimately brought its reward as the dictator's body was left twitching in his car by a burst of gunfire. The plotters were not, however, dedicated Leftists, as first thought, so much as erstwhile friends and associates who had fallen foul of his ruthlessness. With covert support from the CIA, who had begun to fear that Trujillo's high-handedness might open the way for the full-scale Left-Wing revolt a la Cuba, they brought him down with US-made carbines. Nonetheless, Trujillo's death was not enough to upset the status quo, at least not immediately. His son Ramfi assumed control the following day and a period of bloodletting was to follow as the plotters, their families and associates paid the price, many committing suicide rather than face Trujillo's torturers. In November of that year, Ramfi fled the country under pressure, but only after having the last six of the assassins tied up, cut to pieces and fed to the sharks in the ocean alongside his home.

For Dominicans, this huge convulsion in their country's history did not lead to democracy. On the contrary, Trujillo's removal opened the way for a prolonged period of administrative chaos and civil unrest. Four military coups were insufficient to stem the onset of civil war, which was brought under control only when US marines landed in the Dominican Republic in April, 1965, followed a few months later by troops from the Organisation of American States. Since then, the Dominican Republic has made uncertain progress with US help. But its 'success', such as it is, is described as such only in relation to the continuing hopelessness of its near neighbour. Alongside Haiti, everywhere is a success, with the possible exception of the most egregious of African failures like Zimbabwe and Rwanda.

With Batista and Trujillo now best-forgotten backnumbers of Caribbean politics, Duvalier was driven to extreme measures in shoring up his own defences, recognising that both possessed characteristics remarkably similar to his own. The plight of Dr Gerard A Ferere, a former Haitian naval officer who had voiced doubts about Duvalier early in his reign, is a good indicator of how Papa Doc approached this next crucial phase of his strategy for survival in an increasingly sceptical and threatening world. The catalyst for the great Duvalier purge of May, 1963, was an attempt to kidnap the President's corpulent son, Jean-Claude, who was later to be his dynastic successor. The lumbering, over-indulged Baby Doc was on his way to school on April 26, 1963, when anti-Duvalierists tried to snatch him off the street. Papa Doc, by now aploplectic with rage at the impudence of his opponents, reacted with what can only be termed irrational fury, leaving literally thousands of innocent citizens dead in the wake of a string of Tontons atrocities. Dr Ferere was but one of many known opponents of the regime to fall foul of Duvalier's rage. As far back as 1958, Ferere had been a marked man, largely for his expressed displeasure over what he termed the rigged Presidential Election which brought Duvalier to power. It is possible that Ferere was lulled into false feelings of security by the relatively benign Magloire years.

When Duvalier first arrived on the scene, he looked anything but a political hardman. However, Ferere, along with thousands of others, was soon to learn the truth, that Papa Doc's malevolence knew no bounds. He found out soon enough that he was earmarked for execution by the Macoute as they scoured the capital for anyone harbouring anti-Duvalierist thoughts. In what was to become a classic reaction of Duvalier dissenters, he took refuge in the Chilean Embassy in Port-au-Prince, having been harassed by the regime several times before. Ferere told the website Fordi9.com — which has done a sterling job in compiling lists of Duvalier victims — that he was dismissed from the navy and victimised repeatedly for his outspokenness, being thrown into jail no fewer than five times between 1958 and 1963. When he and his wife, Nancy sought diplomatic refuge with the Chileans, they thought it would be a short-term expedient for staying out of harm's way because Duvalier appeared by then to be tottering under the weight of international opprobrium. However, pressure from the Organisation of American States failed to dislodge Papa Doc. As the heat intensified, he tightened his grip on power. The more insistent his detractors became, the more obstinate he proved to be.

The Fereres, like many Haitian intellectuals to follow, realised that exile was the only alternative to persecution and death, so made plans to cut loose and run. The US Consul General, Robert Maule, helped the process along by producing immigrant visas for the couple, who were forced to abandon their two children as they fled to freedom. As Dr Ferere told Fordi9.com, this decision was the most painful of their lives, but it ultimately led to a reunion of parents and offspring in the United States, where they have lived until the present day, never having felt in the interim that Haiti had anything to offer them. Initially, at their Florida base, the Fereres still had many months of uncertainty to endure, and especially when Mrs Ferere's four brothers were arrested by the Macoutes. However, the babies were saved by their grandmother who, with Mr Maule's help, was able to transfer them to the States in September of that year. Dr Ferere was then able to pursue a successful academic career, retiring in 1998 as Professor Emeritus from St Joseph's University in Philadelphia which, he said, gave him and his family the happiest years of their lives.

In exile, however, Dr Ferere never allowed his academic progress in a foreign land to divert him from his abiding interest in Haiti and its political affairs. He continued to lobby against Duvalier, and became part of the exiled movement, which sought to unseat him throughout the 1960s, until the dictator's death in 1971. In Philadelphia, he helped to form an organisation dedicated to the welfare of Haitian refugees, and continued to promote his homeland's culture to all who would listen. More than once during his encounters with Duvalier's henchmen in the late 1950s and early 1960s, Dr Ferere looked death in the eye. During one period of incarceration at Casernes Dessalines, Duvalier actually ordered his execution along with several other military personnel. Only the intervention of his first cousin, General Marc Arty, saved him from the firing squad. Little wonder that he has devoted so much energy since then to discrediting the Duvaliers and everything they stood for.

Businessman and former banker, Frank Simon was another caught up in the aftermath of the Jean-Claude kidnap attempt. With schools and businesses forced to close, as the Macoute swept the city for the would-be kidnappers, Simon found himself being snatched and abducted outside his mother's home at Ruelle Cameau. His mother, Elia Dupont Simon, watched helplessly as he was driven away in a Tontons car. He was never seen again. By now the extremities of oppression had become common-place in Port-au-Prince. Graham Greene's ire was most aroused by the fate of Clement Jumelle, a 1957 presidential candidate, whose corpse was snatched by the Macoute as it was being taken by hearse to the cemetery. A Tontons car halted the funeral procession soon after it had left the home of Dr Gaston Jumelle, one of the deceased's brothers, and an offi-cer (John Beauvoir) commandeered the vehicle, vanishing with the hearse, coffin, body and all, leaving the Jumelle family in a traumatised state.

This was not merely a disruptive measure to upset the Jumelle family. The idea was that Papa Doc would be able to consult the corpse — and specifically the brain — of a man known to have special intellectual qualities. By using Jumelle's body in various voodoo rituals, Duvalier would be able to plumb the intricacies of an exceptional mind and possibly even determine the intentions of his foes. If this sounds bizarre to western minds, it is important to stress that it was no more than normal for people of Duvalier's kind. As a voodoo adept — a *houngan* — he was fully committed to mystical practices whose centuries-old origins lay in Africa, long before his forebears were forced to endure The Middle Passage and the indignities of the slave trade. It is now believed that Jumelle's remains were stolen on his personal instructions. In any event, they were delivered to the National Palace, where Duvalier was enraged to find that vital organs were already missing, rendering the corpse useless for his arcane rituals. Whatever secrets he had hoped to uncover about Jumelle, the Jumelles already knew enough about him to thwart his objectives. Jumelle's coffin was later buried with no body inside. Greene found this astounding, and very disturbing, but it was a tame enough enterprise when set alongside some of Duvalier's more outrageous acts in years to come.

The dictator was merely finding his feet. With the Bay of Pigs 'invasion' of Cuba of 1961, and the Cuban Missile Crisis of 1962 — when the world came to the brink of war as the Soviet Union tried to establish a missile base in Castro's communist island — Duvalier found himself as a front-row spectator in the most momentous events of the age. More importantly for him, every time communism loomed as a credible threat, his own position became stronger, so long as he could hold his own dissidents in check. Thus, with threats all around, he became increasingly uncompromising towards his foes. Arbitrary executions became commonplace. Tontons torture surfaced as a routine expedient for extracting intelligence from reluctant sources. The walls of the National Palace basement were painted a rich brown to ensure the blood of his opponents did not show up too much. Sometimes, in the dead of night, screams and murmurs could be heard from these lower chambers. The Macoute began hanging corpses in the streets as warnings to the politically ambitious. The Hippocratic Oath had by now lost its meaning for the rural physician whose stethoscope had been replaced by a six-shooter. Appalled as Washington was at Papa Doc's brutality, it was reluctant to do anything that might destabilise his regime.

With Cuba already a national obsession, the US was not prepared to allow communist infiltration of Haiti, and so connived at the dictator's behaviour, at least for a time. Post-assassination unrest in the Dominican Republic ultimately left the democratic Leftist regime of Juan Bosch in charge. But he, too, fell victim to unruly forces within and was overthrown in September, 1963. As with the killing of Trujillo, the CIA was heavily implicated. Having eliminated the strongman for his growing business interests, and, therefore, his threat to corporate America, they were now involved in unseating the Leftist Bosch, whose relatively liberal policies were also inimical to US interests. From this period of turmoil emerged a series of anti-Haitian incursions, with potential revolutionaries taking advantage of the Dominican Republic's state of chaos to storm Haiti's eastern defences. As stated earlier, it was fortunate for Duvalier that his opponents were so poorly equipped and — when it came to the crunch — so fundamentally undisciplined and disunited. The disaffected General Leon Cantave led a succession of attacks across the border in that late summer of 1963, but his campaigns were undermined by internal dissent and unseemly power struggles among his men. For Duvalier, however, every attack was significant because it kept him in a state of perpetual anxiety. Fifty per cent of the national budget was now said to be directed into defence. The Tontons, though supposedly unpaid, gathered force as more and more Duvalierists sought the power that membership of the militia bestowed. By the mid-point of Papa Doc's reign, the Macoute outnumbered the army two-to-one. The thugs in blue were now effectively the dominant armed force in the land.

By far the most important attempted coup of that year came, however, from none other than Clement Barbot, once the trusted henchman of the President, now the out-of-favour former Tontons chief with a grudge to settle. Apart from being involved in financial chicanery, Barbot committed the unpardonable sin of questioning Duvalier's sanity. From as early as his 1959 illness, he maintained, Papa Doc had been operating in virtually a delusional state. After serving time in Fort Dimanche, Barbot emerged to reinforce his doubts about the President with assertive action against the regime. It was a plot with all the features of a Shakespearean tragedy, and an extraordinary conclusion which might even have tested the Bard's remarkable imaginative powers.

Barbot and his brother, Harry, conspired in a kidnap plot which, they hoped, would culminate with the assassination of Duvalier inside the National Palace. The kidnap target was the Minister of Information, Georges Figaro, whose co-operation would then be sought to allow access into the inner sanctum for a Tontons murder squad loyal to Barbot. These men, twenty in all, would inveigle their way through Papa Doc's tight defences inside the palace walls and despatch the President in short order, leaving the way clear for Barbot to declare himself in charge of national affairs. Seductive as the plot appeared to all concerned, they overlooked the simple things, including an indignant peasant who had resented being shot at by Barbot, on the day when Duvalier was to be overthrown. The peasant alerted authorities to Barbot's whereabouts, and troops of Macoute were sent to the scene. When Barbot and his followers took refuge in a field of sugar-cane, the militia set the crop ablaze, and picked off the conspirators as they tried to escape the smoke and flames. It was a turkey shoot, with Macoute riflemen relishing the ease of their mission. Barbot and his men, disorientated and helpless, fell like game birds as smoke swirled around them. Barbot's grim death might have confirmed the mounting impression that ex-friends of Duvalier were a doomed breed, but it did nothing to halt the groundswell of anti-Duvalier feeling now threatening to engulf the regime.

Barbot's body was hardly cold when a rebellious horde led by Hector Riobe tried to succeed where he had failed. Riobe, lusting for revenge after his father was gunned down in the street by Macoute thugs, made his bid for glory in a kind of improvised mini-tank. This armour-plated car was fitted with a flame-thrower which was meant to scorch everything in its path. However, his enterprise took on the spirit of hopelessness that seemed to infect every endeavour by anti-Duvalierists. Rolling through Petionville, the ungainly vehicle broke down right outside the police station. Thinking the rebels were a military patrol, police at first offered help, but a twitchy tyro guerilla fighter let loose with a burst of gunfire, alerting officers to their true purpose. Riobe and his men were thus forced to flee into the hills, where they took over an army post at Kenscoff and then fought off a Tontons assault. For several days, Riobe's unit holed up in a cave and resisted every attempt to dislodge them, until Duvalier eventually sent the rebel's mother along to dissuade him from further action. Riobe is said to have responded by shooting himself, the last survivor of another forlorn adventure.

Though Barbot and Riobe joined a long line of failed would-be usurpers in Haiti, their legacy inspired others to action, notably the afore-mentioned Cantave, whose formation of a peasant force, in the summer of 1963, was to lead to menacing incursions from the east. Operating in extremely inhospitable terrain just over the Dominican border, Cantave was intent on picking off Haitian military positions in a gradual but determined onslaught on Port-au-Prince, gathering support as he went. Having been supplied with battle fatigues by the Dominicans, the Haitians certainly looked the part, but they were constantly bedevilled by their own shortcomings, as they first marched on Derac and then Fort Liberte after crossing the Massacre River. Raw, illiterate recruits from Haitian hill settlements were not, in truth, ideal material for clandestine military ventures against a fearsome enemy. Occasionally, they would get nervous and fire off rounds, making surprise attacks on Duvalierists virtually an impossibility. Eventually, jammed weaponry proved Cantave's downfall as he attacked Fort Liberte. He and his men were forced into retreat and eventually scrambled back over the Dominican border is disarray. A support group under Rene Leon lost its guns in the river, bringing the operation to an inglorious end. One tragic but inevitable postscript of this ill-starred campaign was the fate of an army commander suspected of complicity with the invaders. He was executed in public, cut down by a fusillade of bullets in full view of the peasantry. As his bloody corpse lay twitching, the poor were reminded again that their President — once a seemingly kindly man of compassion — was now something else entirely.

At the palace, Papa Doc received news of the event with what must have been measured amusement, though he didn't show it. Six years into his reign, and he was still firmly in charge, even though the fixed-term pro-visions of the constitution decreed his tenure to be officially at an end. In the circumstances, Papa Doc was in no mood for going anywhere. Cantave did not despair at his initial failure. During August and September of 1963, he led two more incursions into Haitian territory from the Dominican Republic, ably assisted by his sidekick Colonel Leon. Though relatively insignificant in themselves, these actions served to reinforce Cantave's credibility within the CIA, as a potential coup leader with genuine public support. They also emboldened potential rebel fighters among the rural populace. Each time the invaders scored minor hits on Papa Doc's military, the rebel force grew in size, with young desperadoes eager for the fight. By September 22, Cantave was ready for another try, this time leading about two hundred men in an early morning assault on the small town of Ouanaminthe. The barracks commander had been fore-warned and took up positions outside his garrison walls. Though a fire-fight ensued, Cantave's unit was again neutralised by confusion and dis-order in the ranks. With a Haitian machine-gun rattling at them from behind, the raiders were again obliged to retreat back into the Dominican Republic.

Duvalier, meanwhile, was now trying to look two ways at once, fearful of Cubans penetrating Haiti from the west and the likes of Cantave launching attacks from the east. Following his latest failure, however, Cantave found himself detained by the Dominicans while they engaged in revolutionary activities of their own, unseating Leftist Juan Bosch in favour of a civil junta. Dispirited, Cantave was finally freed to flee to New York. His small army disintegrated in his wake. Having been cut off by the Vatican, Duvalier was seen by Haiti's persecuted and marginalised Catholic priests as Satan incarnate. It was inevitable, therefore, that men of the cloth would soon find themselves engaged in the crusade to unseat him. In the opening months of 1964, Father Jean-Baptiste Theovges and Father Jean-Claude Bajeaux were at the centre of yet another invasion attempt, this time involving exiles from the Dominican Republic and else-where. For several weeks, the unit underwent intensive drilling in rural hideaways in preparation for a high summer assault on Duvalier. Calling themselves the Camoquins, the rebels landed by boat in western Haiti on June 27, 1964. Typically, two died even before hitting dry land, drowning off Saltrou when a dinghy full of guns turned turtle. Like so many exile assaults before it, this one went nowhere. According to most informed observers, no fewer than seven invasions had been tried and aborted up until May 20, 1967. That was exactly one year before the air-and-land attack from Inagua which left David Knox arguing for his life in a Port-au-Prince courtroom. The pattern of failure was attributable to many things, including poor planning, lack of funding and a fact not readily acknowledged, that Duvalier had eyes and ears everywhere in Haiti's forbidding hills. Whatever his faults, there was a hard core of support for the President during the early and mid-1960s, mostly among low-ranking Macoute and simple villagers frightened into compliance by the militia's nocturnal rampages on their communities. If Duvalier failed to inspire love, his people at least accorded him a solemn respect induced by sheer terror. That much is beyond dispute.

CHAPTER 19

PRESIDENT-FOR-LIFE

With his foes apparently in disarray, and international events evolving to buttress his status as an anti-communist hero, Papa Doc had good reason to feel that spiritual forces were on his side. Using his voodoo powers to summon destruction for his enemies, and seemingly obtaining the right results, he no longer felt beholden to the white man's God. With the Roman Catholic Church now implacably against him, and international opinion recoiling from his excesses with distaste, Duvalier was becoming an isolated figure on the world stage. To white western democrats, he was a godless tyrant under the control of dark, satanic forces. To his people, he was a potential saviour transmuted by power into an ogre. To the Americans, he was a gruesome menace to be endured. As Papa Doc sat in his bath consulting the severed heads of his enemies, he had good reason to feel everyone but the voodoo deities was against him. With his constitutionally decreed presidential term now over, he was faced with the unsettling proposition that he should stand down and make way for an elected successor. By now, though, Papa Doc no longer felt subject to a document so often revised that it bore more deletions, amendments and additions than a poorly written second-form essay. His predecessors had cut-and-pasted Haiti's constitution so often that he saw no reason to grant it even cursory respect. Such matters were, to him, the preoccupations of the 'material' world. As he was immaterial, spectral, a deity in possession of strange but vital powers, there was no longer a need to offer obeisance to white men's ways. Instead, he followed the urgings of the one white man he listened to, Gerard de Catalogne, and opted for a system of dynastic succession. He would become President-for-

Life, thus ridding Haiti of the disruptive and usually thoroughly suspect attempts at democracy it had experienced in the past. Like England's King Charles I, Duvalier felt his mandate was afforded by divine power, a concept mere mortals could not be expected to understand. He was also influenced by the conviction that the modern concept of democracy was for white men, and that his origins lay in tribal societies where a single strongman called the shots.

For those among the Haitian intelligentsia who had hoped against hope that the end of the six-year constitutional term might see the back of the dreaded Papa Doc, his decision to become President-for-Life was a resounding blow. Under his control, a country which had never known true political peace had somehow descended into new realms of misery and despair. They needed him out of power. With life expectancy at a little over forty, annual per capita income at a pitiful $250, and disease running rampant through the rural communities, Haiti was almost totally at odds with a world which was now beginning to ride on the back of a post-war economic boom. For the west, the 1960s were a seminal decade, liberalising old orders, offering hope to the suppressed, and overturning many of the rigid assumptions of the past. Haiti, however, found itself paralysed by fear and at the mercy of a crazed ruler. Papa Doc's declaration of an extended term — possibly into what would seem an unbearable eternity — deepened their despondency and destroyed their hopes. The times were a'changin' for all but them. Duvalier loomed over his people like a malevolent monolith, immoveable now in the face of ineffectual gestures by exiled rebels, and the impotence of his detractors at the United Nations and elsewhere. To dislodge him could destabilise the entire north Caribbean area, and extend the influence of Castro and the Soviet Union, throughout the region. Left where he was, Duvalier at least served as a stopper in what could prove to be a highly toxic and volatile brew.

As Duvalier manoeuvred himself towards the moment when his intentions would become known, a cataclysmic event occurred which he once again interpreted as manna from the Gods. The assassination of US President John F Kennedy in Dallas, Texas, on November 22, 1963, was carried out by an embittered loner with Left-Wing sentiments called Lee Harvey Oswald, a man so weird in his obsessions that even his Soviet heroes turned their backs on him. After a period of self-imposed exile in the Soviet Union, Oswald returned to America with a Russian wife, but was still essentially the isolated and inconsequential no-hoper he had always been. Hence, on that sunny fall day in Dallas, he positioned himself at an upstairs window at the downtown book depository, where he worked, and made his stunning but successful bid for recognition, in what he had always seen as a hostile and uncaring world. He removed the top of the President's head with the last of three rifle shots, spraying his brains on his limo's paintwork and creating a freeze-frame image that will live in American minds forever. It was inevitable, that conspiracy theorists would soon be linking Oswald, a committed communist, with Moscow and Havana. Though latest theories appear to support the view that Oswald acted alone — a Left-Wing misfit with a grudge against society but an unerring marksman's eye — it is still hard to resist the insistent cry that Kennedy's death was part of a much larger tableau. America was so traumatised by the killing that anti-communist sentiments congealed into rabid hatred in some quarters.

For Duvalier, this was heartening news: so long as Washington reviled the Left, and so long as the US Government's attention was turned elsewhere, his own position would remain pretty well inviolable. For local consumption, he peddled the legend that he had brought about Kennedy's demise, an uncompromising response to a cut-back in US aid and a reminder to all that Haiti was not to be trifled with. No-one outside Haiti believed it for a moment. Castro, triumphantly chewing cigars in Havana, was considered by observers to be a much likelier candidate. To this day, however, no-one is certain who arranged and carried out the shooting of John F Kennedy. All we know is that it remains a defining moment in US history, and an event that left the western world in deep shock. The date of Kennedy's murder also excited the superstitions of Duvalier's people. The number twenty-two had long been talismanic for Papa Doc, especially as he had been 'elected' on September 22 in 1957. He encouraged them to believe that voodoo spirits had been working on his behalf when Oswald's bullets struck Kennedy's skull. It was a yarn the credulous peasants swallowed whole.

Students of the Duvalier era cite two periods when Tonton terror purges reached new heights: the years 1963-64, when the President was gearing up to make his tenure permanent, and in 1969, when assaults on his regime gained new impetus. The 1963-64 atrocities eliminated entire families, including intellectuals and professionals who could no longer restrain their cries of despair and indignation. They were thrown into cells at Casernes Dessalines before transfer to Fort Dimanche. Most were never seen again. Interestingly, the 1964 Haitian constitution made specific reference to human rights in a form of words which seemed wildly at variance with everyday reality. "The life and liberty of Haitians are sacred and must be respected by individuals and by the State," it said.

At about the time this travesty was being committed to paper, an internationally-known footballer, Joseph Nicholas Gaetjens, was arrested by Lieutenant Edouard Guillot, a uniformed officer, and two armed plainclothes men in front of witnesses. Seven years later, his 'arbitrary detention' was officially condemned by the Inter-American Commission on Human Rights, whose attempts to extract information from the Haitian Government about Gaetjens proved fruitless. The commission concluded that the football star was dead, presumably despatched under Article Twenty-Five of the same constitution, which stated that 'capital punishment may not be imposed for any capital offence except treason', with treason defined as 'taking up arms against the Republic of Haiti, joining avowed enemies of Haiti, and giving them aid and comfort.' The commission, however, was seemingly unaware of any offence committed by Gaetjens. Whatever he did, it displeased Papa Doc, whose thugs whisked him away at 10am on July 8, 1964, to an uncertain fate. He did not stand trial, but was never seen again.

Another person spirited away and killed in undetermined circumstances was Roland Chassagne, who was last seen on April 26, 1963, in the custody of four Macoutes being driven towards the National Palace. His brother Georges, who petitioned the Ministry of the Interior for information, was never given an explanation of Roland's fate. Positive evidence of his death did not emerge until the late 1970s, when the commission noted his name on requests for death certificates. Once again, the Haitian Government would not provide details of his demise, though the suspicion is that he perished in the palace basement, where Tontons torturers did much of their gruesome work. By now, Duvalier's hunger for power and money was unrestrained. Luckner Cambronne's Duvalierville fund-raising efforts were, in truth, no more than an excuse for wholesale extortion. His National Renovation Movement became the means by which Haitians were pressured for money they could ill-afford.

Capitalising on the upsurge in Leftisim, Duvalier cried out for more aid, even though he and Simone — now transformed from taciturn bumpkin into the rapacious Mama Doc — were stashing huge sums of misappropriated cash into foreign bank accounts along with jewellery, precious artefacts and other plundered treasures. The British Ambassador to Haiti, Gerald Corley-Smith, was ultimately to express the collective distaste of the diplomatic corps in Port-au-Prince, having been elected for the task by fellow envoys who appreciated his capacity for telling the undiluted truth. Duvalier was so appalled by Corley-Smith's effrontery in calling the NRM into question, and specifically his claim that ordinary Haitians were being pressured into subscribing by fear of the Tontons, that he demanded his recall. London, in turn, called for withdrawal of Haiti's Ambassador to Britain. As Duvalier now faced the suppressed wrath of foreign embassies, the US was caught up in a diplomatic fan-dance of its own making, insisting that financial aid did not imply endorsement of the regime and reminding Papa Doc that May 15, 1963, was the official end of his constitutional term as President. To drive home the point, the US and several other embassies boycotted Haiti's 'Day of National Sovereignty', undermining Duvalier's attempts to use the occasion for unashamed propaganda purposes.

In the weeks and months preceding the Kennedy assassination, Washington and Port-au-Prince were locking horns over the succession, with Duvalier citing the so-called 're-election' of 1961 as the beginning of another term, and Kennedy insisting that May, 1963, was Papa Doc's departure date. This diplomatic stand-off was known to all informed Haitians. Little wonder, then, that Duvalier was later to cite Kennedy's demise as further evidence of his own enormous mystical powers. Simple-minded Haitians were led to believe that even the truly mighty — the all-powerful blancs in Washington — were no match for Papa Doc and his voodoo gods. When Duvalier studiously ignored calls for a presidential election in February, 1963, resentment simmered in the streets. Though Haitians had grown used to palace high-handedness in the past, they were unhappy at having to witness impotently such flagrant abuse of their constitutional rights. Previous presidents who had tried to flout due process to extend their tenures were dealt with accordingly, usually by military intervention. However, Duvalier had by now neutralised the army by skilful deployment of his Macoute murder squads. Only the exceptionally courageous now dared to speak out.

On the day elections should have been held, three young Leftists engaged in an after-dark graffiti campaign against the President. Scrawled slogans appeared everywhere in Port-au-Prince. 'Death to Duvalier' was one, itself an act of high treason in Papa Doc's eyes. More insultingly, he was referred to as 'Caca Doc'. Unhappy at being likened to excrement, Duvalier ordered the culprits to be tortured Tonton-style, a process which could include limb-lopping, eye-gouging or even sustained abuse of the genital region, including castration. One young man died from the Macoute's mauling. Another was released after a few months in a filthy cell, having suffered the distinction of being tortured personally by Papa Doc himself.

As international opprobrium mounted, Duvalier grew increasingly reclusive. Yet while he was acutely aware of First World disapproval, he was unwilling to be fazed by it. In his eyes, Haiti required special treatment, an exclusive form of democracy which only people like him could understand. Sometimes he made brief appearances on the palace balcony, his huge spectacles peering out from amid a phalanx of Macoute heavies, all armed with a devastating array of weaponry. There was something extremely comical about these shows of strength: for all his excesses, his innate evil, Papa Doc was a conspicuously small man, and individual bystanders were bound to ask how he exercised such power in light of his physical slightness. Nonetheless, he did and as calls for him to relinquish the presidency grew, he harangued his detractors by asserting the special characteristics of Haitian democracy, which now evidently included his right to rule by decree if the occasion demanded it. He told his people that no outside force would deter him in his mission. If Haiti were to be consumed by flames, he said, 'no power in the world can come and give us a lesson in democracy.' Duvalier's determination to retain the Presidency for Life had been provoked, to some extent, by the almost incessant plotting of his foes, many of them ambitious young army officers who saw themselves as custodians of Haiti's future.

Typical of these in-house conspiracies was the failed assassination attempt by Colonel Lionel Honorat, whose family had traditionally been fervent Duvalierists. Honorat and fellow plotters had decided on a pre-dawn strike — a time, they figured, when the President and his wife would be asleep. Unfortunately for Honorat, he needed to secure guns and ammunition from Casernes Dessalines, and attempting to gain access to the arsenal led to exposure of the scheme. Alerted to this fact, Honorat and three associates sought refuge in the Brazilian Embassy, leaving another colonel, Charles Tournier, to take the flak. He was arrested, hauled off to Casernes Dessalines and was brutally murdered, his shot-up corpse left on the barracks parade square, where it served as a warning to others. This was followed by another 'assault' from the Dominican Republic, when a small plane flew over Port-au-Prince dropping leaflets, warning of a full-scale air attack on the palace. Haitians were warned to leave the area and foreigners — especially diplomats accredited by the regime — told to evacuate or be caught up in the revolution to follow. Duvalier responded with a propaganda offensive in which 'supporters' were ordered to declare openly their appreciation and approval of him. The President's family doctor, Jacques Fourquand, was quick to respond and warmed to the theme in alarming detail. Any attack on the regime, he said, would set Haiti ablaze again, creating a 'Himalaya of corpses' with blood flowing 'as never before.' Given Haiti's past — and particularly the circumstances of its hellish birth — this was a prediction to be feared.

As a long line of Duvalierists lauded their master in public speeches, de Catalogne's philosophy of dynastic succession began to take shape. The idea was even floated that Duvalier would become emperor, like Dessalines, or king, like Christophe. Supporters who saw the President as Haiti's best long-term bet began arming themselves with rifles and cutlasses, anticipating invasion at any time. Meanwhile Duvalier, for the most part, stayed indoors, raging at the world with what he saw as a blanc-inspired crusade to unseat him. If there was one event during this trying period which did most to harden Duvalier's resolve to become President-for-Life, it was the aforementioned plot by his old friend Barbot, and his suspected involvement in the move to kidnap the Duvalier children, Jean-Claude and Simone. Oddly, Jean-Claude was not, in any sense, like his father. While the President was physically slight and mentally bright, his son was a roly-poly boy with measured responses, whose proportions were the product of sustained over-indulgence. As he progressed through his teenage years, this over-indulgence became ever more apparent as his belly and thighs stretched his suits to the limit. He developed a spoilt-brat obsession with material wealth and a routine contempt for his underlings. Despite their greed, the senior Duvaliers were not ostentatious, but Jean-Claude was. He acquired a taste for sleek, fast cars and exotic, expensive food. Reared in the hothouse of the National Palace, he became furtive and suspicious. Nonetheless, whatever his faults, Francois and Simone Duvalier adored him. Baby Doc was to grow up believing he was exceptional in every sense, a view those closest to him found difficult to share. The attempt to kidnap Jean-Claude and his sister was, therefore, a traumatic event in the life of Papa and Mama Doc, as the people now referred to the stone-faced First Lady. Though power had driven them to extremes of brutality and insensitivity — Mama Doc was never seen as anything other than a willing accomplice in everything her husband did — they remained extremely solicitous in the protection of their own.

The morning of April 26, 1963, was, therefore, to prove one of the most shocking of their lives, as gunmen opened fire on the children's bodyguards outside the Methodist College in Port-au-Prince. The guards had just delivered the children to the school steps in the chauffeur-driven limousine when bullets started flying. All three men died in the fusillade, which Duvalier saw as an act of treachery without equal. Reprisals came immediately, and triggered off a spate of bloodletting that was to prove very much in line with events of Haiti's distant past. Hundreds, some say thousands, were to die in the horrific aftermath of this event. Duvalier's immediate response was to order a neighbourhood sweep. Then he instigated a witchhunt among all those considered suspect. The precision of the shooting which took out the chauffeur and bodyguards hinted at exceptional marksmanship and firearms expertise. Hence, Duvalier's baleful gaze fell upon the noted head of the army rifle squad, Francois Benoit, a junior commissioned officer whose noble and striking countenance made him one of the pin-up boys of the Haitian military. As army officers rarely acted alone in enterprises of this kind, Duvalier ordered the arrest of all those army personnel known to have associations with Benoit.

Meanwhile, having convinced himself that the army was behind the kidnap plot, Papa Doc mobilised the militia, giving them carte blanche to do whatever needed to be done to exact revenge. When Duvalier's uniformed thugs finally arrived at Benoit's door, the young lieutenant fled through a rear window to take refuge in the Dominican Embassy. Benoit's decision to flee was interpreted as evidence of guilt. Duvalier was now convinced of the Benoit family's complicity and what happened next was to become a defining landmark of the regime. The President's men launched a military-style assault on their Bois Verna home, machine-gunning Francois's elderly parents as they stood unsuspectingly on their porch, then slaughtering the household servants, blasting one in the back as he tried to escape. The wooden Benoit home was then raked by a long burst of machine-gun fire. Hundreds of bullets shattered windows, splintered louvres and punctured walls. At the end the building was torched, burning to death Francois' baby son Gerald, who was lying in his crib upstairs. The Macoute then turned their attention on the rest of the Benoit family elsewhere. Francois's pregnant wife, Jacqueline, fled in advance of the Tontons as they stormed the school where she worked as a teacher. It was later discovered that they intended to dismember her in front of her colleagues, cutting her unborn child out of her womb. Though Jacqueline reached sanctuary in the Equador Embassy, others in the Benoit family were not so fortunate. The name 'Benoit' became an obscenity on the tongues of the Tontons, and everyone of that name they could find was thrown, without hint at due process, into prison.

Outside the Dominican Embassy, where Francois now took refuge, Macoutes set up machine-gun posts, in the branches of surrounding poinciana trees, to await the appearance of their prey. In the streets, peasants looked on warily as Macoutes rounded up all former army officers — as per Papa Doc's orders — and took them directly to the palace torture chambers or the grim cells of Fort Dimanche. The scores of 'suspects' arrested that day — in fact, the number probably ran into several hundreds — were never seen again. Speculation persists as to their fate. The likeliest explanation is that they died at the hands of their torturers or were exterminated by the Dimanche firing squads and clubbers, the Duvalierists who quietly despatched enemies of the regime by beating them to death in an area behind the prison. The victims have, in any event, entered the annals of concerned exiles who, to this day, continue to chart the extent of the Duvalier atrocities. In response to the murder and mayhem, Port-au-Prince fell into a state of panic. Foreigners were warned by their embassies to hunker down, hurricane-style, stockpiling food and barricading doors until the danger had passed. At nights, the streets fell silent. Only the rampaging Tontons were free men in this city of fear and terror.

Papa Doc, meanwhile, seems to have taken leave of his senses. He was overtaken by bloodlust and became indiscriminate in exacting reprisals. Anyone even faintly suspected of having anti-Duvalier feelings was now in fear of his or her life. The Macoute gunned down dissenters with reckless glee. Age, gender and social standing were of no account: in defence of the regime, they were prepared to be pitiless beyond reason. Papa Doc's purges did not go unnoticed by the outside world. The Dominicans, who for generations had tolerated the insane behaviour of their near neighbour, complained bitterly about violation of their diplomatic territory in Port-au-Prince. Tensions grew so rapidly that the Dominican Government even threatened to bomb the National Palace. They demanded safe passage of Benoit and other asylum-seekers in the Dominican Embassy and threatened severe military action if the ultimatum went unheeded. President Juan Bosch even characterised Duvalier's regime as 'a government of savages and criminals', a description which was to prove increasingly apt as time went on.

The ensuing stand-off between Haiti and the Dominican Republic prompted intervention of the Organisation of American States, which was told in no uncertain terms that Santo Domingo was ready to send a flotilla of gunboats to attack Port-au-Prince, if the problem was not resolved. As Haiti vowed to defend itself, the OAS voted overwhelmingly to take action against Duvalier to ensure he conformed to the expectations of the international community. For the United States, Duvalier was now emerging as the hemisphere's poisoned dwarf, a man so vicious, inept and corrupt that support for him in any form could no longer be countenanced. President Kennedy, despite the many important global issues now on his desk in the Oval Office during the final months of his life, had to divert valuable time into his administration's posture towards a nation which, though small and inconsequential in itself, was creating havoc because of the unconscionable behaviour of its irrational dictator. Kennedy, acutely conscious of Duvalier's value as an anti-communist bulwark, had to square his own liberal stance on human rights, against the horrendous abuses of power now commonplace in Port-au-Prince. In addition, while seeking to liberalise Latin America in an attempt to stop the spread of Castroism, he had to find ways of neutralising Duvalier, without creating the kind of power vacuum the Leftists were poised to exploit. No wonder he was under stress.

The people of Port-au-Prince were, meanwhile, under siege as the Macoute set up roadblocks and searched everyone in a sustained effort to unmask the plotters. With their guns cocked for action, the Macoute were an unnerving presence. Those foreigners who were able to do so began packing their belongings and flying out. Long-suffering business and professional folk found themselves under daily interrogation. Meanwhile, corpses became a common sight on the streets. Flea-bitten dogs, grubby hogs and even inquisitive urchins lingered round every new crop of cadavers when they were illuminated by the rising sun. In the night hours, the Macoutes entered neighbourhoods, took away everyone under suspicion and despatched them right there, a process of arbitrary murder with a rich provenance in Haiti, dating all the way back to Boukman and beyond. These were terrible times for a land which had known many terrible times. The city took on the aura of a police state. The Tontons had subverted all others to become symbolic of presidential oppression.

While Papa Doc sat in his study, as phlegmatic and apparently unmoved as a bullfrog, President Bosch declared Haiti a major hazard for the entire region and began assembling his warships for action. Young Dominicans rushed to enlist for the armed forces. But the tiny dictator remained defiant. Whatever happened, it seemed, Duvalier would remain steadfast in his belief that the mystical forces propelling his fortunes would prevail against any foe. "That was part of the man," an observer was to remark later,"Duvalier always felt he was right and that he was the beneficiary of supernatural powers." When the OAS sent a delegation to Portau-Prince to appraise the situation, Duvalier's defiance was nigh palpable. As I was to discover a few years later, when I interviewed him at the National Palace, he was capable of sitting silent for long periods, during which his brain seemed to be clunking out a form of words that would maintain his presidential dignity, while preserving whatever interests he needed to preserve in the outside world. Before the foreigners arrived, Duvalier told his troops to clear away the remains of the Benoit home, where the corpses of Francois' parents, a visitor who had been calling on them at the time, and two servants still lay among the cinders. Leaving the decaying trophies of his brutality on public view was not unusual for Duvalier. It was part of his modus operandi to leave human remains on view for the frightened citizenry to peruse at leisure. This appetite for cowing the populace by showing them what he was capable of, reached a new low when he ordered the televising of a public execution, ensuring children were allowed time away from lessons to witness the spectacle. More of that later. A cursory clean-up in time for the OAS delegation was, at least, an acknowledgment that Haiti's standards were not necessarily shared by others. It is doubtful, though, that it implied guilt, for guilt was not part of Duvalier's thinking when it came to preserving power. The end justified the means, however foul.

The assembled ambassadors did not, however, get much by way of a cordial reception. Duvalier's attitude towards them when they were ushered into his presence at the National Palace was far from effusive. Through those reptilian eyes, magnified by his thick spectacles, he showed only quiet contempt for his critics. For Duvalier, this was another example of international interference in Haiti's sovereign affairs. He was less than amused. In an attempt to confound all their preconceived notions, he deployed the Macoute in a cynical piece of crowd manipulation. Rum was distributed liberally among the peasants, who were soon fired up into a riotous display of pro-Duvalier fervour. Whatever their parlous everyday state, the poor were soon prompted into displays of affection for their Papa Doc by spontaneous gestures of largesse, which usually involved the languid tossing of coins into the street, or the circulation of copious quantities of rough rum. Within hours, Port-au-Prince was in festive mood, with peasant women wriggling their backsides as drums beat out intoxicating rhythms. Under Tontons' coaxing, the revellers converged on the palace to fill the lawns at just the moment Papa Doc appeared on the balcony with the OAS delegation. Press observers noted the orchestration of events. In such a disorganised land, it was remarkable how large groups of people could somehow materialise from the slums on cue. As a piece of classically stage-managed theatre, it was hard to fault. Hollywood producers could hardly have done better. It was a memorable example of Papa Doc's power to control the populace. No ruler of Haiti before or since — and that includes a later palace incumbent, Jean-Bertrand Aristide, another champion of the people who was corrupted by power — was able to achieve it with such apparent ease. Whatever their faults, the Macoute got things done.

From the balcony, Duvalierist officials lambasted the US for its recent decision to cut aid. The mood was not, however, that of needy supplicants, but defiant freedom fighters. This was, however, only the warm-up act for the main event — a speech of measured calm from Papa Doc himself, who seemed to adopt his 'other world' persona to electrifying effect in proclaiming himself Haiti's ruler for eternity. As the crowd listened intently, and foreign newsmen clicked cameras on the lawns below, Duvalier stood bolt upright, his huge hands at his side, and proceeded to articulate his belief in dynastic succession. Portraying himself as 'the symbol of an idea', he said he and the Fatherland were indivisible, and that he represented a moment in their history as an independent people. "God and the people are the source of all power. I have twice been given the power. I have taken it, and damn it, I will keep it forever," he said. Then he returned to the kidnap attempt on his children, using the incident to reinforce impressions of his own invincibility. He said guns did not frighten him, and no foreign power would ever dictate to him. Asking the people to 'allow the blood of Dessalines to flow in your veins,' he declared himself the long-dead emperor's natural successor, a man born to lead Haiti into a free and proud future. By far the most significant words he uttered, though, were those hinting at his spectral existence. "I am already an immaterial being," he said. The speech, delivered in a peculiar mixture of French and Creole, was notable for its apparent calm, for in truth Duvalier was filled with fury that day. But it had the desired effect. As he turned and disappeared into the darkness of his apartments within, the crowd turned away in a triumphant transfixed state, as though they had just witnessed a celestial revelation.

Reaching back three centuries or more, before the Europeans subjected them to the indignities of The Middle Passage, the crowds acknowledged their tribal origins by hailing the chieftain. Papa Doc was their tribal father, their God-given leader, the embodiment of their national pride. The mood was euphoric and they left the palace grounds murmuring their appreciation of a miracle. However, when the effects of the rum wore off, they were compelled to confront the everyday reality. Poverty and deprivation were deepening and Papa Doc's power was being exercised ruthlessly by the Macoute. To utter dissent was to invite summary liquidation. When the OAS departed, corpses began to appear again on the streets of Port-au-Prince, crowded tap-taps manoeuvred round them as curs and urchins leapt clear. The madhouse was, it seems, beyond the help of outside forces.

CHAPTER 20
A STATE OF TENSION

During one of my many walks around Port-au-Prince in the late summer of 1968, I was photographed (presumably by my colleague, Bill Cole, though I have no clear recollection of the event) standing alongside the waterfront statue of Christopher Columbus, whose expeditions in the late 15th Century were eventually to produce the horrors of modern Haiti. The picture is no more than a snapshot betraying the first signs of a beer paunch whose origins lay in my days as a junior journalist in Nottingham, when two pubs were effectively annexes of the Evening Post's newsroom. For me, though, it remains a memento of an interesting phase of my newspaper life. The monument struck me then as an incongruity, for there was hardly a soul in Port-au-Prince, apart from the mulatto elite, who regarded Columbus as anything other than an exploitative adventurer, whose mercenary activities had eventually led millions into lives of misery. The statue's presence reminded me of the smaller version of Nelson's Column which once stood in the middle of O'Connell Street in Dublin. This, too, was symbolic of times best forgotten, but the Irish never thought to remove it until Easter, 1966, the fiftieth anniversary of the famous Rising. A necklace of explosives did the trick, though the IRA's unsure handling of such material in those days also actually led to shop windows being blown out all the way along the street. As Nelson fell, so did the last blatantly visible vestige of British imperialism. Republicans wondered why they hadn't thought of it before. Similarly, I wondered why Columbus was allowed to preside proprietorially over Port-au-Prince waterfront. There was nothing about the man or his endeavours that modern Haiti needed to celebrate. His intervention in the lives of Hispaniola's indigenous Indians was hardly an auspicious event, either for the Indians themselves, or the unfortunates from Africa who were to succeed them in the mines and on the plantations. Only the imperialists had good cause to laud him, and they had been ejected in 1804.

Years after I stood next to the statue (it was featured in *The Comedians* by Graham Greene, rendezvous for an assignation, as I recall) Haitians finally acknowledged the absurdity of its presence, tore it down and threw it into the sea. In a city so given to expressions of anger, it was remarkable that he had lasted so long. The feeling sweeping the byways of Port-au-Prince after the OAS visit was that Duvalier would not enjoy anything approaching Columbus's longevity. Urged along by the now frequent anti-Duvalier proclamations of President Bosch of the Dominican Republic, international opinion was united in expressions of open revulsion. While Papa Doc himself imposed yet another shoot-on-sight curfew, with loiterers near the palace fence being rewarded with bullets in the head, Bosch threatened to invade his neighbour with no further reference to international organisations. Duvalier, he declared, was 'a menace to the peace of the hemisphere', but more specifically to the Dominican Republic itself, which had once been Haitian territory. Bosch clearly feared a reprise of earlier incursions by its pestilential neighbour, and called for a coalition of Latin American forces to rid the region of the sinister despot once and for all. Meanwhile, Dominican troops were massed along the common border between the two countries. It is, indeed, likely that the indignant Bosch might well have carried out his threat, had it not been for persistent reports out of Port-au-Prince that Papa Doc was about to throw in the towel. It seemed that the dictator was, in spite of enraged rhetoric to the contrary, on the verge of bowing to international pressure and flying into exile. The idea, it seems, was that the entire Duvalier family, plus the faithful Luckner Cambronne, would head for Paris, where it was felt that French authorities would accommodate them.

There was something ironic in this: Paris was emblematic of the old oppressor, the European exploiters, yet its salons, its perfumeries and couteriers were deemed infinitely preferable to the now grand Duvaliers than the wastelands of Guinea or the Congo, the Africa of their distant past. Though vocal in propounding the joys of negritude, and in denouncing the vileness of white colonialism, Duvalier knew where the good life lay in the event of his removal. While all this was going on, Washington became convinced that the Duvalier regime was in its death throes. US officials began planning a mass evacuation of its personnel as everyday life on the streets became more hazardous. Opponents of the regime sought asylum in the foreign embassies, Clement Barbot's wife and children among them. Papa Doc's spokesmen began to repeat the by now tired old mantra that Haiti was being persecuted by international racists, that the world's first black republic was being wounded by old-style imperialists. The more exasperated the outside world became, the more insane Duvalier appeared to be. As if taking a cue from his neighbour to the west, Fidel Castro, he declared himself to be a revolutionary of 'the hard kind', a ruler in the tradition of armed usurpers of the past. In reality, Duvalier's power as a military commander was strictly limited by the size and quality of his armed forces. Unlike the Dominican Republic, Haiti had nothing resembling a formidable military set-up. Its 6,000 strong army consisted largely of raw recruits with unreliable weaponry. Among officers, there were sizeable pockets of genuine resentment. As a revenue-earner, and a means of engendering popular support, Papa Doc functionaries began selling plaster images of 'The Great One' on the streets, an exercise given impetus by the glowers of the Macoute. The threat from Bosch fizzled out, largely because of growing domestic preoccupations of his own, and international indignation quietened down with time.

For Duvalier, the real threat was once again to come from his own countrymen inside and outside Haiti. Old foes, Daniel Fignole and Louis Defoie, formed a Haitian government in exile based in San Juan, Puerto Rico, with a properly constituted parliamentary assembly in waiting. In the Bahamas, Cuba and the Dominican Republic itself, units of Haitian resistance took shape and awaited their opportunity to strike. Several ultimately abortive invasion plans were already in train, but Papa Doc was going nowhere. At a hastily arranged press conference in the palace, Duvalier reiterated his position that international groups like the OAS had no right to interfere in his country's internal strife. He then went on to draw wholly credible comparisons with the civil rights problems being experienced by the United States, citing Birmingham, Alabama, as a flashpoint for the kind of civil upheaval he was trying to prevent. To the dispassionate observer, Duvalier's arguments were plausible, if not persuasive. Astoundingly, the old gnome had outflanked his critics with the kind of logic they found hard to counter.

In the streets of Port-au-Prince and among the shanty settlements in the hills, the bloodletting continued. By now, the Macoute permeated every area of Haitian life. In rural areas, local leaders were almost invariably Tontons militiamen. Cab-drivers, tap-tap owners, voodoo priests, and even schoolteachers were enlisted into the 10,000-strong group that now held the entire nation in its grip. The rank-and-file were slum people, empowered for the first time. With unlimited powers to terrorise and murder, they ran riot, settling old scores with an abandon horrifying to behold. In their ragged denims and bright bandanas, they were the instantly recognisable enforcers of the President's will in the hills outside Port-au-Prince.

In my own childhood, older adults warned of 'nine o'clock horses' carrying off naughty children into the night. In Haiti, before Duvalier, 'Tontons Macoute' were the bogeymen of childhood, rewarding the good and punishing the bad. It was part of Christmas folklore, with 'Uncle Knapsack' carrying off recalcitrant children in a bag to an uncertain fate. Under Duvalier, the legend became reality. Men, women and children really did disappear into the night, never to be seen again. And this was no Christmas ritual. It was a year-round ordeal which left few families unaffected. The essence of Macoute power is best exemplified by one Ti Bobo, whose very presence could send crowds fleeing. He enjoyed his notoriety to the extent that he swaggered into communities expecting, and receiving, instant obeisance. If he wanted food or fruit from a stall, he took it. If he wanted to ravish a woman, he did so. If he wanted to take over a man's home, or coveted his car, he purloined them, usually with a warning that anti-Duvalier remarks had been attributed to the victim. Anyone showing resistance would either be savagely beaten or summarily executed. Ti Bobo would pull a gun and fire a bullet straight through a dissenter's head. Family members would look on helplessly, with no recourse to justice, and no way of calling authority down upon the killer's head. The problem was that Ti Bobo, and many more like him, WERE authority in Duvalier's Haiti. In addition to killing indiscriminately, Ti Bobo and his men forced businessmen into exile, taking over their property in orgies of greed.

Macoutes in the public service drew multiple cheques, and corrupted regulations to their own advantage. For Ti Bobo, excess led to obliteration. His physical enormity made him an intimidating presence, but also a tempting target. One day, a soldier who had suffered at his hands grabbed a machine-gun from the Casernes Dessalines weapons office and hunted down the towering militiaman. Ti Bobo expired in a storm of bullets, his body almost cut in half by the blast. However, Ti Bobo's well-deserved fate was the exception: it was on the foundation of Macoute loyalty, their willingness to kill even their own families in pursuit of the cause, that Duvalier built what he came to see as his own unassailability.

In the first three years of his administration, he used his militia to silence dissenters, neutralise the press, and exile or imprison recognised political opponents. Throughout this tumultuous period, Duvalier would often vanish for weeks on end into the dark inner offices of the palace, while his country fell into an advanced state of disrepair. At the time of US occupation, roads and bridges were renovated, infrastructure improved beyond all recognition, and docks taken to pristine heights. But by the time the mid-1960s arrived, the country was back to its old chaotic self, the treasury sacked, the education system installed by the Americans effectively dismantled, and more than ninety per cent of the people illiterate. Far from uplifting the masses, Duvalier oversaw their worsening descent into hopelessness and despair. By the end of 1963, more than half of the national budget was being spent on maintaining the 500-strong presidential guard and the dreaded Macoute, who were at the core of Haiti's decline into widespread and wholly destructive corruption. Under their menacing supervision, business carried on with the government was almost entirely dependent on kickbacks. It was virtually impossible to get a licence for anything without paying something directly into the pockets of Macoute enforcers.

The result of all this, of course, was to increase financial pressure on the poor, who fell victim to the avarice of predatory government officials and their Macoute protectors. If the burning of the Benoit household, the killing of its inhabitants, and even the slaughter of its pet dogs was to prove one of the most egregious of Duvalier's reprisals, it was to be exceeded in savagery by the events of summer, 1964, when the exile group, Jeunes Haiti, attempted an invasion of its own close to the south-western city of Jeremie. Again the 'force', such as it was, was pitifully inadequate for the task at hand. Only thirteen young mulattoes landed that fateful day with the hope of capitalising on mounting discontent and sparking an insurrection.

Unfortunately for them, Duvalier's system of repression was insufficient, in itself, to overcome the long-held suspicions of the black peasantry. The problem was that prosperous Jeremie mulattoes, in their grand colonial-style homes, were not seen as natural allies of the downtrodden poor. Restored to power, the blacks suspected the mulattoes would revert to their elitist ways and continue the system of paternalism and patronage which had so disabled Haiti's progress in the past. Hence, when Jeunes Haiti stormed ashore, the uprising didn't happen. Instead, the young idealists were left at the mercy of the Tontons, who hunted them like rabbits, gunning them down in a series of brief, one-sided exchanges. Only two survived, and that was their misfortune. They were taken to Port-au-Prince, tortured for weeks at Fort Dimanche, and then executed against the wall of the National Cemetery in full view of crowds of schoolchildren, who had been brought from their classrooms on Duvalier's orders, to witness the demise of people he decried as misguided traitors.

As mentioned earlier, the entire gruesome ritual was televised in another distasteful attempt to browbeat the populace. If that had been the end of the matter, it would have been bad enough, but Papa Doc wasn't finished yet. In time-honoured fashion, he now turned his attention to the invaders' relatives. Jeremie was purged of its wealthy mulatto families, who were stripped naked and forced to march through the city's elegant streets. With crowds jeering at their humiliation, the doomed European-educated *brahmins* of Haitian society were taken to the airport to be massacred. The Tontons did the job systematically, first knifing the children to death in front of their parents, then slaughtering the women in front of their menfolk, and finally despatching the enraged menfolk as the poor of Jeremie looted the now empty, balconied mansions. Occasionally, it seemed, Duvalier's brutality worked in favour of some, if not all, of his people.

When I arrived to work in the Bahamas, two years after the massacre of Jeremie, one of my sources, in all stories relating to the Haitian immigration problem, was Father Guy Sansariq, a mulatto priest who was a gentle presence among the sad souls who fled north for their lives. The Drouin family, the Villedrouins and the Sansariqs were among those most affected by the Jeremie atrocity. Father Guy never spoke of it, at least not to me, but his intense understanding of 'The Haitian Problem' was, I now know, the product of harsh and harrowing experience. His kin had felt the pain of Duvalierism. Worse still, though, was the recognition that Haiti was now almost beyond hope. Having formally declared himself President-for-Life, putting the Haitian constitution to rest in the process, and having again proclaimed himself the sacred ruler of the Fatherland, Duvalier battened down for the long haul. He cursorily acknowledged the role of 'God' in his elevation, but paid more sincere homage to the voodoo spirits whose power, he said, sprang from Africa. There would, he said, be no more disruptive presidential elections on Haitian soil, just a ritualistic acknowledgment by all that he was 'lord and master' of Haiti, in much the same way that de Gaulle was unchallenged leader of France, Sukarno of Indonesia and Mao Tse Tung of China. These casual allusions to big-league leaders in reference to his own standing in world affairs became more common once his status had been confirmed. He depicted his own inscrutability as evidence of his durability under fire: he invited the Macoute and others to draw strength from his unshakeable resolve.

At his official inauguration on June 22, 1964, crowds danced round a monstrous monument in Port-au-Prince, marking the eternal nature of his regime while Duvalier himself took upon himself a long list of grandiose titles, 'Uncontestable Leader of the Revolution' and 'Worthy Heir of the Founders of the Haitian Nation' among them. More bizarrely, he also declared himself to be a physical, and spiritual coalescence, of some great names from the past. In his mind, at least, Toussaint, Dessalines, Petion, Christophe and Estime had all been resurrected to produce the ultimate deity called Duvalier. The Dominican President, Juan Bosch, was not the only one who felt psychiatric help might well have been appropriate at this stage. But who would tell Duvalier? To top off the absurdity of his delusions, Papa Doc rewrote the Lord's Prayer: 'Our Doc who art in the National Palace for life, hallowed be thy name by present and future generations, thy will be done at Port-au-Prince and in the provinces. Give us this day our new Haiti and never forgive the trespasses of the anti-patriots who spit every day on our country; let them succumb to temptation, and under the weight of their venom, deliver them not from any evil.' The Vatican, presented with such a sacreligious tract, must have felt more than vindicated in withdrawing the papal nuncio from beneath the nose of the Haitian tyrant, who was now being viewed by even the most circumspect of the diplomatic community as a megalomaniac of quite exceptional dimensions. Here was a man whose self-belief — if genuine — was quite unnerving. But was it, in truth, evidence of fundamental insecurity?

For the next few months, military activity among the exiles quietened down. There were rumblings in the Dominican Republic, where up to 50,000 Haitians were living in dreadful conditions around the sugar plantations. A Catholic priest began raising money in South America to fund a liberation army to overthrow Duvalier. Small training camps were set up in isolated areas to get volunteers up to scratch militarily. But the prospect of revolution continued to seem remote, even though the Camoquin units in the hills scored occasional minor successes against Duvalierist forces. Meanwhile, Duvalier was prepared to leave the guerrillas to their fate in the denuded hills, where food was in short supply, while he concentrated on suspected collaborators in the suburbs and lowlands. Any peasant found with anything more than a tattered gourde or two on his person was summarily shot, the Macoute taking the view that banknotes in Haiti's crippled economy could only be generated among the poor if betrayal was afoot.

To those who fell victim to Duvalier's deadly whims, it seemed that every fit of rage, every explosion of indignation, brought with it a new purge of suspected families. Some of these killings appeared to be entirely arbitrary, the elimination of oil executive, Maurice Duchatelier being a case in point. True, his wife was sister-in-law of the marksman Francois Benoit, who was still enduring miserable exile in the Dominican Embassy, but the Duchatelier family's links with the suspected plotter were considered tenuous. Nonetheless, Duchatelier, his wife and their infant child vanished into the President's murder machine, exact fate unknown. Only the Jeune Haiti initiative in the rural areas near Jeremie, a quaint old market town with an air of dereliction about it, had shown any real sign of success, but the thirteen young men at its core, most of them thrusting mulatto intellectuals with a burning sense of mission to liberate their homeland from a monster, were ultimately to die for the cause.

As mentioned earlier, the body of Yvan Laraque — shot while tossing grenades at advancing Duvalierists — was hauled to Port-au-Prince to be displayed outside the international airport in an armchair. For half a week, it grew increasingly hideous and malodorous, a feast for meat flies and rats. Eventually, foreign diplomats began complaining to the palace about this latest manifestation of presidential barbarism, with black

222

envoys, in particular, taking issue with the possible negative fall-out on people of African descent. Duvalier, though, had little time for niceties. The heads of three rebels were photographed being held up by triumphant Duvalierists, so that local newspapers could publish yet more graphic evidence of the President's control of events, while the two survivors, Drouin and Numa, were prepared for the main feature, a carefully stage-managed public execution on November 12, 1964, with hundreds of schoolchildren in attendance. The televised killing by firing squad of this gutsy pair was shown on Haitian television for a week, lest anyone should have missed the spectacle, and the lesson it taught. Before the nine-man squad fired, the lanky black Numa and the stocky mulatto Drouin yelled defiance as they stood, eyes masked, bound to poles. Their voices were stilled by bullets only after they called damnation down upon Duvalier. Witnesses said afterwards how impressed they were by the pair's courage. Struck by gunfire, the men shook and twitched in their final throes, two more victims of Haiti's unending nightmare.

While all this was going on, Duvalier's resident philosopher, guru and confidant Gerard de Catalogne, was using silken words to convince the world that Haiti remained one of the great tourist destinations. "Of course Haiti is safe," he told visiting correspondents, blaming the press and the likes of Graham Greene for Haiti's poor image. Long before Nixon, Clinton and the Bushes perfected the art of spin, Duvalier and de Catalogne were a bravura double act. Even a Tontons raid on a Catholic church, and the savage beating of the priests and congregation, were explained away as an aberration — an effort to halt a black mass at which God's help was being sought to destroy Papa Doc and the ghouls who kept him in power. Finally, the Dominican Republic's civil war of 1965 muddied the revolutionary efforts in Haiti. Intervention by US troops rendered the entire island of Hispaniola unsuitable terrain for rebel military activity. Disunity — an unwillingness among disparate groups to co-operate in joint operations against Duvalier — was eventually to cripple the cause and bolster Papa Doc's might. It seemed now that the only hope the regime's opponents had was to turn the people's minds by propaganda.

A New York-based group called the Haitian Coalition beamed radio broadcasts into Haiti every day, not only denouncing the President and his armed thugs, but also actively inciting the people to rise up against the evil men of the night. At the head of this group was an urbane young Haitian anthropologist called Raymond Joseph, whose eternal optimism — "Papa Doc is about to fall," he told me repeatedly in the year that Knox was tried and convicted in Port-au-Prince — became the lietmotif of an organisation obsessed with Duvalier's removal. I travelled to New York in 1969 to interview him. My article, used extensively by US features agencies, began with a paragraph which must have given Haitian exiles a scintilla of hope. "Sitting high above the teeming streets of Manhattan," it said, "is a young man who could conceivably be the next President of Haiti." Alas, it was not to be. Joseph's predictions of doom for the Duvaliers were not to be fulfilled for seventeen years. The Coalition's exhortations rattled the airwaves day after day to little effect. Compatriots in Haiti tuned in if they dared (Tontons reprisals were typically brutal for anyone caught doing so) but the calls to rise up for their freedom went largely unheeded.

Papa Doc's hold was complete. Through the severed heads of his foes, he used his voodoo powers to keep track of their intentions. Whatever spirits he summoned up during his incantations at the palace, they served him well.   Light relief for Duvalier during these grim days was in short supply. He maintained as near normal a family life in the palace as he could, but there was little cause for amusement as he and the dreaded Simone continued to twitch at the possibility of a full-scale rebellion. In purely military terms, Haiti was an easy target. It's literally true to say that a unit of, say, one hundred highly-trained troops could have toppled the regime any day of the week. Duvalier's unkempt forces were no match for anything resembling an organised invasion under expert military leadership. And the Macoute, in real terms, were only capable of terrorising a fearful, defenceless peasantry. Against real opposition, they would have been exposed as a shambolic band of brigands, little more. Yet exiled foes of Duvalier were never able to summon up the expertise, or the numbers, to make a really decisive impact on the President and his protectors.

In one sense, however, Duvalier was outflanked — by a smooth-talking Arab, who one distant day would become the owner of the prestigious Harrods store in London, and the putative father-in-law of the iconic but doomed Princess Diana. Mohammed Fayed flew into Haiti for the first time on June 12, 1964, a time when Duvalier was transfixed by the alarming events happening all around him. Later, Fayed would add the embellishment 'al' to his name, but as an ambitious thirty-five-year-old fixer with deals on his mind, he was unconcerned about such fripperies at the time. For him, the deeply troubled land of Haiti was a commercial opportunity. His six-month sojourn was to be talked about for decades afterwards. In essence, Fayed was remembered as the man who first bewitched, and then tricked, the Duvalier family, reportedly seducing one of the daughters in the process. The story goes that the plausible former Coca Cola salesman left Haiti a good deal richer than when he arrived, a remarkable achievement given that the nation was so broke that it had to panhandle its way from one month to the next, buying arms it could ill-afford to repulse foes who continued to harass the regime.

It's unclear why Fayed was attracted to Haiti, but he was introduced to the Duvaliers by a shipping executive called Dabinovic, and first flew into Port-au-Prince to assess the prospects for whatever scheme he had in mind. Among those despatched to meet him at the airport was Aubelin Jolicoeur, the prancing boulevardier, who would not only record Fayed's presence in his scribblings for *Le Nouvelliste*, but would also report back to Duvalier with his impressions of the visitor, and whatever dirt he could dig up on him. In the event, Jolicoeur was impressed enough to describe him as 'the eminent Kuwaiti sheikh', and Fayed was accorded the most lavish welcome Haiti could run to at the time. Whatever the exact nature of the relationship between them, one thing is clear: each wanted something from the other. In this particular battle of wits, it seems Fayed was the victor. From Haiti's viewpoint, Fayed's appeal was obvious. With his aura of wealth, bolstered by tales of untold oil riches in his 'homeland', Fayed was viewed as an investor with the potential to turn the nation's fortunes. For Fayed, it seemed, Haiti was a backward black country whose people knew nothing and whose ruler was desperate. All in all, it was a heaven-made situation for a man who told anyone who would listen that he was there to explore Haiti's oil-producing capabilities. After his initial exploratory trip, Fayed returned within a few weeks to establish himself, ostensibly at least, as a businessman, having been offered accommodation in the spacious home of the ill-fated Macoute chief, Clement Barbot. By smoothing his way into Port-au-Prince's higher circles, and captivating Duvalier, Fayed quickly secured Haiti's oil exploration concessions and control of the capital's docks, which were the hub of the national economy.

The deals he secured in both cases were, by all accounts, extremely favourable – to him.

Duvalier was enchanted by the Arab's easy charm and was sufficiently confident of his ability to make him the oil and docks supremo. Sceptics were discouraged from comment by Fayed's close links with the President, a relationship which enabled the Arab to acquire citizenship, by presidential decree, within three months instead of the legally required ten years. He also received a diplomatic passport, enabling him to leave and enter Haiti with none of the usual irritating and burdensome formalities. Like much else in Haiti, the Fayed association was to end in farce. The 'black gold' found seeping out of the Haitian soil was discovered to be crude molasses, residue of a long-abandoned sugar plantation. That was the end of the oil boom hopes. The sweet deal Fayed secured on the docks collapsed after concerted pressure by foreign shipping lines serving Port-au-Prince. Fayed was later to deny suggestions that he had made off with a fortune from his brief brush with the land of darkness, claiming he had invested two million dollars of his own money in Haiti and was then pressured by Duvalier to stump up another five million.

When Fayed was suddenly deprived of his personal bodyguard – a heavyset minder provided by the President – he took the hint and flew out. Sensibly, he recognised that Fort Dimanche might well have been his next home in Port-au-Prince and that the fate of Clement Barbot might also have been his. Today, those who recall Fayed's Haitian adventure accord him legendary status as one who tangled with Papa Doc and somehow escaped with his life.

CHAPTER 21

THE LION OF JUDAH

B y the spring of 1966, Duvalier's regime had taken on an aura of invincibility. The President had repelled seven 'invasions', all in their different ways lamentably inept military exercises, in which ambition had far outstripped resources and know-how, and was now adding credence to the increasingly widespread view that he was sustained by the gods and spirits of a distant past. The structure of the government now rested not only on the fear instilled by the Macoute, but also the growing belief that Papa Doc had been willed on the people by the voodoo deities, and that his enemies were impotent against the supernatural forces guiding him. Whatever the truth behind the uneasy relationship with Washington, the Haitian people interpreted Duvalier's resilience as proof of his uncanny qualities, which had enabled him to defy the world's greatest power, eliminate the anti-patriots within Haiti, show contempt for the exiles in New York and Florida, and acquire, in the process, an image which made him the most instantly recognisable Third World leader of the age. Whatever his deficiencies, Papa Doc was actually emerging as a quite impressive incumbent of the most difficult political job in the Americas. The fact that Haiti itself had made no progress during his tenure, and had suffered countless bloody convulsions because of his uncompromising methods, did not detract from his single most remarkable achievement: he had been President of Haiti longer than anyone else, and looked set to reign for years to come. The official visit to Haiti of Emperor Haile Selassie, Ethiopia's Lion of Judah, undoubtedly added to his lustre during what was, in truth, a period of continuing difficulty. Duvalier's reverence for Africa as the original homeland, and his belief in the innate nobility of the negro, were always dominant themes of his thinking. Selassie's one-day visit that spring was, therefore, seen by Duvalier as an international imprimatur: an acknowledgment of Haiti's special place in African thinking and the negro experience. Selassie was, of course, a God-figure for many blacks. Rastafarians see him, even today, long after his death, as representing the great African civilisations of the past, a living link with sophisticated black societies once predominant in the cradle of humanity. The intense self-loathing many New World blacks feel in the post-slavery era is countered, to some extent, by the reassurance to be gained from Ethiopia, a country whose majestic past set it above the more humble tribal societies of sub-Saharan Africa. Hence, to be graced by the Emperor's presence, however short his stay, was to be seen as something other than the bleak hell-hole Haiti represented in the minds of western whites. In Haiti, Selassie saw a land with a proud history of defiance, an independent streak uninhibited by the scepticism and active discouragement of the First World. At the airport, decked out with bunting for the occasion, Duvalier led a welcoming delegation consisting of his own family and some of his most loyal allies. The President himself wore a top hat and tails, while Simone Duvalier turned out in some of her most elegant finery. When the uniformed, heavily bemedalled Selassie appeared, with his handsomely sculpted ebony countenance and trimmed dark beard, Duvalier was almost overcome with emotion. It was as though Haiti's umbilical cord had been re-attached. The main road into the city, and all subsidiary routes along which the Emperor would pass, were resurfaced for the occasion. One was actually named Haile Selassie Avenue. Crowds lined the route to hail this noble personage from afar, Port-au-Prince itself taking on a festive air for what was, by any reckoning, a very unusual happening in Haiti. Few national leaders wanted to be associated with the Caribbean's pariah nation and its demented ruler. Selassie's implied support could not be taken lightly. The visit, part of a wider Caribbean tour, lasted only twelve hours, but Duvalier extracted from it every squeeze of positive spin he could manage. In his mind, at least, he had 'arrived' as a leader, confounding the doubters.

Selassie's visit to the region embraced three countries and was the direct result of an invitation handed out the previous year, during an offi-cial visit to Ethiopia, by Trinidad's leader, Dr Eric Williams. In Jamaica, he was greeted by hundreds of the Rastafarian fraternity, who managed to generate so much marijuana smoke in their excitement that it filled the air at the airport. Selassie, alarmed at the placard-wielding throng, retreated immediately into his aircraft, demanding that extra security be laid on. The dreadlocked hordes carried signs declaring Selassie to be 'King of Kings' and 'God Anointed'. Some even declared outright that he was a reincarnation of Jesus Christ. With formalities trimmed to the bone, Selassie was whisked away in a limousine flanked by outriders to a reception organised by Prime Minister Sir Alexander Bustamante, later accepting an honorary degree from the University of the West Indies and addressing the Jamaican Parliament. Accompanying Selassie were two members of His Imperial Majesty's family, Her Royal Highness Imebet Sofiya Desta, the Emperor's grand-daughter, and His Highness Prince Mikael, a grandson. The Ethiopian Ambassador to Haiti and Selassie's personal physician were also among the sixteen-strong entourage as they descended from the aircraft on a hot, wet day at Norman Manley International Airport.

This was followed by four days of almost incessant adulation from the Rastafari community, who felt themselves to be in the presence of 'the Messiah'. Fuelled by ganja, buoyed up by the coming of the saviour, the crowds were in a euphoric stupor for the best part of a week. In Haiti, Selassie's reception also entailed as much grandeur as the regime could muster. A fleet of black limousines and sedans was assembled for the official convoy, some of them commandeered from indignant taxi-drivers and prosperous families. As the cars swept away from Francois Duvalier International Airport, and barrelled towards the city, crowds shrieked their delight at seeing these two iconic black supermen in the flesh. For Haitians, it was as though King Christophe and Emperor Jean-Jacques Dessalines had been resurrected. Their joy was unrestrained. At the airport and during the drive back into the city, the Duvaliers were under the close guard of the Tontons Macoute. The shaded heavies, most armed with machine-guns, were far removed from the pristinely uniformed armed forces Selassie was used to seeing on such occasions. However, this was no ordinary state visit: it was a whistlestop call at what was, in effect, a gangster-run fiefdom, a slum nation under the control of sinister forces. It was probably the unpredictable nature of Haiti, and specifically its crazy dictator, that prompted the Emperor to opt for a short stay. Having spent three days in Trinidad, and three more in Jamaica, he had decided not to 'overnight' in the land of darkness. For him, no doubt, this was little more than a token visit, a gesture of fraternal feelings between an ancient African civilisation and a New World satellite. For Duvalier, though he was slightly put out by the shortness of the visit, this was momentous, an underpinning of his credibility, and he made the most of it. The two leaders lunched privately together at the palace, after which a state reception was arranged in the palace ballroom. The African royals were feted extravagantly, with Haiti eager to make an impression in its unfamiliar role as host. Few international leaders included Port-au-Prince on their itinerary: the fact that Selassie had chosen to do so seemed to seal Duvalier's legitimacy, certainly in the eyes of himself and his followers. Duvalier's minions prepared a Petionville mansion for Selassie's use. It was here that the 'King of Kings' freshened up and changed clothing. By its own standards, Haiti had mounted quite a show: peasants waved tiny flags — supplied gratis by the government — at the airport, along the route into the city, and outside the palace perimeter fence. It was amazing how quickly the crowds could be cajoled into displays of affection for Papa Doc when the Macoute were orchestrating events. In its way, it was touchingly impressive, as though the President and his people were united in a war against First World propagandists and mischief-makers. The reality, however, was somewhat different. Duvalier's prime reason for exploiting Selassie's visit for all it was worth was, as usual, economic. By emphasising his country's desire for international peace, and proclaiming the fundamental legitimacy of his position — not only as President of Haiti but 'leader of the Haitian people' — Duvalier was again pitching for aid, which he saw as the crucial element in the nation's recovery. It was a time, also, when he chose to attack the media's demonisation of his administration, in the process adopting conciliatory postures towards Haitians living abroad. Haiti's home-grown talent was, he said, badly needed in Port-au-Prince, where it could help in the considerable task of reviving a crippled country and its moribund economy. Once again, it seemed, Duvalier was detached from reality: having driven out Haiti's best brains, it was unrealistic to expect them to return while he continued to torture and kill with impunity, but the rhetoric was intended for Washington DC and he managed to make it sound sincere. In the background, however, disenchantment continued to fizz away ready to detonate, helped along by the Coalition's continuing broadcasts from New York. With so much butchery behind it, so much intimidation, persecution and treachery, the regime was too discredited to turn opinion in its favour at this late stage.

The desire to see Duvalier fall was now gathering pace: Selassie's visit did little more than provide a cosmetic flourish to a regime that was, in truth, ugly beyond redemption, sullied beyond salvation. The Diederich-Burt biography of Duvalier (1969) charted the President's almost desperate pleas for understanding at this time, quoting from his Independence Day address of 1966, when he called for 'an era of collaboration, both national and international' so that Haiti's economic woes could be tackled with at least some chance of success. "To all Haitians, I repeat my patriotic call for reconcilation, agreement, concord, to valiantly face the battle for construction of a new Haiti." At this time, Diederich and Burt recall, Duvalier put aside his differences with the international media, and began to make overtures as part of a carefully orchestrated public relations offensive inspired, at least partly, by the solicitous de Catalogne. Diederich and Burt were in better positions than most to describe the horrors of Haiti, especially in its relations with the press. Diederich, as correspondent for several leading US publications, including the *New York Times*, was jailed repeatedly in Haiti from 1961 onwards, finally being ejected from the country in 1963. Burt, of *The Miami Herald*, was expelled the same year, after writing a series of controversial dispatches about the May crisis. They were, therefore, obliged to witness Papa Doc's newly-minted posture of accommodation from afar. Duvalier used the Selassie visit to help dispel some of what he regarded as the sinister, devilish myths besmirching his reign. He invited reporters en masse into his palace, an unheard-of gesture of friendship towards his tormentors, and allowed them to see first-hand the avuncular family man who languished beneath the ghoulish image of popular renown. The result was a softened approach, a more questioning note, in their reporting, at least for a time. Some journalists now sensed that Duvalier's brutality was, in truth, a pragmatic handling of a country which understood little else. Others felt his messianic image was a necessary expedient in attempting to control a land that was, at base, uncontrollable. For a few glorious months, the beleaguered Duvalier began to enjoy the benefit of the doubt in some of the West's most prestigious titles. As Diederich and Burt record, *The Washington Post* even carried the headline: 'Duvalier — Devil or Messiah?' It's a question that had never previously been asked. His reputation as the devil incarnate had been taken as read. Whatever the press's posture, however, it did little to fragment the reality, which was that Haitian exiles were continuing to use every means they could muster to loosen Duvalier's hold. Once again, the Bahamas was implicated, with guerrillas being filtered from Florida through the island chain to within sixty miles of Haiti's northern shoreline. For the Bahamas Government, which was about to undergo convulsions of its own, this activity was unwelcome. In the months preceding the 'bloodless revolution' of January 10, 1967, when the Bahamas moved to black majority rule, Haitians were turning up in Nassau in increasing numbers, herded on to the dock by baton-wielding police. From August, 1966, onwards I witnessed these disturbing events, appalled at the terror and resignation in the eyes of the refugees as they were hauled out of filthy sloops, in which they had defecated and vomited for days on end during their voyages to freedom.

The great exodus from Haiti was already well underway, and the Bahamas would bear the brunt of it right into the 21st Century. This time the prime plotter was Henri Vixamar, an African idealist who felt that Duvalier's brutality was thwarting black development, and in the process reinforcing white prejudice against those of African descent. Vixamor felt that Duvalier's behaviour was not only unconscionable but deeply damaging to the Civil Rights Movement in America and the global drive for acceptance by aspirational blacks everywhere. Once again, the revolutionary and counter-revolutionary ambitions of Haitians and Cubans were entwined. The Cuban rebel, Roland Masferrer entered into a deal with Vixamar: we'll help you to topple Duvalier if you allow us to use a newly-liberated Haiti as a base from which to unseat the communist tyrant, Fidel Castro. Raymond Joseph, from his Manhatten headquarters, began to lay the foundation for a new order. His broadcasts promoted the thesis that Duvalier was a retardant element in Haiti's development, a power not for good, but bad, with the prospect of irretrievable damage to the economy and eternal obstruction of much-needed social development. Nassau was identified as a prime source of rebellious elements. Duvalier, with typical heavy-handedness, ordered the liquidation of anyone landing in the northern ports — Port-de-Paix, Cap Haitien and Gonaives — from the Bahamian capital. As a result, Macoute summarily executed six evidently blameless Haitians on a visit home to Cap Haitian, hauling them off the boat and eliminating them without ceremony.

Duvalier's actions once again took on an edge of desperation. International organisations interpreted the tactics of the trigger-happy Tontons as indicative of a government in trouble. In Washington, contingency plans were formulated for a collapse of the regime, with media commentators predicting a crisis greater than anything since the turmoil of 1963. The deteriorating situation was given impetus by Britain's decision to withdraw its diplomatic mission from Port-au-Prince. This was a staggering loss, for Britain was then still a major player in world events. Envoys moved to Kingston, Jamaica, from which the Ambassador Dalton Murray and diplomat Charles Sanderson were despatched when David Knox was arrested two years later.

For the image-conscious Papa Doc, it was bad news that one of the world's most respected and prestigious nations should take its leave. London, however, considered the Port-au-Prince government's irrational approach to diplomacy unacceptable. Its diplomats could make no headway in its dealings with the tyrant. Officially, however, the reason given for withdrawal was financial. In 1967, Britain's Labour Government devalued the pound. Diplomatic missions in inconsequential Third World outposts were no longer sustainable. Britain's departure came at a time when the diplomatic consensus suggested that a combination of rampant corruption, growing internal unrest, arbitrary arrests and executions, and increased restiveness in the army was exerting unprecedented pressure on the palace. Unexplained disappearances continued, some of them to be resolved only many years after the Duvalier dynasty had ended. The roll-call of the missing lengthened alarmingly: behind each name was a tragic tale, with families wrecked and children orphaned in their hundreds. The Fordi9.com gallery compiled by Patrick Lemoine offers grim reminders of the kind of people who died at Duvalier's hands.

The unrecorded peasantry, the supposed beneficiaries of Duvalierism, had their share of suffering, but it was the more confrontational middle-class, and especially the troublesome mulattoes, who were most subject to Macoute reprisals. Mostly, they were citizens of quality whose courage was founded on an earnest belief in a better Haiti, a fervent desire for happier times ahead. Lucette Ambroise was one: this feisty sister of Monsignor Joseph Lafontant, Bishop of Port-au-Prince, was married to the communist professor Jean-Jacques Ambroise. Macoute officer, Elois Maitre and two army lieutenants, Eduard Guillot and Gregoire Figaro, smashed their way into her home in search of her husband and dragged away the entire family. Lucette, seven months pregnant, vanished into the night. It's thought she was executed within hours of the swoop. Jean-Jacques, who was driven off in the boot of Figaro's car, was interrogated and tortured by Maitre and Captain Jean Tassy, a Barbot protege in the black arts of death. His broken body was tossed into a cell, where he died the same day. Civil rights advocate Hubert Legros was penalised for being a constant irritant to the regime by being incarcerated, first at the National Penitentiary, then at Fort Dimanche, where he was eventually to die in the mid-1970s, leaving behind a family of four. The Estiverne family suffered, too, with Charisna Estiverne losing her husband, Pierre, and three sons (Frank, Prosper and Gerard) to Fort Dimanche in 1969. Lemoine's tireless efforts to chart the obscene record of Papa Doc's atrocities are helping to flesh out the bald statistics.

Heroes and heroines of all the main drives against the dictator have now found a permanent Internet memorial for the world's perusal. Among them are the brave thirteen of Jeune Haiti and the eight desperadoes caught up in the Florida deputies' attempt at insurrection six years earlier. It's heartening to learn that Louis Drouin, the defiant mulatto selected for public execution on November 16, 1964, after being wounded by the army at Ravine Roches, managed to spit in the face of the Fort Dimanche commandant, Francois Delva, before he died. And that Charles Tournier, whose face was slapped by Duvalier after the deputies' debacle, managed to shoot a volley of spittle into the President's startled face before being gunned down in the parade yard of Casernes Dessalines. While the bloodletting continued through 1966 and 1967, Duvalier insisted that he was a democrat, not a dictator, telling US newspapers that he was the only man capable of ruling Haiti, and persisting with the myth that imprisonment and executions were not part of his policy for taking Haiti forward. Meanwhile, incredibly, the Catholic Church rescinded his excommunication and began adopting a more positive stance in what they saw as a 'period of consolidation', even allowing the President a role in selecting a home-grown church hierarchy.

From afar, those who cared took stock of a decade of Duvalierism, concluding that the tyrant had done little to promote the welfare of the peasantry, but had reinforced the entrenched elite with an expanded black middle-class. Mulatto business leaders were now beginning to feel that Duvalier, for all his faults, was not inimical to their interests. In fact, his rigid approach to wages and labour relations provided the right climate for them to prosper. There was no redrafting of the social order, no elimination of the slum neighbourhoods, just an extension of privileges to those who were sympathetic to Duvalierism. In fact, it was probably mulatto lobbying that led to the Vatican's revised approach to the President. Bad as he was, they reasoned, Papa Doc wasn't as bad as he might have been. Having repulsed his foes with such assurance, Duvalier was beginning to symbolise something Haiti had never enjoyed: a constancy of tenure, the prospect of things being the same next week as they were today. In a land of mayhem, this was not be taken lightly.

CHAPTER 22

SOLDIER OF FORTUNE

I recall the year 1967 primarily for two pop records - *A Whiter Shade of Pale* by Procol Harum and *San Francisco* by Scott MacKenzie. I used to sit on the balcony of my poolside apartment in Nassau, Bahamas, listening to these bewitching anthems of youth as I relaxed with a Camel cigarette, something by Hemingway and a Dewars with ginger ale on the rocks. It was the year when black majority rule came to the Bahamas in a momentous election and flower power reigned in Haight-Ashbury, San Francisco. Anything was possible in 1967. Civil rights, self-determination, the rule of youth were defining movements of the age. I was a young reporter in the thick of it, rattling out prose for *The Nassau Guardian* and feeling life was on a roll. It was a very good year for me.

For Francois Duvalier, however, 1967 brought much of what had gone before: periods of unshakeable self-belief interspersed by whispers of treachery which left him feeling unsettled and misunderstood. At the National Palace, there was little by way of serenity. Jean-Claude raced round inside the perimeter fence on a motor-cycle his father bought him (the latest of many such indulgences) in sight of ever-vigilant guards, Mama Doc engaged in frequent verbal spats with her twitchy and some-times unnervingly irascible husband, and the Duvalier daughters twittered around their apartments in what they saw as a comfortable but confining life, with parents whose existence now seemed permanently under siege. There must have been times when Duvalier looked at his presidential chair and wondered whether it was, indeed, a jinxed artefact of Haiti's haunted and tumultuous past. Certainly, it had rarely afforded true comfort for its occupants, only the continuing unease of the beleaguered. From the palace windows, the city streets were as hectic as ever, a maelstrom of supplicants

236

whose scramble for survival was always an unsettling reality for those in power.

Two figures were to loom large in Duvalier's consciousness during the latter months of 1966 and the opening weeks of 1967, as I savoured the best of Bahamas life in my poolside home. One was part of his own family circle, a genial giant he saw everyday, the other a bantam-sized soldier of fortune who sold arms for a living from his sixty-acre estate in Georgia. Papa Doc's towering son-in-law, Colonel Max Dominique, a charismatic officer in the Haitian Army, had until then never seemed anything other than an affable addition to a rather sombre family. During 1967, however, his relationship with his father-in-law would take some unexpectedly threatening turns, with horrendous consequences. More of this later. The other figure, Mitchell Livingston Werbell, was unknown to Duvalier in person, but would become part of yet another scheme to topple the regime. In their different ways, these men would help to make 1967 a memorable one for Papa Doc, but not in a sense that could have left him with any residual pleasure.

Werbell, the son of a Czarist cavalry officer, was to emerge during the 1960s and 1970s as one of the world's most fascinating figures in the field of arms dealing and counter-insurgency. He was a swaggering, moustachioed, menacing character whose military adventures had taken him to a variety of international hotspots, including Vietnam, riotous areas of Africa and — if all the rumours about him are to be believed — Dallas, Texas, on the day John F Kennedy died. It's almost literally true to say that, where there was trouble, there also was Mitchell Werbell, a bellicose terrier of a man who traded in death, and expended much of his considerable intelligence on ways to achieve the elimination of enemies, with highly sophisticated hardware.

My interest in Werbell was twofold: firstly, for his alleged involvement in trying to assassinate Papa Doc, an objective never actually fulfilled; secondly, for his role in trying to help the Bahama island of Abaco secede from the rest of the archipelago nation when independence was in prospect during the early 1970s. It was during the latter venture that I met Werbell personally at his Powder Springs Estate outside Atlanta. Lunch with the disconcertingly unpredictable Mitch and his lovely wife, Hildegarde gave me one of the most memorable experiences of my life. I recall it here only because it offers an insight into a highly complex personality, whose considerable expertise was being directed towards the National Palace in Port-au-Prince, at a time when flower power was preaching the virtues of love and peace as the prevailing credo. Mitch Werbell was not, however, attuned to the times. That much he would frankly admit. In an article I wrote about him in 1973 I described him as "a dedicated commie-killer who likes war-war not jaw-jaw." In fact, killing communists was a prime objective of Werbell and his private army of hard-headed veterans. But it was not his only aim. If the money was right, mercenary Mitch could be persuaded to turn his destructive talents to any cause. Ideology in itself was no impediment to his unusual but eternally intriguing business.

My introduction came after he had been 'appointed' the military supremo of the Abaconian secessionists. These were a group of pro-colonial extremists who believed that Abaco — a straggly isle in the north-eastern Bahamas covered by bush and pine barrens — should remain a British Crown Colony when the rest of the country declared independence in July, 1973. Born of loyalist stock, suspicious of black radicals, the fiery Abaconians were ready to take up their hog-hunting guns in anger if the Bahamian Prime Minister, Lynden Pindling, were to insist they join the movement to part company with the motherland. For them, the Union Jack represented solidity, stability and security in an uncertain world. Two centuries before, their forebears had rejected the blandishments of the American revolutionaries in the Carolinas and opted to stay with the Crown. As the original colonies of the United States seized freedom from Britain, the loyalists and their slaves headed for Abaco, the nearest out-crop of British-ruled soil they could find. The island had provided them not only with a refuge, but also a livelihood of sorts which, by the 1970s, had bloomed into a quite buoyant economy. They were in no mood to squander their heritage on what they considered an ill-advised bid for nationhood by Mr Pindling and his political cohorts.

In their own simple way, the Abaco freedom fighters had expected London's support for their proposed breakaway. In fact, they were encouraged in these beliefs by a small group of Right-Wing British MPs, including one Ronald Bell and an ex-soldier turned parliamentarian called Colin 'Mad Mitch' Mitchell, a veteran of several campaigns during the twilight years of the British Empire. It's odd that two prominent warriors of reactionary persuasion called 'Mitch' should have become embroiled in Abaco's bizarre bid for freedom, but in truth it was almost inevitable that they should.

Abaco, an elongated limestone rock flanked to the east by a shallow sea, had always been more fervently loyal to the Crown than the rest of the Bahama isles, partly because of its people's origins, and partly because its economy was sufficiently robust to suggest that it could function as a separate entity. The plan was not that Abaco should become just another parasitic British dependency, but a loyal colony enjoying London's protection while paying its own way in the world. There was something undoubtedly seductive about this proposition to everyone concerned except the indignant Mr Pindling and the British Government. While Ronald Bell and Colin Mitchell considered Abaco's move as a telling blow for a dying empire, more realistic politicians at Westminster saw the Bahamas as just another expensive appendage they would rather be rid of. Abaco's secession attempt was not to their taste at all. It was during the relatively short period, when Abaco thought it might get London's support, that Mitchell Werbell came on the scene as the proposed military commander who would lead Abaco's guerrillas to victory over Pindling's police force. On reflection, the proposed scenario seems absurd, with the police storming Abaco's beaches against Werbell's mercenary army and a shambolic battalion of wild-eyed hog-hunters. However, that's the way Werbell and Abaconian leaders like the former police officer, Errington Watkins saw things panning out. And for a brief time it seemed it could, indeed, come to pass.

The Abaco cause was just the kind of madcap adventure Werbell liked. Seeing Pindling and his party as radicals — and possibly communists in disguise — Werbell became quite enthusiastic about the mission ahead. During our meeting at his estate, we discussed the vague outline of his intentions with some intensity, for it was impossible not to be caught up in his passion for the cause. After a convivial lunch, we went on to Werbell's firing range, where I was invited to unload a compact Ingram machine-gun into a man-shaped figure made of lead standing next to a hard mudbank. He was less than impressed with my performance. As bullets began ricocheting off the bank, Werbell's Doberman Pinschers scattered in all directions, realising that the man with the gun was a donkey in military terms and a hazard to behold. I have never handled a gun since. Back inside the house, we enjoyed a coffee together — Hildegarde as solicitous as ever — and prepared to part company. "By the way, John," Werbell said suddenly, looking me coldly in the eye, "If this story goes wrong, we'll catch up with you." I had no doubt he meant what he said. Somewhere in rural England, I thought, Werbell heavies in battle fatigues would track me down, cutting me in half with machine-gun fire. Not a pleasant thought. What I didn't know then — and I wished I had — was that Werbell had been implicated not only in the assassination of John F Kennedy in 1963, but also a proposed 1967 insurrection against Papa Doc. With his waxed moustache, his cocksure demeanour, and eyes as glacial as ice-shards, I thought him capable of anything. But it would have been interesting to ask the questions, even had it meant being taken outside and stood against a bunker wall.

The Kennedy hit story is as nebulous as most theories surrounding the President's killing. It relies heavily on the three or four-shot conspiracy version of events in Dallas that bright fall day. Werbell is suspected of providing his own custom-built silencers for the weaponry that took off the President's head, thus creating the considerable confusion, which prevails to this day, about the number and location of the gunmen. That Werbell detested Kennedy is beyond reasonable doubt. As a liberal-minded democrat, Kennedy was not Werbell's type. With a mindset some way right of Benito Mussolini, Mitch was not a man with much sympathy for pinko thinking. Odd, though, that he should get involved with a committed communist like Lee Harvey Oswald, especially as his own father was a White Russian officer with deep Czarist sympathies. The proposed attempt on Duvalier's life was more his line, even though Papa Doc was conspicuously engaged in anti-communist campaigns of his own. Though I have no direct evidence to support this theory, I suspect Werbell was anti-black. His dislike of Kennedy — of all the Kennedys — was probably as much to do with their liberal civil rights, anti-Mob attitudes as anything else. For anyone as rabidly Right-Wing as Werbell, anything pink was suspect. And pro-black was pink thinking as far as he was concerned. Thus, Duvalier fell into Werbell's sights. Had he known, Haiti's dictator would have been even more uneasy than he was during those difficult months. To be targeted by an internationally-known hitman like Werbell was no joke. To be a red splat on Mitch's campaign map was to be a dead man in waiting.

Werbell is worth examining in detail. Of all the anti-Duvalier conspirators, he was the one with real, copper-bottomed experience in military affairs. Born in Philadelphia in 1918, he was the off-spring of fervent anti-Bolshevists, presumably refugees from the 1917 upheavals in Russia, so he was congenitally inclined to resist Leftist revolutionaries of all kinds. Most of his military adventures were markedly Anti-Left though, as mentioned earlier, not all fitted exactly into the Right-Wing profile. It's true he worked covertly for Fulgencio Batista in Cuba in 1958, just prior to Castro's takeover, at a time when he was also heavily into arms dealing. It's also true that he did covert work inside the Dominican Republic and Vietnam. All these campaigns gelled well with his sentiment that 'the only good Commie is a dead Commie', but Project Nassau — the anti-Duvalier invasion plot — was something else. I am not privy to Werbell's thinking at this time, but it's possible his plan was to take out Duvalier — by then considered an ogre by all shades of political opinion in the western world — so that Haiti could be used as a permanent base for the harassment and ultimate overthrow of the Castro regime in Cuba.

Though Duvalier was making a big show of his anti-communist sentiments at the time, diplomatic circles were not fooled. This was a Duvalier stratagem to shake down the West for aid. If Duvalier could be replaced by a non-communist regime, he would be no loss to the anti-Red cause, just another vicious tyrant out of harm's way. The Project Nassau exercise was, in fact, a combined effort by Cuban and Haitian exiles which, if successful, would lead to more extensive co-operation between their respective regimes in years to come. If they could jointly remove both Duvalier and Castro, then work for the common good of both Haiti and Cuba, they would have changed the political landscape of the northern Caribbean in one sweep.

For Werbell, the lure of such an enterprise was irresistible. In a National Archives website interview, Werbell is reported to have admitted having been involved in several attempts on Castro's life. Although the worse for drink at the time, Werbell is alleged to have slurred, "There's a helluva lot I ain't said yet — and there's a helluva lot I ain't gonna say yet" before admitting his involvement in plots against Castro. "I was sitting in Miami with a goddamned million dollars in cash for the guy who was gonna take Fidel out," he told the interviewer, though he disclaimed knowledge of the Kennedy killing and denied being involved in gun smuggling deals with Jack Ruby, the man who was to gain infamy as the killer of Lee Harvey Oswald. "Now I didn't like Jack Kennedy," Werbell is reported to have said, "I thought he was a shit to begin with, but I was certain not to be involved in the assassination of an American president for Chrissakes." Whatever the truth of Werbell's supposed involvement, he was never subpoenaed to appear before the House Assassinations Committee.

In both the Abaco and Haiti campaigns, however, his footprints are more pronounced. As a former OSS secret agent during the Second World War, and a CIA operative in China in the 1950s, Werbell was well-versed in international espionage and covert operations of all kinds. During the 1960s, he was sent to Vietnam as a weapons adviser and helped lay the foundations for the 1965 invasion of the Dominican Republic. In between he initiated several madcap raids on Cuba, usually at night in boats flying the Confederate flag. Whether Werbell was entirely sober during these nocturnal excursions to the Cuban coast is not known, for he is said to have played bagpipes while speeding over the Caribbean waters, some-times yelling anti-communist slogans between blasts on the chanter. Though he was articulate enough during my encounter with him in 1973, he apparently became increasingly erratic, and forgetful, during the final years of his life, (he died of cancer in 1983) and even mixed up his various adventures when trying to recall his past. This blurring of memory was not helped by a copious intake of alcohol.

His 'New Country Project' for Abaco was devised in much the same way that Project Nassau had been seven years earlier. It is claimed he received tacit CIA and State Department approval for the Abaco venture, the only proviso being that there would be no violence. In fact, Werbell was convinced that Pindling's 'army', such as it was, would back off without a shot being fired, having no taste for the hell Werbell and his Vietnam vets could lay on them. With machine-gun nests on the beaches, and a bazooka or two to make the point, the rebels would be free to hoist the Union Jack in triumph, creating a colony of casino resorts, wealthy enclaves and a racial profile of which well-heeled Caucasian investors could approve. Meanwhile, Nassau under its new black government would be left to make its uncertain way in the world.

For the Abaco venture, Werbell signed up soldier of fortune Robert K Brown, who in turn hand-picked a dozen or more former Vietnam hardmen, who would become the island's full-time army. No doubt a few eager Abaconian volunteers would have been drafted, if only to make them feel good, to add numerical might to this unlikely unit. However, the Abaco rebellion didn't happen because Britain made it clear it would not entertain the island as a Crown colony. As far as London was concerned, the Bahamas chain was being given its independence en bloc with no dissenters. To add to the disappointment, Werbell himself was indicted on charges — later dropped — that he was aggressively marketing the Ingram machine-gun, a foldaway killing machine he had been distributing with his partner Gordon Ingram since 1967. Werbell and his arms company, Defence Services, were also indicted for trying to sell such guns to a federal undercover agent and the international financier, Robert Vesco, in Costa Rica. Again the charges came to nought, but the court actions were enough to divert Werbell's mind from other matters at hand.

The Abaco rebellion collapsed in ignominy, leaving the so-called secessionists to swallow their pride and throw in their hand with Pindling and his newly-independent Bahamas. Seven years earlier, as Werbell and his men plotted against Duvalier, the law intervened again. A Federal Grand Jury heard a two-count indictment against Cuban counter-revolutionary, Roland Masferrer and six other defendants, including Werbell. All seven were among a 75-strong invasion group arrested at Marathon, Florida, on January 2, 1967. When Customs agents swooped, the men were setting off for Haiti, where plans were in hand to spark a full-scale insurrection. Leading the expedition was the priest Jean Baptiste Georges, along with Antonio Leon Rojas, Rene Juares Leon and several more key conspirators. According to court documents, all had been planning since May, 1966, to launch a military action against Haiti, assembling fighting men and weaponry for deployment from the quaintly-named Coco Plum Beach in Florida. The defendants were a mixed bag. Masferrer, a Miami resident, was a former senator in the Batista government. He was still deeply irritated that Castro had not only imposed an austere communist regime on his once colourful and vibrant land, but also that his own status and lifestyle had been so impudently undermined. Jean Baptiste Georges was one of many disaffected Catholic priests in Haiti, since the excommunication and reinstatement of Duvalier by the Vatican. He was, however, among the very few men of the cloth ready to take up arms in pursuit of an overthrow. As a former Minister of Education in Haiti, he was indignant at being forced into exile in Florida, and wanted desperately to restore sane government to a land where it had traditionally been in very short supply. Rene Juares Leon, only 33 at the time of his arrest, was a palace guard commander under President Paul Magloire, having attended military training school at Fort Benning, Georgia, in 1956. He, too, wanted restoration of something akin to Magloire's relatively benign regime.

In the court papers, Werbell was described as a self-employed public relations man, a peculiar designation for an arms dealer and military adviser. But there was always more than one facet to this complicated and unfathomable character, whose genetic roots lay east of the Urals. In fact, it was the PR aspect of Project Nassau that appealed most to Mitch: here was a chance to engage in a popular cause with full television exposure, for CBS News was keen to film the invasion as it happened. In the run-up to the operation itself, Werbell and his fellow would-be invaders met the producer, film crews, freelance journalists and others who would record the overthrow of Papa Doc, which would include the reading of a proclamation to the Haitian people from the headquarters of the 'revolutionary army'. CBS's role in the enterprise was later to be the subject of congressional hearings because US politicians wanted to be sure that major networks were not actively financing revolutions in the Americas. For Werbell, however, the motives for his own involvement were clear enough. Project Nassau, which was also referred to as Operation Istanbul, was a potentially high-profile military expedition, with a strong anti-communist element, aimed at overthrowing the most reprehensible ghoul in the Caribbean. Add to all this the prospect of hard currency revenue for his company and you have an alluring scenario for a soldier of fortune.

The prospect of joint Cuban-Haitian exile forces storming the beaches, alongside seasoned mercenaries, promised exciting footage for the media team and peak-time viewing for television audiences across America. Cuban Information Archives hold the full text of the revolutionary proclamation, which was to be read in French, once the military operation had been successfully completed. In it, civilians and armed forces were to be urged to end nine years of 'unfeeling dictatorship' which had — in its words —

inflicted humiliation on Haiti. Urging disaffected soldiers and unhappy civilians to join the cause, it promised liberty to the oppressed supported by military firepower which the Duvalierists would find hard to counter. It all sounded high-minded and, superficially, quite impressive. The problem was that the television team included government agency informants who scuppered the project before it had cleared the Florida beaches. Instead of a gung-ho march on Port-au-Prince with all its attendant fanfares, Werbell and his team had to make do with dispiriting court appearances, in which they were depicted as rather woebegone wannabes. Thus ended another 'invasion' of Haiti and 'predicted collapse' of Papa Doc.

CHAPTER 23

DEATH BY FIRING SQUAD

From Nassau, Haiti's growing tension was being felt second-hand during the early months of 1967. The haunting melody of *A Whiter Shade of Pale* and the love message of the flower people were finding their way round the world, but no-one expected them to make much headway in Haiti, where hatred was the prevailing emotion as Papa Doc dug in for the long haul. The wide-eyed refugees herded ashore at Prince George Wharf on Nassau's waterfront were only part of the story. In the bush, where Haitians were cobbling together makeshift homes out of galvanised tin and discarded doors, conspiracies were being hatched against the man in the palace in Port-au-Prince, the author of their misfortune.

In *The Nassau Guardian*, I wrote a feature headed 'On the Run From Papa Doc', recording the tribulations of the suffering. Father Guy Sansariq, who tended the spiritual needs of the homeless hordes, who had managed to evade Bahamian police and join the exiled communities, was eloquent in describing the ongoing plight of Haiti. For him, a mulatto pained by the decimation of the Sansariqs at Jeremie in 1964, Duvalier's domination of a tormented people was a seemingly endless trauma. "They come here in desperation," he told me, "they would rather die on the high seas than live there under that terrible regime." As rough-hewn, overladen sloops set sail from the rocky shores near Port-de-Paix, and some turned turtle in the churning straits to the north, the Bahamas braced itself for the unwelcome migration.

By the summer, the situation was so bad that a six-man delegation headed by the Bahamas Government's Chief Secretary William Sweeting, was sent to Port-au-Prince to find out ways of regulating the influx. In June and July that year, nearly 3,000 hungry and terrified Haitians had been repatriated after fleeing to the Bahamas. "The talks were held in an atmosphere of cordiality and mutual understanding," said a Bahamas Government statement. A reception was arranged in the National Palace, with Papa Doc presiding, and the Bahamas team reciprocated by hosting dinner for the Haitian negotiators at Port-au-Prince's Sans Souci Hotel. At the end, little was concluded, other than that unscrupulous Haitian boat captains were capitalising on the illegal trafficking and that tough sanctions should be taken against them. While this sounded high-minded and commendable, it did not address the underlying issues. The opportunistic skippers were responding to economic forces: Papa Doc's horrific government was creating a demand which they were happy to supply. The Bahamas delegation's visit, while well-intentioned, did not and could not address the source of the refugees' woes, who happened to be the grizzled host, his ruthless militia and the social chaos over which they presided.

In early July, the Bahamas faced more trouble as fighting broke out on board the Nassau Government's rickety vessel, the Ena K, as she plied through the Exumas on her way to Haiti with 200 fractious deportees. The eight-man crew and their four-man police escort, faced with a possible full-scale mutiny, turned the boat round and headed home. Meanwhile, hatch-covers were smashed and bottles thrown as the normally easy-going Bahamians received a taste of Haitian volatility. "They were really desperate and I believe they would rather have been killed than go back," said Captain Stanley Hollingworth on his return to Nassau. "Those people were really vicious. Nothing would have got in their way." Then he added bitterly: "If I had my way, every illegal immigrant here would have had his head chopped off." During the melee, Captain Hollingworth had to fire a flare gun over the Haitians' heads to quieten them down. "Their language was foul and they were shouting and screaming at us," he said. Finally, the armed guards forced the angry Haitians below deck in scenes eerily reminiscent of the ravages of The Middle Passage, two centuries before.

In Nassau, there were rumblings that deportees were being tortured and shot in Haiti on their return, but the Haitian Consul-General in the Bahamas, Julio Bordes, denied it. He issued a statement to The Tribune saying those fleeing on boats were being brainwashed by the captains, who told them there was work waiting for them in the Bahamas, which was not so.

Subsequent events would prove that Mr Bordes was not entirely accurate in his assessment: Haitians wanted to escape their homeland because they were impoverished and oppressed. It was a process that would continue for decades to come, all begun by the excesses of the Duvalier dynasty. For Duvalier himself, there was nothing auspicious about the dawn of another year. Though 1967 marked a decade in power, he was unable to look back over the 1960s with any sense of real achievement, other than the satisfaction of having hung in where others might not, and in eliminating some of his most insistent foes. With the Coalition continuing to agitate from afar, turbulent Catholic priests hatching plots against him, and continuing unease within Haiti's armed forces, life at the National Palace was far from serene. The Bahamas group, sipping drinks in the ballroom, would have known nothing about the undercurrents now swirling round the President and his family. However, the heavily-armed Macoutes lurking in the corridors and on the staircases would have offered some potent clues.

Protracted siege conditions made the Duvaliers irritable, not only towards their detractors, but also each other. Mama Doc, the President's increasingly formidable spouse, was hardly a tranquil presence: power had made her rapacious and hard-edged, with a venomous tongue. If Duvalier was beginning to feel unwell at this point, and his health undoubtedly went into a tailspin from around this time, then the pressures exerted by the harridan Simone were undoubtedly a factor. Duvalier was sometimes curt with her, anxious to assert his authority in his own home, but she in turn was dogged and relentless in her strictures. Though united in the cause of self-preservation, the Duvaliers were far from being a mutually supportive Darby and Joan. The Presidency undoubtedly heaped pressures upon them which took their toll. Meanwhile, daughter Marie-Denise was preoccupied by conflicting loyalties. She was besotted by her enormous husband, Max Dominique, a fact which did little to comfort her parents. Over the coming months, Dominique's huge frame would cast long shadows in the palace and do little to encourage anything akin to harmony in the Duvalier household. In fact, Dominique was to become the central figure in what Haitian historians now see as the most defining, and disturbing, event in the entire Duvalier era.

After ten years of Papa Doc, the Haitian people had much to look back on, but none of it with anything approaching satisfaction. Many fine

Haitian people had vanished into the jaws of Fort Dimanche. The kidnap crisis of 1963 had sparked a deadly witch-hunt, including the burning of the Benoit home and the slaughter of the family. The Jeremie massacre in 1964 had marked another low point, not to mention the televised public execution of defiant rebels and the public exhibition of a bloated cadaver. There had been the parading of heads in Port-au-Prince, the dockside massacre of peasants by Tontons Macoute and the nocturnal disappearances of entire families. In the hills, mothers were prepared to sell their babies for a few pence. A Haitian priest in Nassau, tending a refugee who was forced to abandon his family, leaving them with only three dollars to survive on, was quoted by Associated Press as saying: "Haiti is easily the most miserable country in the western hemisphere." Duvalier, forever suspicious of soldiers, began looking askance at Casernes Dessalines and the ambitious young military men who marched up and down its parade yard everyday. Among them were headstrong elements with a rebellious turn of mind. Having been on his guard for so long, the President had developed instincts about those who would be by his side in the most extreme circumstances. Max Dominique was not among them. In spite of the familial connections, Duvalier now began to see the mountainous Max as a prospective conspirator.

Big trouble was afoot, with family divisions adding to the President's burden. Wherever there are three or four wilful women under the same roof, turmoil invariably reigns. At the palace, the Duvaliers were torn by petty jealousy, family rivalries, the usual ups and downs of sibling conflict. The President's pride and joy, Marie-Denise, was immensely proud of her Max, a captain in the palace guard, whose entry into the ruling family brought instant promotion to colonel and the approval of his new mother-in-law. The dumpy but perky Nicole wed the mulatto agronomist Luc Foucard, brother of Duvalier's private secretary, Mme France Saint-Victor, who wielded rather more power than Mama Doc thought good for her. Hence, two distinct factions formed in this incestuous hothouse menage, with the Dominiques on one side (supported by Mama Doc) and the Foucards on the other.

Observers have noted that Max Dominique and Luc Foucard were far from being bosom pals. On the contrary, each saw the other as a rival for power in the family hierarchy. Both were from the north — Dominique from Cap Haitien, Foucard from Port-de-Paix — and therefore reared in a region traditionally suspicious of the metropolitan elite. Of the two, Foucard was more attuned to the President's cultural pretensions. Alongside the relatively prosaic Dominique, Foucard came over as something of a mixed-blooded sophisticate. Duvalier, in spite of himself, was quite impressed by that. Mama Doc, though, preferred the strikingly imposing Max. Naturally, sisterly rivalry coalesced round the two sons-in-law, while Mama Doc and Mme Saint-Victor could barely stand the sight of each other. All in all, this was far from being a scene of domestic bliss. During celebrations of Papa Doc's sixtieth birthday (April 14 and 15, 1967), trouble erupted, with two explosions rocking the palace from just outside the perimeter fence. This was soon after Foucard had been appointed Minister of Tourism, the bombs thus blowing holes in his promotional efforts. Papa Doc, ever suspicious of Dominique, felt treachery was afoot, with the soldier trying to discredit his rival. When a third explosion occurred at the International Casino, it was interpreted as Foucard's revenge. A confectionary vendor was blown to pieces in this tit-for-tat exchange, victim of what would now be termed collateral damage. The fall-out was, as usual, drastic, with Duvalier full of rage, engaging Foucard's support in rooting out plotters within the palace guard. Several young officers were initially banished to the provinces, only to be recalled and despatched to Fort Dimanche. Dominique was under presidential scrutiny as a wide-ranging purge of senior soldiers and militia got underway, not just in the capital, but Cap Haitien itself, where Dominique was suspected of harbouring co-conspirators.

Macoute hardmen were sent north to do their worst: homes were ransacked as suspects headed for the hills. Some were never heard of again, among them the former Trujillo henchman, Johnny Garcia, a committed Duvalierist whose wife and children also disappeared. In Port-au-Prince, there was panic among young army officers, and other erstwhile Duvalierists, when it became known that Dominique was under threat. Many headed for the city's embassies, among them the much-feared Colonel Jean Tassy and the Palace Chaplain, the Rev Luc Hilaire. Meanwhile, nineteen young officers, all friends and colleagues of Dominique, were arrested and taken to Fort Dimanche, where Papa Doc was to stage one of the most horrific dramas of his Presidential career.

On the eve of June 8, 1967, while the flower people preached love and peace in Europe and the USA, Duvalier took lead role in an orgy of revenge, that even Shakespeare himself might have considered beyond the pale for one of his tragedies. Summoning an extraordinary meeting of his general staff, including Max Dominique himself, Papa Doc laid the ground for what was to prove a deeply disturbing event for all who took part in it. Under escort by heavily-armed Macoute militiament, the officers were driven to Fort Dimanche, where the nineteen men were already tied to stakes at the far end of the firing range. When Duvalier himself appeared in army helmet to supervise the slaughter, the officers knew where things were headed. With Tontons machine-guns at their backs, the officers formed a firing squad and despatched their friends and colleagues in short order. Dominique, too, was ordered to fire on his friends. As a show of force, it was as sickeningly dramatic as anything in the annals of Latin American politics and warfare. That the President himself should have been present, revolver in hand, added a flourish which shocked the diplomatic community and proved, once again, that Haiti lived by no rules that international opinion could begin to understand. The victims had been subjected to a swift judicial process before being sentenced to death, but it's likely that some, if not most, of those who died that day were as bemused by their fate as everyone else. Among them were noted Duvalierists like Major Sonny Borges, Mama Doc's ADC Joseph Laroche, the Monestime brothers, who had been key members of the palace guard, and Major Pierre Thomas, unjustly branded an American spy.

At the palace, family tensions were at their height. Had Papa Doc had his way, Dominique himself would have been shot. Only Mama Doc secured his reprieve, an intervention which provoked the President into a frenzied rage. Mama Doc, on the other hand, was distraught over the killing of Laroche, who had accompanied her on family visits and become a faithful and ever-present protector. As he looked down the firing range at the officers being issued with rifles, so that they could fire at the President's command, Laroche must have wondered how Haiti's madness could have reached this pitch. A little over a year later, my acquaintance, David Knox would fall foul of the regime in circumstances in which he could expect no mercy.

A few days after the mass execution, Duvalier summoned the peasantry to the city and read a gruesome roll-call. With barely concealed glee, Papa Doc recited names of men who had shown loyalty to him for a whole decade, but who finally fell to his capricious nature. "Where are you?" he asked after each name, "Come to your benefactor..." Of course, none responded. As the crowd's eyes widened in horror, Duvalier said: "All have been shot." It was an incredibly effective exercise in mass intimidation. Among the names were senior Tontons militiamen who had fallen out of favour. No-one, but no-one, was immune to the President's wrath. The Foucard faction of the Duvalier family must have experienced quiet satisfaction as the Dominiques toppled so dramatically from grace. With Mama Doc lobbying for his life, Dominique faced formal treason charges based on the President's suspicion that he was behind an assassination plot aimed at provoking a full-scale insurrection. But his punishment was confined to exile in Europe.

Open conflict erupted between the President and his wife, with Duvalier resorting to foul-mouthed abuse as she urged restraint for the sake of the family. Thus, both were at Francois Duvalier International Airport to see off Marie-Denise, her younger sister Simone and the some-what shell-shocked Max Dominique who, having been cashiered from the army, now found himself Haiti's Ambassador to Spain. Settled in his seat, lifting off from Port-au-Prince, the ex-colonel would not have been aware that his bodyguards and chauffeur were being seized by the Tontons, and shot without ceremony. This was Papa Doc's way of ensuring this particular rebellious 'cell' was conclusively eliminated. It left no loose ends, no aggravating residual resentment to contend with. Meanwhile, the President and his agitated wife were driven back to the palace, where they resumed their bickering. Eventually, Papa Doc's anger got out of hand. As he struck his wife, the corpulent Jean-Claude intervened, locking his father in a room for three hours while his temper abated. Despite his bravado, his attempts to draw comparisons with great revolutionary leaders of the past — Lenin, Ataturk and Nkrumah had now joined his list of imagined political soulmates — Duvalier was beginning to tire.

From 1967 onwards, the President's physical frailty became more apparent. With diabetes and heart problems setting in, the President looked more than his sixty years, and by the time I met him in the fall of

1968, he looked seventy at least, even allowing for the fact that the young always think their seniors are a good deal older than they are. Whatever Duvalier had intended for Haiti when he grabbed power by nefarious means in 1957, it's unlikely he achieved it, even by his own reckoning. Though the peasantry were seen as 'my people' the poor in truth did not prosper under his rule. Like many Third World leaders before and since, Duvalier in economic terms fell into a rather unsatisfactory stereotype, enlarging the black middle-class and aligning with the whites and mulattoes to keep the masses down. Whether this was achieved unwittingly, or by design, it had emerged as an unchallengeable truth by the time my plane circled Port-au-Prince and touched down in the land of darkness in 1968.

To mark his decade in power, Papa Doc issued golden postage stamps bearing his own motif, a guinea hen on a conchshell. He tried to orchestrate a carnival atmosphere to gloss over the unpalatable reality of a nation in crisis. Talking big and achieving little is a Third World trait as post-colonial governments sink in a mire of corruption, dishonesty, kickbacks and double-dealing. Duvalier was no exception. But the stamps, a special minting of gold coins, and publication of his *Little Red Book* of political philosophy, were all intended as grand gestures to conceal the squalid truth, which was that the Haitian people were still desperately poor and their country near bankruptcy, unable to pay its way in the world and subject of international contempt and despair. For the people, malnutrition and poor education continued to be ever-present features of rural life. Income was down to around $85 to $100 per year in some areas and age expectancy hovered around forty years. Coffee continued to be Haiti's premier crop, but it was insufficient to sustain some six or seven million souls. Tourism had potential, considering the country's astonishing beauty and deep culture, but it was constantly bedevilled by the unpredictable political situation and persistent press reports of gratuitous violence and unexplained killings. As Haiti's brightest and best flew to jobs in North America, Europe and, in some instances, Africa, the most enterprising of its poor continued to invest their 'savings' into sloop voyages north, usually to the Bahamas and, for the very fortunate, Florida. Among the professionals who fled were journalists, engineers, doctors, attorneys and academics: it was a serious leakage of the nation's intelligentsia which accelerated into a heavy flow. Add to all this Haiti's unfortunate location in 'Hurricane

Alley' — the Caribbean region most prone to killer storms — and it was easy to concur with the Bahamian claim that this unhappy land was being persecuted by an unforgiving God.

In 1966, shortly after I arrived in Nassau, I lived through the terrifying fringe storms of Hurricane Inez, but only after it had raked Haiti's hills and left the country in a state of virtual devastation. Following Flora in 1963 and Cleo in 1964, Inez wiped out crops and left vast areas waterlogged. The country's economic woes deepened. In this dispirited, demoralised state, Haiti was vulnerable to whatever the exiles could throw at it in 1968. When the New Year came, Duvalier would have been unaware that the island of Inagua, at the southern extremity of the Bahamas chain, would feature in another attempt on his life. But it was from there, home of the homicidal George and Willis Duvalier in the 1930s, that another rebel force would launch itself against a regime seemingly in its death throes.

CHAPTER 24

A RAID ON THE PALACE

By the early summer of 1968, I had left *The Nassau Guardian*, where I worked as a political reporter for two years, to join its evening rival, *The Tribune*. Within weeks, it became clear that Haiti was again to loom large in Bahamas newspapers, not only because the refugees were continuing to flee north, but also because exiles were already at work in Nassau and Grand Bahama to deal the killer blow to the Duvalier regime. The last time I saw David Knox before his departure on his 'lost weekend' he seemed buoyant enough. He was his usual brisk, efficient self, slightly contemptuous of young reporters who bugged him daily for information, but conscientious enough in his duties. Of course, I didn't know then that 'every woman in Nassau was in love with him' – a claim made more than once by his contemporaries, who assure me it was close to being true – or that he had an insatiable appetite for Oriental women, which was the supposed reason for his 'trip to Jamaica', which turned out to be an ill-starred excursion to Haiti. There was certainly nothing in his demeanour to suggest he was an anti-Duvalierist conspirator, or indeed much of a political animal at all.

On reflection, if pressed, I would describe the David Knox of 1968 as the archetypal lotus-eater, a bon vivant who bounced from one fly-blown imperial outpost to another, with few objectives outside of absorbing the sun, eating and drinking well, and bedding as many compliant females as he could lay hands on. However, I didn't know him well enough to substantiate anything I felt about him, or to confirm the view which has since gained credence, that he was a literary wannabe with fanciful notions about his own image as an urbane man-of-the-world and the quality of his writing talent, which seems rarely to have found expression. If it's true that, before his departure, he was liaising with Haitian exiles in Nassau and Inagua to become link man in the May 20 invasion attempt, then there was a good deal more to him than I gave him credit for. As a former soldier who felt he had fallen short in the Second World War, Knox was probably subject to psychological pressures I could not be expected to understand. Having missed out on glory, and now in his mid-forties, it was just possible that Knox was in the throes of a serious mid-life crisis. Craving Chinese nymphets, and stuck with the rather magisterial Phillippa, it's just possible that Knox was driven to one last adventure before he settled into premature senility in Madiera. We shall never know. At this distance in time, we are left with only two possibilities — that he was a very sad character in search of a cosmetic scar, or a closet revolutionary who used his humdrum civil service job to cloak his real purpose in life, which was to unseat the most dreadful tyrant of the age.

What we know for sure is that US-based rebels, liaising with contacts in the Bahamas, acquired a Second World War B-25 bomber for a blitzing mission over the National Palace in Port-au-Prince. If the Haitian Coalition's propaganda was to be believed, and Raymond Joseph insisted it was true, Duvalier was now in such a state of failing health, with deep depression and diabetes combining to undermine his resolve, that one devastating blow was all it needed to precipitate collapse. Whatever the reality, the 'one devastating blow' did not materialise due, it must be said, to the spectacular ineptitude of the exiled raiders. Knox, according to the witness Toussaint, was at the training base in Inagua shortly before the attack was launched, a claim Knox subsequently denied. If true, this evidence opens up intriguing possibilities about our hero and his intentions. It also adds a devilish dimension to his reputation as the most loved man in Nassau. There are at least two variations on the story of the May 20 raid. Neither attributes much by way of military expertise to the invaders. Essentially, this was another tale of commendable ideals, poor planning, inadequate resources and lamentable execution: in other words, it was a monumental botch-up with the usual calamitous consequences. What's known for sure is that the exiles gunned up the B-25 at Inagua for the 'bombing run' on Port-au-Prince. None of the Inaguans I have spoken to over the years admits knowledge of this operation, but news reports of the time insisted it was here — traditional home of the Bahamian Duvaliers —that the plane took off on a perfect early summer morning with a mission to end the reign of Papa Doc.

The twin-engined B-25 Mitchell was a respected air warrior of the 1940s which, heavily armed with machine-guns and cannon, proved a formidable foe for the Japanese in the Pacific War. It was a medium bomber which could be adapted for multiple roles, but essentially was a reliable journeyman of the skies which, though not the biggest, fastest or most stylish of US aircraft, proved popular with aircrew. With a maximum speed of 285mph and a top range of 2,200 miles, it enjoyed what aviation experts described as a 'colourful career' as an Army 'War Dog', to use a senior officer's expression. Apart from its many military escapades, the B-25 gained unwanted notoriety after a 'C' version of the plane crashed into the Empire State Building in 1945. However, the aircraft has proved durable in various roles. Since production halted at the end of the war, the B-25 in its many forms has been adapted to do all kinds of work, with one named 'Heavenly Body' remaining an ageing star of airshows right up to the present day.

The Haiti raid failed to add another glorious chapter to B-25 combat history, but it did give the old warhorse another splash of press exposure. The version of events circulating in Nassau at the time was that the bomber, on arrival over the Haitian capital, banked menacingly towards the palace in a way calculated to cause most public panic. As it zoomed low over Port-au-Prince, peasants scattered in fear, and tap-taps veered off-course, as their drivers were diverted from their task. From the plane's underbelly fell a large cylinder, believed to be a bomb, which bounced off the palace lawn. The B-25 then banked again, coming in for a second pass, dropping another cylinder as it skimmed over the palace. Once more, it fell harmlessly on the lawn. In Diederich and Burt's account of the raid, the details differed somewhat, but the outcome was the same. Describing another 'off-key aria' in the comic opera of anti-Duvalier military might, they say the first 'bomb' struck the street outside the palace, creating 'one more pot-hole' in a road system already well-blessed with them. This was accompanied by a carton of leaflets which failed to open after striking the palace a glancing blow. During the next pass, a second 'bomb' fell harmlessly to the ground, failing to explode. It is difficult even now to guess at the motives behind this inadequate air raid, for several hours elapsed before anything else happened. Then, during the early afternoon, a Cessna Skybus appeared from the north heading towards Cap Haitien. After requesting landing permission, it unloaded a squad of desperadoes armed with machine-guns. Immediately, the twitchy invaders began shooting up the control tower, where surprised Haitian airport staff were enjoying a siesta. Then the B-25, having loaded an invasion force back in Inagua, touched down with about two dozen hardmen in battle fatigues, who joined the struggle for Haiti's liberation.

By now, Duvalier's troops in the area had been alerted to the commotion and descended on the airport to engage the invaders. It proved to be an unequal match. In short order, the rebels were routed and captured before being whisked off to Port-au-Prince for questioning by Duvalier himself. As we now know, some were killed and beheaded in the action. At least one, the aforementioned Toussaint, was to testify against the 'co-conspirator' David Knox at the military tribunal. Some are said to have disappeared in the time-honoured fashion, while others, the younger ones, were freed as misguided adventurers who had been influenced by sinister forces. Via his Ambassador, Arthur Bonhomme, Duvalier lodged complaints with the United Nations and Organisation of American States and began pitching for aid, by depicting the attack as another Castro-inspired assault on Haiti, part of Cuba's campaign to spread the poison of communism throughout the Caribbean.

For the Bahamas, news that Inagua had served as the launch-pad for the attack proved an embarrassment. The new Prime Minister, Lynden Pindling, had no desire to be seen as a hostile neighbour, especially as Duvalier had so warmly welcomed the election triumph of the Bahamian blacks only the year before. At a point when Pindling was still offering assurances that such rebel activity on Bahamian soil would be discouraged, his Director of Information, David Knox, was setting off for his 'lost week-end'. Close friends were under the impression that he was chasing Chinese women in Jamaica, taking advantage of Phillippa's absence from Nassau. In fact, he was bound for Haiti. Soon, we were to learn that he was in the hands of the Tontons Macoute, having booked himself into a hotel room within machine-gun distance of the National Palace.

I was on holiday in Britain when the call came through, from the Bahamas, saying I was needed in Port-au-Prince to cover the trial of David

Knox. I flew from London to the land of darkness via Miami, receiving some quizzical glances as I checked in for the final leg. "Mmmmmm... Haiti? On business, sir?" "Yes, business." "Rather you than me, sir." "Thank you." And then by Pan Am jet to who knew what? I was bound for the only country in the western world where the President was known to consult the severed heads of his foes, and scrutinise their entrails. Where evil militiamen struck terror into an already cowed and uncomprehending people, and where civilisation as I knew it existed only in tiny scented enclaves on the slopes around Port-au-Prince, a city whose history had not only been written in blood but scorched into the ground by a thousand fires. It was here that sticks were run through people's hair, during the slave uprising, so that true negroes could be spared at the expense of the hated mulattoes. "If the stick got tangled in the thick curls of a negro, that meant freedom. If the stick passed easily through the straighter hair of a mixed blood Haitian, that meant death," I was told by a student of Haitian history.

Compromise had never figured largely in the continuing nightmare of the Haitian nation. I recall the debilitating heat as I walked through the arrivals hall, the shaded Tontons assessing every passenger as we made our uncertain way through Haiti's immigration formalities. Then out into the sun again and the beseeching humanity: countless outstretched hands and cries of "Papa, Papa!" The taximen fought off the beggars as I was ushered to a car. The air was heavy, electric, a thick stew of Haitian smells. The few arriving passengers looked slightly alarmed. Only two Catholic priests remained serene, but they had God on their side and I didn't. Less than two weeks after David Knox was sentenced to death by firing squad, Papa Doc — in an unfamiliar gesture of compassion — decided to let him go. It was, of course, less to do with compassion than his desperate need for aid, but Knox's reprieve brought deep relief to me and others who had felt somehow implicated in the fate that befell him. Duvalier wanted to show the world that, whatever Graham Greene and other detractors thought of him, there was another aspect to the ghoulish persona of popular renown. British Ambassador Dalton Murray said Knox was 'profoundly grateful' to Duvalier for the clemency shown to him. Premier Lynden Pindling also expressed gratitude "that the President of Haiti should so readily have acceded to the representations that were made on behalf of Mr David Knox", who was described in the letter as misguided.

Knox flew back to Nassau via Jamaica and Miami, and was met by the long-suffering Phillippa, who must by that time have been engulfed by a multitude of conflicting emotions. At Nassau International Airport, Knox stepped down from the plane with some uncertainty to what I described in *The Tribune* as 'a hero's welcome', hardly an original phrase but one I stick by to this day, in spite of the sneering of some Bahamian politicians at the time. This was no Beatles-style reception with groupies screeching from the rooftops, but in its own sedate way, a smallish gathering was offering goodwill to a prodigal who had defied the odds. Maybe 'an anti-hero's welcome' would have been more apt, especially as anti-heroes were very much in vogue at the time, but I'm not sure my Bahamian readers would have understood. Wearing the same biege suit and chukka boots he left in five months before, Knox was a somewhat chastened, and diminished, version of his former self, a man who had almost died ignominiously with his hands bound to a stake in a stinking Caribbean compound. It was all a far cry from what he had hoped for himself as a young soldier in North Africa, and a writer in waiting.

At the airport, the couple were taken quickly to a car and driven off to a hideaway, where they would have an opportunity to make up for lost months and confront a few unpalatable truths. For most of the Bahamas press, it was the end of the story. But not for me. There were still one or two pressing questions hanging over Knox's head: why was he really in Haiti? Why was his face really scarred? Was he truly a Walter Mitty wannabe or a real-life conspirator? Was he really at the Inagua training camp, or was that a figment of a dishonest man's mind? If the cosmetic scar story has any credence at all, then it's because Knox is suspected of having been involved in such a bizarre escapade before. Everyone who knew Knox well, including one or two of the Nassau women who reputedly loved him, claim he had a distinct scar on his face before he went off on his Haitian jaunt. This scar, he had supposedly alleged, was the result of a fight he once had in Macau, when he was 'defending the honour of a Chinese prostitute'. The tallness of the story was made taller still by his claim that the weapon involved was a scimitar: nothing so prosaic as a flick-knife for the ever-romantic David. "In truth, though," a friend once told me, "it's suspected he fell over while drunk and cut his face on a Heineken bottle."

Knox and Phillippa went to ground. Only a very few close friends knew their whereabouts, but shrewd calculations eventually took Malcolm Keogh of *The Daily Mirror* and myself to their door. They were holed up in the suburban home of the Attorney General, who was away on holiday at the time. We drew up in a car and I told Malcolm to get his foot in the door first because the sight of me was guaranteed to make them wary. He loped across the lawn and knocked on the door. After a minute or so, Phillippa appeared, holding the door only slightly ajar. Initially, she told him to clear off, but he told her he had flown all the way from New York and wanted only a minute or two of David's time. At the precise moment she relented, I dashed out of the car to join them. Phillippa went pyrotechnic with rage. "Not you, you f......g murderer!" she yelled, blaming me for her husband's plight. "You almost had David shot!" By this time, Keogh's shoe was firmly wedged inside the threshold. Knox, hearing the commotion, came downstairs and, very reasonably to my mind, asked Phillippa to be more forgiving. "No recriminations," he said, tiredly, "Let them in." Thus, Keogh and I found ourselves in the sitting room sharing a bottle of Scotch with the man who had been spared by Papa Doc, with a still visibly annoyed Phillippa sitting bolt upright nearby, to block awkward questions and spare Knox any possible indiscretions. "I'm not sure you should answer that one, David," she said at one point.

Knox himself seemed to bear no grudges. After all, his name had been splashed across some of the world's most illustrious newspapers and, in a sense, he had sprung from the obscurity he loathed and grabbed a slice of fleeting glamour. "Who are you doing this for?" he asked me languidly. "*Reuters, The Mail...*" I said, hoping to earn a dollar or two from the linage. "But most of all for *The Tribune*. They'll splash it tomorrow." Knox didn't say much. The terms of his release included a few constraints on what he revealed. "They treated me well," he claimed, choosing not to go into detail. In my story, I quoted him as saying: "When I was sentenced to death in Haiti, it came as a surprise. I never expected the death sentence — I had never even thought of it." This was a surprising comment for many reasons, but most obviously because of Franck Romain's constant calls for the death penalty in court. Skirting all the most penetrating questions, Knox said: "Everyone from the prison commandant down was extremely kind to me." Although fed on maize and rice for a time, Knox said he was given vitamins regularly and also a typhoid injection. He again expressed gratitude for Duvalier's decision to release him.

For me, the Knox case brought one or two interesting repercussions. In the Bahamas House of Assembly, I was attacked verbally by back-bencher Arthur Foulkes who — in a general onslaught on the 'callous' Bahamas press — said: "One of them even went to the extent of trying to execute David Knox." It wasn't the last time I was vilified in this way, though I bear Arthur no grudges now. He was later to become a diplomat and a knight and is now an elder statesman and esteemed political commentator in Nassau. In a reflective piece in *The Tribune*, I wrote: 'Doctor Duvalier, the shuffling little man who has declared himself President of Haiti for as long as he lives, freed David Knox to show the world that novelist Graham Greene was wrong. But by then he had already proved him irrefutably right.' And in an uncompromising dismissal of the trial as a distorted exercise in justice, I wrote: "The Knox trial has harmed Haiti irreparably because, far from being a fair hearing, it was as squalid as the festering streets of Port-au-Prince, as lopsided as maimed beggars who lope alongside tourists pleading for a dime. It was a trial that never was — a travesty remarkable for calculated injustice and rabid racial hatred." Ramming the point home, I added: "In presenting the prosecution case against Knox, Haiti boiled up a variety of unrelated incidents, sprinkled them with irrelevancies, flavoured them with innuendoes, garnished them with absurd emotional outbursts, and ended up with a hotpot of hatred which left a very bad taste in the mouth." In attacking Romain, I wrote: "He drew verbal encouragement from the soldiers at the back of the courtroom, despite the frenzied ringing of a dinner-bell by Laroche (the chairman) aimed at calling the court to order." And, in hitting out at Britain's apologetic attitude towards Duvalier, I ended on an indignant note. "Britain has, seemingly, allowed herself to be bullied by Duvalier on an issue which a gunboat could have settled in a day." Perhaps I was the personification of British imperialism after all.

CHAPTER 25

A DICTATOR IN DECLINE

With Knox out of his hair, the nineteen rebellious army officers safely dead, and Max Dominique now far away in Spain, Papa Doc began a renewed purge of communists, who by 1966 were mobilising as part of a growing global alliance. Two distinct factions jostled for power in Haiti, a reflection of the Sino-Soviet schism which forever seemed to bedevil the spread of pure Marxism worldwide at this time. Cuba, which was positioning itself alongside Moscow, began broadcasting Leftist propaganda into Haiti. This, together with the Coalition's broadcasting activities and the increasing spread of communist publications, gave the ordinary Haitian more access to information than he had ever enjoyed.

Haitian newspapers that were allowed to survive peddled an unvarying diet of pro-Duvalier propaganda, often accompanied by large photographs of the President himself, while the underground press offered different fare in limited and sporadically distributed portions. Now readers who dared were given access to contrary views, read at the risk of arrest and punishment. Books on Marxist-Leninist doctrine had been circulating in Haiti since 1963, but observers felt most of those influenced by Leftist literature were more preoccupied with their different interpretations of communist ideology than with any concrete plan for insurrection. This was essentially an intellectual movement without an army. In the midsummer of 1966, however, an explosion in a Petionville home exposed the more proactive intentions of at least one Leftist faction. The leader of the PPLN group, Professor Jean-Jacques Ambroise, and his wife were tortured and killed by the Macoute in the aftermath of this event. Another respected academic, Professor Mario Rameau, also died at the hands of the Tontons as Leftist colleagues fled Duvalier's clutches into exile. As a result, communist resolve hardened, and the PEP group – the PPLN's rival faction – was to claim responsibility for the bombs that upset Papa Doc's sixtieth birthday celebrations the following year. Nonetheless, as 1969 dawned, Duvalier looked as entrenched as ever. The army, having lost Dominique and nineteen of its finest young officers, was in disarray. Raymond Joseph and his Coalition forces were still ranting ineffectually in Manhattan, while would-be invaders in Miami and the Dominican Republic remained essentially a divided force, at odds on practically every aspect of anti-Duvalier strategy. Most of those regarded as irritants by the President – the Haitian professional elite – were now reduced to baying from the sidelines in Montreal or Paris.

Haitian newspapers opposed to the regime had been closed down by the Macoute, and committed Duvalierists were now in key positions throughout the government service. The legislature was no more than a rubber-stamping authority made up of frightened tailwaggers while the Catholic Church itself had been infiltrated by ordained militiamen. It would be hard to imagine a situation anywhere with such strong presidential representation at every level of public life. By mid-1969, Duvalier's physical deterioration became more apparent. This panicked the now enlarged black middle-class and the mulatto merchant elite into pressing for consolidation of all that Papa Doc had achieved on their behalf. Fearing that the president's death would lead to an unravelling of a governmental structure they had come to appreciate, the elite and church combined to encourage implementation of what now became Duvalier's priority project – obliteration of every trace of the communist movement, the only credible threat left to the President's power base.

In June, 1969, Duvalier's thugs raided a property in Avenue Martin Luther King, killing not only the party's central committee but also 'trophy' prisoners bussed into the city from Fort Dimanche. As journalist Mark Danner related in a New Yorker article in 1989, by the time New York Governor, Nelson Rockefeller visited Port-au-Prince a month later, Papa Doc was able to assure him of Haiti's success in eliminating any threat from the Left. A press photograph circulated at the time showed Papa Doc, visibly ailing, leaning on Rockefeller for support. According to Danner, 'the rapprochement with the United States had begun', followed in short order by the appointment of a new black US Ambassador to Haiti. For Raymond Joseph and other anti-Duvalierists, the President's appearance during the Rockefeller visit was encouraging, and probably inspiring.

In *The Tribune*, I recorded this air of jubilation after visiting the secret Coalition Headquarters high above the Manhattan streets, saying predictions of his death 'can no longer be regarded as mere wishful thinking, on the part of those who yearn for his downfall.' The article added: "The Coalition, meanwhile, is keeping its adherents up-to-date with health reports which are so authorititative that they appear to come from right inside the Presidential Palace walls". *Le Combattant Haitien*, the Coalition bulletin, rarely allows itself to get hysterical over possibilities of Duvalier's demise. With an almost impudent restraint, it announced recently: "The condition of Dr Duvalier, a diabetic and a victim of a 1959 heart attack, is complicated. The pleural cavities of the old man have been filling up with a surplus of fluid. That's what has caused the shortage of breath. The doctors have been literally pumping the chief dry. The only question now is how often they will have to pump him. If the cavities continue to fill up, let us say, every three weeks, we might as well prepare to say goodbye to Papa" Then, cheekily parenthesised, is the comment: "Sounds like a leaky battleship that must be bilged to keep it afloat."

Interestingly, while discussing possible immediate successors, Joseph mentioned neither himself nor Jean-Claude Duvalier, the teenage pretender, but Max Dominique, who by the final months of 1969, was in the process of rehabilitating himself within presidential circles, having returned from his Spanish exile a few months before. Joseph expected Dominique to head a military junta, during an uncertain post-Duvalier period, in which organisations like the Coalition would be able to stake their claims. "We have laid the psychological terrain," he said. On coming to power, he added, the Coalition would lay the foundation for a real democracy, having conducted its own affairs on the basis of consensus. "As far as democracy is concerned, we shall start from nothing, but we have got to try. We will have a lot to catch up, but it can be done," he said. At the time of our interview, Joseph was under death sentence in absentia in Haiti and listed as an undesirable in the Bahamas. Neither status seemed to trouble him. But, alas, his hopes for a Haitian democracy were to come to nought in the short term. The elimination of the communists was to be the last serious blast from Duvalier in a presidential reign which, by any calculation, was extraordinary in its capacity to survive against an array of seen and unseen forces.

In April, 1970, all five vessels of the Haitian Coast Guard unleashed a volley of bullets at the National Palace, but there was something pathetic about their gesture. It was a Parthian's Shot which achieved nothing as they fled into exile at Cuba's Guantanamo Bay. Typically, Duvalier's troops were unable to respond effectively because their weaponry did not have the range to reach the retreating gunboats. Militarily, every attempt on Papa Doc's rule bore the hallmarks of pure comedy. This final flourish was no exception.

Twelve months later, exactly one week after his sixty-fourth birthday, Papa Doc died of the combined effects of diabetes and heart disease. Most of the family were there for his passing, which in itself was a substantial triumph for the little tyrant. Few if any Haitian presidents before him had died peacefully in bed while still in office, and most had concluded their tenure either by fleeing the country or being torn apart by the mob. It is not recorded whether a smile played on his lips as he breathed his last, but it's likely that there was no small measure of self-satisfaction in his passing.

During that final year, Duvalier had erected the dynastic framework suggested by de Catalogne and groomed the unlikely Jean-Claude as his successor. The portly Baby Doc, as he became known, was in no way suited to the task, largely because he appeared to lack the charisma, character and brainpower necessary to keep a notoriously volcanic nation in check. Even so, Papa Doc would not be diverted from his objective, and, in January, 1971, just three months before his death, announced to a surprised nation that the over-indulged fat boy — known until then only for his love of fast cars and loose girls — would be his successor. As Danner noted in his *New Yorker* piece, Jean-Claude was referred to by his schoolpals as Tete-Panier (Baskethead), but that did not prevent Papa Doc drawing ludicrous comparisons with Caesar Augustus who — also at just nineteen years of age — was declared leader of the mighty Roman Empire. Exactly where the parallels lay is hard to discern, but it's to Papa Doc's credit that this unexpected transition took place without the bloodletting and mayhem that by now had become a traditional part of Haitian political life. Having achieved a degree of constancy via the father, Haiti's main institutions — including the army and the church — were ready to concur with the President's wishes, at least for the time being.

Jean-Claude himself, supported by his doting mother, recognised the logic behind the move, even if his personal commitment to the task was somewhat doubtful at the time. It was, he noted in a missive to his father, to "avoid fratricidal fights...and assure the perenniality of the revolution." In de Catalogne's estimation, this is how it should be: even the ponderous Jean-Claude was preferable to an untried upstart with no background in governance. On the day of Duvalier's death, Mama Doc called in the United States Ambassador and asked for protection of Haiti's shoreline. It was feared that exiled rebels, thwarted for so long, would take this opportunity to catch the nation unaware and stage a full-scale invasion.

At the funeral three days later, bells tolled solemnly as Papa Doc was laid to rest with Haitians wailing and swooning all around. Whether this mass demonstration of public grief was orchestrated by the Macoute is unclear, but those who witnessed it were impressed by its apparent sincerity, given all that had gone before. Many of the bereft wailers panicked when a fierce wind blew up, seeing it as the dramatic departure of the President's soul. Right up to, and even after his death, Papa Doc was able to capitalise on the absurd superstitions of his people.

When Jean-Claude was officially declared Haiti's new President, thus ensuring the transfer of power to youth, as Papa Doc desired, few thought he would last. But, with Simone Duvalier's help in the early years (she instilled as much fear into the populace as her husband), the callow youth grew into the job and, incredibly, endured for fifteen years, thus outstripping his father for presidential longevity. It would be heartening to record that life improved for the Haitian people during this time. However, Baby Doc retained much of the apparatus of power his father had used so effectively. The Tontons Macoute continued to hang over people's lives like a huge shadow until Jean-Claude was finally ousted in 1986. According to a BBC report at the time, Baby Doc was still torturing and killing enemies in the palace basement on the very day he and his family took their leave. Having looted Haiti's treasury, they flew to Paris to live the grand life in exile.

No sooner had their aircraft faded into the eastern sky than the Haitians began exacting revenge. Known Macoutes, many of whom fled into the hills and sought to adopt new identities, were tracked down and slaughtered. Some were literally cut to pieces in the streets, echoing the fates of Dessalines and Sam. Others were 'necklaced' with burning tyres, left to roast in front of baying crowds. Some of the lucky ones fled by boat to the Bahamas, where known pockets of Macoute live on today. Bahamians are complaining that vicious elements of Haitian society have infiltrated the shanty communities, where the more deferential early refugees settled in the early 1960s. "At first we got only peace-loving country folk," said one Bahamian who campaigns against the spread of the makeshift settlements, "now we are getting fiercer urban Haitians, elements of the Tontons who began to leave the country after Baby Doc left."

During a big blaze at The Mud Settlement in Marsh Harbour, Abaco, in 2005, hostile Haitian youths began to threaten firefighters with knives and cutlasses. It was a disturbing manifestation of changing attitudes among the settlers. For four decades, Haitian volatility had lain dormant in the Bahamas. Now it was all too apparent among headstrong Haitian youths. Though Mama Doc died in France more than a decade after their flight into exile, Baby Doc continues to live in France to the present day (June, 2006) but is by all accounts a good deal poorer than he was. In his maturity, he still yearns for Haiti where, he is happy to tell anyone who will listen, things have gone downhill since his day. Unfortunately for all concerned, he is right.

Graham Greene was mistaken when he said it was "impossible to deepen that night" in describing Papa Doc's regime, for Haiti's nightmare by 2005 was deeper and darker than it ever was. The legacy left by the Duvaliers led to another long succession of false dawns. Maybe their excesses, added to all that went before, caused wounds that can never heal. The rise and fall of the Catholic priest, Jean-Bertrand Aristide, were propelled by the same racial and social dynamics that have always been at the base of Haiti's troubles, dating all the way back to Dessalines, but that's another story for another time. Suffice to say that, after Aristide's flight into exile, in the 200th year of the Haitian Revolution, things deteriorated so badly in Port-au-Prince that murders and kidnappings became commonplace. Instead of the calculated killing of the Macoute, death was dispensed in spasms of reckless gunfire. The city's morgues were stacked high with corpses which, left to rot in Haiti's perpetual heat, heaved with maggots and rats. United Nations peacekeepers patrolled the streets, but armed gangs held the real power, simply by virtue of being out of control in the urban slums, where rivers of filth ran between shacks made of corrugated iron and board. People were shot in the alleyways for no good reason other than that they were in the wrong place at the wrong time. Another corpse on the road was as unremarkable as a multi-coloured tap-tap truck or a woman with a turkey on her head.

The election of Rene Preval as President, in 2006, ended two years of bloody chaos following the rebellion that ousted Aristide, but analysts wondered how long it would be before the desperate people of this troubled land took to the streets again. As I write, hope lives once more in Haiti, but its chances of survival are still rated slim to none in the long term. Mr Preval begins his task with the goodwill of the western world behind him, but will it be enough?

When the Duvalier dynasty collapsed in 1986, Haitians descended on Papa Doc's marble tomb, intent on dismembering his corpse in a savage reprise of the Dessalines, Leconte and Sam episodes of former times. It will surprise no-one to learn that, when the vandals smashed their way into the inner chamber, Duvalier had already taken his leave. There was no body, only the faint mustiness of death. "I am already immaterial," Papa Doc had boasted in life. In death, he made the point even more emphatically, spirited away no doubt by the voodoo deities. Exasperated and enraged, the crowd turned its fury on the mausoleum of a leading Duvalierist instead. Thus, the cadaver of General Gracia Jacques was dumped from its coffin and beaten and kicked by angry Haitians. It was the kind of irrational violence that followed the American withdrawal in the 1930s when crowds tore up infrastructure the occupiers had left behind. Little had changed over fifty years. Papa Doc himself once said that the Haitian people were meant to suffer. He was more aware than anyone of their propensity for self-destruction. "They people crazy," said my Haitian friend after the upheaval of 2004, when Aristide fled amid chaos. "Crazy, crazy, crazy..."

The National Palace in Port-au-Prince, Papa Doc's seat of power.

(Tribune photograph)

The Oloffson Hotel renowned haunt for writers, featured in the *Comedians*
by Graham Greene.

(Tribune photograph)

Jean-Claude Duvalier also known
as Baby Doc with his wife Michelle.
(Tribune photograph)

Lady Marguerite Pindling, wife of Bahamas
Prime Minsiter Sir Lynden Pindling, with
Jean-Claude Duvalier

(Tribune photograph)

The soccer star Pele pins a medallion on Papa Doc just a few weeks before the President's death.

A visiting ailing Papa Doc promotes his son, Jean Claude, as his successor as Haiti's President-for-Life.

Jean-Claude Duvalier and his mother view the body of Papa Doc during the funeral services in Port-au-Prince in April, 1971.

POSTSCRIPT

Simone 'Mama Doc' Duvalier spent the last twelve years of her life in exile in France. She died in her mid-80s of 'undisclosed causes' at a Paris clinic just after Christmas in 1997. Larry Rohter of *The New York Times* noted that Simone "was often regarded as a power behind the throne" during the regimes of her husband and son. Moreover, she "cultivated the image of a benefactor" in spite of the dread she inspired among the masses. Like other Third World presidential wives before and since, 'Mama Doc' promoted palace favourites, and undermined those she disliked, as she schemed to keep the Duvalier dynasty alive. Her death provoked few tears.

Jean-Claude married and later divorced Michele Bennett, a woman whose extravagant tastes reportedly exceeded even those of 'Mama Doc' herself. Subsequently, he and his mother were said to have lived in severely reduced circumstances in France, while pining for an eventual return to Haiti. In fact, there are still a significant number of Duvalierists who believe Baby Doc could yet prove to be his country's salvation. He has more than once expressed hope of reconciliation with the country he fled in disgrace.

Franck Romain, the vicious prosecutor at the trial of David Knox, became not only the leader of the Tontons Macoute, but also Mayor of Port-au-Prince. On September 11, 1988, he was involved in an attack on the Church of St John Bosco, where the anti-Duvalierist priest, Jean-Bertrand Aristide was preaching. Thugs torched the church and terrorised the congregation, leaving fifty dead in an orgy of violence. Romain, unrepentant, said Aristide was "justly punished", adding: "He who sows the wind reaps the storm." In the tumultuous aftermath of this event, Romain was granted safe passage to the Dominican Republic. Aristide was, of course, ultimately to become President of Haiti, only to be forced into exile himself after the 2004 uprising. Like others before him, including Francois Duvalier, he is said to have been transformed by power from an unassuming quiet man of compassion into a raging avenger.

David and Phillippa Knox told me, during our interview following the trial, that they were not sure where they would go in the future. Knox himself never worked for the Bahamas Government again but was paid until the end of his contract. Eventually, instead of settling in Madeira, which was their original plan, they went to the Seychelles, where he found work once again as a government information officer. Nassau friends heard that he frequently 'dined out' on the story of his incarceration and trial, milking the Papa Doc connection for all it was worth. Whatever else he lost, as a result of his detention, he retained his powers as a raconteur. Sadly, he contracted cancer and died at The London Clinic in 1972, never having disclosed the whole truth about that memorable summer of 1968. I believe he was still short of his fiftieth birthday when he passed on.

It's probably appropriate to reveal here one very interesting sidelight of the Knox case in Haiti. If nothing else, it will help to convince press-baiters that there is real honour within the ranks of professional journalists. During the trial, we heard that Phillippa Knox was, in fact, the daughter of the celebrated British spy chief, Maurice Buckmaster, who during World War II was head of the French section of the Special Operations Executive, providing military support to the French Resistance, in their clandestine activities against Hitler. Buckmaster, one-time newspaper reporter and banker, was an old Etonian who at the start of the war, was part of the British Expeditionary Force which was forced to retreat from Dunkirk, in the summer of 1940. When he joined the SOE the following year, he had a tremendous opportunity to strike back at the Nazi regime through his network of continental spy contacts. It was the kind of romantic assignment Knox would have relished, and Buckmaster himself gained legendary status among his contemporaries in the world of espionage.

When this information was made known to us in Haiti, the British press entered a pact not to disclose it in our stories. This is because we felt it would seriously jeopardise Knox's position, and give the Haitian authorities more weaponry in trying to establish a case against him. Alongside the MI5 references, the Buckmaster connection might just have tipped the balance in favour of Romain, in his quest to besmirch Knox's name. To this day, I am unsure whether the Buckmaster link was significant. Certainly, Knox himself might have felt somewhat inferior alongside his illustrious father-in-law, especially as Buckmaster managed to cap his wartime career with a senior executive position in the Ford Motor Company.

By comparison, Knox's own wartime exploits were less than impressive, a point which would have become all too obvious whenever such matters were raised in family circles. Buckmaster's Etonian past might also have had an impact on a man who wanted so much to be an English gentleman. Did Buckmaster's success, and presumably Phillippa's pride in her father, prompt Knox to engage in what his friend Paul Bower characterised as a last bid for glory? No-one knows for sure, though there seems little doubt that Knox would have been mightily impressed by Buckmaster's exploits, especially as these were recounted in two post-war autobiographical books. As a respected spy chief, company boss and a published author to boot, Buckmaster was all the things Knox might have wished to be himself. Minor civil service postings and an unfulfilled literary career were scant fare alongside the Buckmaster story. Was the Haiti adventure an attempt to redress the balance?

My friend and colleague Bill Cole of *The Nassau Guardian* returned briefly to Britain in the early 1970s, then spent some time as a reporter with *The National Enquirer* in Florida from about 1973 onwards. The last time I saw him, at a restaurant in West Palm Beach, he told me he was once again 'living a dream' by digging dirt on the famous and enjoying access to a lavish expense account. The last I heard, he was supposed to be working on a newspaper in St Louis, but I was never able to confirm that. However, if he's reading this somewhere, maybe we should get together for a drink sometime. If Haiti's safe, the bar of the Oloffson might be a good idea. Jolicoeur, Greene and Capote have long since gone, but the view over Port-au-Prince will be much the same. Mine's a Barbancourt and Coke for old time's sake.

ABOUT THE AUTHOR

JOHN MARQUIS, an award-winning British journalist with nearly half a century of experience on newspapers and magazines, was born in Wigston Magna, Leicestershire, England, in 1943. He entered journalism after winning a newspaper writing competition when he was 16 and has since worked as a prize-winning investigative reporter, an international sports writer and editor of both newspapers and magazines in a career which has included two long spells in The Bahamas, where he is now the highly controversial Managing Editor of the nation's leading daily newspaper, *The Tribune*.

During an eight-year spell in London, he was a sub-editor on *Reuters World Desk* and *London Sports* Editor and Boxing Correspondent for Thomson Regional Newspapers, covering major fights all over the world, including several involving Muhammad Ali. He also worked for more than a decade as editor and publisher of newspapers and magazines in Cornwall. His early career was spent with the *Northampton Chronicle* and *Echo* and the *Nottingham Evening Post* and *Guardian Journal* in the English Midlands. Since then he has worked as a staff journalist for several major organisations and his byline has appeared in many leading newspapers, including *The Washington Post*, *The Scotsman*, *The Western Mail*, *The London Evening Standard*, *The Boston Globe*, The *Dallas Morning News* and the now defunct *Washington Evening Star* among other prominent US and Commonwealth titles.

In 1974, he won the Provincial Journalist of the Year award in the British National Press Awards for a hard-hitting investigation into a major hospital child deaths scandal. Judges described his work as 'utterly compelling'. His first book, *Blood and Fire* — about the wartime murder of Sir Harry

Oakes in Nassau — was published to critical acclaim in 2005. Author Chester Thompson described the book as 'an awesome read' and Marquis as 'a master wordsmith'. In a letter to Marquis in 2002, the best-selling novelist Arthur Hailey — a fan of his journalistic work — wrote: "You are a damned good writer." Marquis and his wife Joan, an artist, have eight children. They divide their lives between their home in Cornwall, England, and Nassau in The Bahamas.

CRITIQUE ON *BLOOD AND FIRE*
THE DUKE OF WINDSOR AND THE STRANGE MURDER OF SIR HARRY OAKES BY JOHN MARQUIS

A master wordsmith...an awesome read (Chester Thompson, author of The Fledgling)

The most entertaining book ever written about the Sir Harry Oakes murder case. His writing is without equal (Paul Bower, chairman, Star Publishing, Nassau)

A riveting, compelling book. I wish it had been 200 pages longer (Ivan Clifford, Mid-Ocean News, Bermuda)

A fantastic read. One of the few books I have read straight through from cover to cover in a long time (Henry Toledano, author of The Bitter Seed and A Sort of Justice)

You're a damned good writer (letter to John Marquis from Arthur Hailey, author of Airport and Hotel, in 2002)

It's a heck of a piece of reporting. I've really enjoyed reading it. (John Perry, King Features, USA)

One of the great unexploited talents of British journalism (Tom Arms, chairman, Future Events News Service, London)

A brilliant craftsman of the English language — a master of his profession (Eileen Dupuch Carron, Publisher, The Tribune, Nassau, Bahamas)

John Marquis has always been a robust and colourful journalist (Andrew Grant-Adamson, journalism lecturer, University of Westminster, London)

Objective, easy to read, a riveting page-turner, and a book I'll keep on my shelf (Art Montague, Canadian crime writer, True Crime Ink)

LaVergne, TN USA
10 September 2010
196625LV00002B/44/A